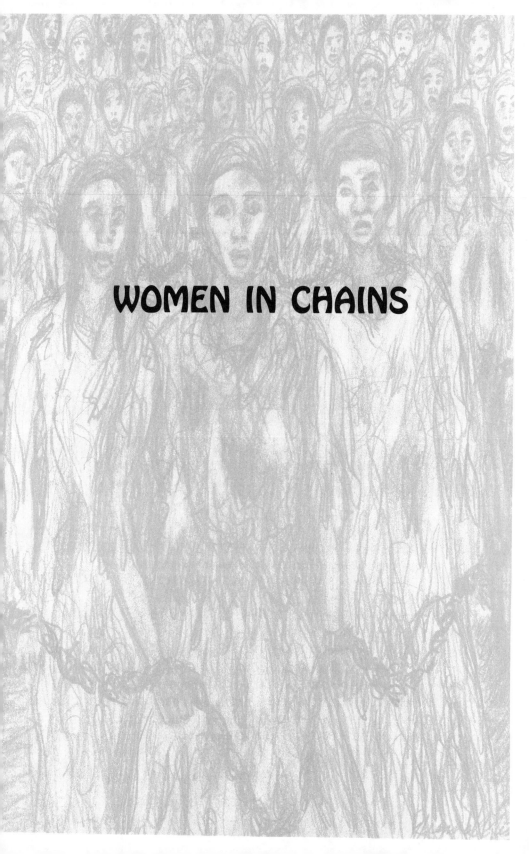

WOMEN IN CHAINS

SUNY series in
Afro-American Studies

John R. Howard and Robert C. Smith, editors

WOMEN IN CHAINS
The Legacy of Slavery
in Black Women's Fiction

Venetria K. Patton

STATE UNIVERSITY OF NEW YORK PRESS

Cover artwork by Regina C. Jeanpierre.

Production by Ruth Fisher
Marketing by Fran Keneston

Published by
State University of New York Press, Albany

For information, address the State University of New York Press,
State University Plaza, Albany, NY 12246

Library of Congress Cataloging-in-Publication Data

Patton, Venetria K., 1968–
    Women in chains : the legacy of slavery in Black women's fiction /
Venetria K. Patton.
        p.   cm. — (SUNY series in Afro-American studies)
    Includes bibliographical references and index.
    ISBN 0-7914-4343-4 (hc : alk. paper). — ISBN 0-7914-4344-2 (pbk.
: alk. paper)
    1. American fiction—Afro-American authors—History and criticism.
    2. Women and literature—United States—History—20th century.
    3. American fiction—Women authors—History and criticism.
    4. Afro-American families in literature.   5. Afro-American women in
literature.   6. Mother and child in literature.   7. Afro-Americans
in literature   8. Motherhood in literature.   9. Slavery in
literature.   I. Title.   II. Series.
    PS374.N4P38   1999
    813'.5099287'08996073—dc21   99-14973
                                                                         CIP

10 9 8 7 6 5 4 3 2 1

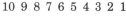

This book is dedicated to my mother, Hildegarde J. Patton
and in memory of my father, Frederick J. Patton

Contents

Acknowledgments

I would like to thank those who provided financial, intellectual, and emotional support for this project. A large portion of this manuscript was completed during my residency at the University of California Humanities Research Institute (HRI). The time and resources provided by HRI in coordination with the Western Interstate Commission for Higher Education greatly enhanced my productivity. Through the various stages and drafts of this manuscript I have received insightful comments and suggestions from Wheeler Dixxon, Emory Elliott, Jennifer Brody, Moira Ferguson, Sherry Harris, Paulette Brown-Hinds, Katherine Kinney, Kimberly Nettles, Kathy Patterson, Walter Rucker, and Carole-Anne Tyler. My research assistant, Sarah Fisher, provided invaluable assistance with all the nitty gritty aspects of the production of this manuscript. I would also like to thank my mother, Hildegarde J. Patton, and my late husband, Rogers Druhet, for their tremendous emotional support.

Introduction

"Feminism" often conjures up idyllic visions of a united sisterhood; however, black feminists such as Hazel Carby and bell hooks, among others, have questioned the existence of a sisterhood of black and white women. Carby states, "Considering the history of the failure of any significant political alliances between black and white women in the nineteenth century, I challenge the impulse in the contemporary women's movement to discover a lost sisterhood and to reestablish feminist solidarity."[1] She implies that contemporary feminists are searching for a sisterhood that is more imagined than real. hooks is even more critical of racism within feminist movements: "Every women's movement in America from its earliest origin to the present day has been built on a racist foundation."[2] They demonstrate that all too often when feminists presume to speak about women, the assumption is that what is true for the white middle-class woman is true for all women. This assumption is evident in the tendency of some feminists to fall into "essentialism." Feminism is based on the belief that women share a common experience of subordination to men; however, in an attempt to identify an "essence" of a "common" experience, there is a tendency to flatten the experience of all women into an image that denies the rich variety of women's experiences. This image then forms a static gender identity in that a woman's femininity or gender is boiled down to some aspect that is deemed to be shared by all women.[3]

However, other aspects of personhood complicate a woman's gender identity and make it difficult to generalize about women as a group. Contemporary feminists have begun to realize the impossibility of separating gender issues from other aspects of identity such as race, class, sexual preference, and nationality, to name a few. However, despite the greater awareness of the problems of essentialism, there is still the desire among many feminists to speak about women as a group, which is connected by some essential factor. For some, this means returning to biology as a common denominator for all women. Shared biology, and particularly maternity, are then seen as sites from which to speak about females, womanhood, and motherhood. This is not to say that this is the only reason for feminist interest in maternity; the interest is much more complex. How one mothers and the way in which mothering is continued in society have many ramifications for gender identity. However, for the purpose of this project, I am focusing on the understandable, yet problematic attraction to maternity as a common bond for all women. While I appreciate the appeal of such a view of maternity, I will argue in the following pages that maternity or mothering is a social construction that must be separated from the biological process of giving birth. While most women are capable of giving birth, all do not and those that do give birth vary in their approach to mothering. Motherhood is not merely an aspect of gender, but also a function of race, class, sexual preference, nationality, et cetera in that each of these things impact the way in which mothering is performed. In other words, mothering is not a stable, static event, but a changing, flexible phenomenon.

This project critiques the notion of maternity and shared biology as a common bond for all women by analyzing the slavery institution. During this period of American history, one sees the separation of the biological process of birthing and the gendered act of mothering. This separation of birthing and mothering was based primarily on race and to a lesser degree on class, as female slaves were excluded from the mothering realm. I argue that the slave system attempted to degender slaves by treating them as chattel. I contend that although slaveowners recognized sex differences by using female slaves as breeders, they did not acknowledge gender differences. My analysis begins by looking at the work of Hortense Spillers and Angela Davis, who note the degendered status of female slaves. While I will follow the lead of Spillers and Davis, I believe changing their frame of reference enhances their arguments. They both present their arguments from the viewpoint of the slave masters, but the slaves probably did not view themselves as degendered. I argue that despite the intentions of the master class, the degendering process was not perfectly realized. Although female slaves could not live by the cult of true womanhood practiced by their mistresses, they were not immune to its effects. Slave narratives record several instances of identification with white femininity. The retention or remembrance of African gender practices often further complicates this identification. The disjunction between the female slave's position and gender expectations of North America and Africa complicated the gender development of the female slave and even her descendants, who continue to be affected by the history of slavery.

In other words, I will argue that their race, history, and enslavement affected female slaves' conception of their gender. Upon arrival in the colonies that would later form the United States, these slaves were not blank slates; they brought direct or indirect knowledge of various African gender traditions that were later placed alongside of American traditions and their frequent exclusion from these traditions based on racial difference. I contend that this situation led to a conflation of various gender systems (African and North American) that were further complicated by the different perceptions of slaves and masters. Thus slaves were often discussed and portrayed in terms that ran counter to their own sense of themselves. This historical scenario developed and transmuted itself across time and continues to have a bearing on black women's lives today. The image others have of black women and black women's self-image continues to be framed and colored by the history of slavery. I would like to clarify here that I am not equating the experience of female slaves with that of black women; however, I am attempting to draw a connection between the past treatment and perceptions of female slaves with later (and continued) impressions of black women. These later impressions do not remain static over time, yet their various permutations seem connected to the history of slavery. Thus the legacy of slavery continues to have currency, as reflected in the writings of black women, past and present.

The legacy of slavery lives on in a different articulation of gender found in the writing of black women. While the observations that follow may be equally true of a variety of genres, I am limiting my discussion to slave narratives and nineteenth- and twentieth-century novels. However, I will use the terms black women's writing and black women writers as shortcuts that include fiction and nonfiction writing and writers which I address explicitly while implicitly suggesting that this may also be true in other genres such as poetry and essays that are not addressed specifically. Often black women writers' articulations of gender are not the same as their white counterparts due to their different experiences as a result of race and the history of slavery. Just as female slaves developed a different conception of gender identity, later black women writers created a different means of approaching the subject. Often black women writers did not find the methods of white women writers fully satisfying because they were working with different ideas about gender as well as different receptions of their gender. This tendency is particularly evident in the work of nineteenth-century black women writers who borrowed from the sentimental novel tradition frequented by white women writers, but strategically changed the format in order to better address race issues. This was necessary not so much because the two groups of writers had different views of nineteenth-century women's gender, but because society had differing views regarding the level of womanhood achieved by black and white women—black women were traditionally regarded as less than their white sisters. This divergence is firmly rooted in the institution of slavery and feelings and beliefs that developed in response to slavery.

The effect of slavery on gender is particularly evident in the realm of maternity. The slavery institution's attempt to degender female slaves and their resistance to such tactics generated different gender constructs. And due to the socially constructed nature of maternity, slave mothers and their descendants formulated different maternal ideals than white mothers. My hope is to stimulate discussion of the relationship between slavery, maternity, and black women's writing; however, I do not purport to cover the vast field of black women writers. Rather, I have selected seven authors and texts, which seem emblematic of a traceable legacy of slavery and gender conventions. I hope to illustrate that slavery continues to be a very real concern even in the twenty-first century. However, slavery does not serve as a static, ahistorical term. Its effect and the response it generates fluctuate. In setting up my discussion of slavery, I am cognizant of the difficulty of generalizing about such a vast period of time and the variety of scenarios across different types of plantations and slave households. I am also aware of the unsettled debate regarding the female slave's role. Therefore, I rely on the work of historians with various viewpoints to develop a generic sense of slave life from which I build my analysis of narratives and literature. It is not my intention to provide an all-encompassing study of slavery or even gender relations within slavery, but instead to point to recurring issues and the various responses of black women writers to these issues. I do not think it is an accident that slavery and motherhood are often linked in the writing of black women. I think these have become significant sites from which to begin discussions of black women's gender.

The black women writers that I address are aware of the history of slavery and its implications for female slaves and later generations. Their depictions of black womanhood are tied to the effects of slavery and represented through the black mother. While the writers' discussions of motherhood are often the means of critiquing notions that equate womanhood with motherhood, the mother is a logical choice for gender analysis because the history of slavery would have one believe that slaves were not and could not be mothers. The depiction of female slaves as mere breeders, and not mothers, was just one manner of attempting to strip female slaves of their gender. Thus the mother figure becomes the means of asserting and critiquing gender.

I argue that writers such as Harriet Jacobs, Harriet E. Wilson, Frances E. W. Harper, and Pauline Hopkins were cognizant of both the cult of true womanhood that defined women as pious, pure, submissive, and domestic and the stereotypes of black women that excluded them from this definition of femininity and related notions of maternity. These writers used their texts as a means to reclaim black womanhood by removing the stigma of sexual promiscuity associated with black womanhood. Although the cult of true womanhood, which was predominant from 1820 to 1860, did not continue to be the governing notion of femininity in the twentieth century, black women have been continuously omitted from North American codes of morality and womanhood that have superseded or developed from it. Twentieth-century black women writers like Toni Morrison, Sherley Anne Williams, and Gayl Jones continue to explore the legacy of slavery in relation to black womanhood and motherhood. While numerous white women have offered critiques of limiting definitions of womanhood, black women writers often believe they must first establish their heroines as women and mothers before beginning their various critiques.

Chapter 1, "The Breeding Ground: The Degendering of Female Slaves," explodes the feminist desire to identify maternity as a shared female identity by illustrating the graphic difference between slave mothers and free mothers. Under slavery, female slaves were relegated to the position of breeders, not mothers. Female slaves were denied the right to traditional feminine gender as constructed in the United States. They were seen as mere chattel, not women; however, this in itself was not sufficient to degender the slaves. Although the slave masters may not have acknowledged gender difference, female slaves were able to create their own sense of gender identity. Yet the institution of slavery necessitated that their conception of gender be different from that of their white mistresses.

The second chapter, "The Cult of True Womanhood and Its Revisions," begins by analyzing the cult of true womanhood that nineteenth century women were expected to live by. This ideal was often addressed in women's sentimental fiction. According to this ideal of femininity, women were expected to maintain the four cardinal virtues of piety, purity, submissiveness, and domesticity. The condition and legacy of slavery, however, made these virtues impossible for female slaves and their descendants to observe. In order to negotiate these expectations, black women writers reconfigured the sentimental novel by incorporating aspects of the slave narrative. This blending of genres is also seen in Harriet

Beecher Stowe's *Uncle Tom's Cabin* (1852). I argue that *Uncle Tom's Cabin* serves as an important precursor for the African American woman's novel in that several nineteenth-century texts appear to offer significant revisions of Stowe's discussion of race and gender, as well as her use of sentimentality.

While the first two chapters lay the groundwork by discussing gender expectations generally, and the cult of true womanhood specifically, the following three chapters address the way several black women writers responded to gender conventions through their texts. Chapter Three, "Reclaiming True Womanhood," examines the impact of the slave narrative tradition in the writing of two black women. Harriet Jacobs' *Incidents in the Life of a Slave Girl* (1861) and Harriet E. Wilson's *Our Nig* (1859) are both stories of single mothers—Linda never married and Frado is widowed. Although Daniel Moynihan would later describe this "matriarchal" pattern as a form of social "pathology," these texts may be seen as a rewriting of female empowerment. The fact that neither of these texts concludes with the sentimental novel's traditional ending of marriage implies a critique of traditional gender expectations. While both texts comment on the limitations of the cult of true womanhood, Jacobs' narrative attempts to dismantle the ideology.

The fourth chapter, "Tragic Mulattas: Inventing Black Womanhood," focuses more on the sentimental tradition as I analyze Frances E. W. Harper's *Iola Leroy or Shadows Uplifted* (1892) and Pauline Hopkins' *Contending Forces* (1900). While the third chapter primarily addresses gender and its relation to motherhood, this chapter is more concerned with the relationship of sexuality and gender. Purity was a central component of the cult of true womanhood, and both of these texts address the stereotype of black women's promiscuity, which is linked to their forced concubinage during slavery. *Iola Leroy* and *Contending Forces* differ significantly from *Incidents* in that they seek to include black women in the cult of true womanhood, while Jacobs attempted to eradicate it. I attribute this difference to the texts' different relation to slavery—Linda is enmeshed in the slave system, while Iola and Sappho are further removed. Despite this difference, both *Iola Leroy* and *Contending Forces* remain critical of the exclusionary nature of the cult of true womanhood.

The concluding chapter, "The Haunting Effects of Slavery," moves into the twentieth century with an examination of Toni Morrison's *Beloved* (1991), Sherley Williams' *Dessa Rose* (1986), and Gayl Jones' *Corregidora* (1975). This chapter brings together the issues of sexuality and motherhood in relation to gender construction. Morrison's Sethe must come to terms with a sense of motherhood that is "too thick" before she can become a complete sexual being. By mothering Desmond, Dessa is able to move beyond the slavery institution's attempt to deny her femininity and therefore her humanity. Dessa's assertion of her rights as a mother are linked to her refusal to be labeled and misidentified by whites. In *Corregidora*, Ursa is instructed to make generations in order to bear witness to the terrors of slavery; however, an accident precludes the possibility of conception, which in turn affects Ursa's ability to feel like a "real" woman. For Ursa, conception, sexuality, and femininity are inextricably linked. All these texts echo the themes found in the earlier texts and serve as fictive examples of the lasting effects of slavery.

In *Playing in the Dark: Whiteness and the Literary Imagination*, Morrison has observed that black women are seen as "natally dead."[4] The belief that black women lack maternal feelings is connected to the history of slavery, which used this myth to justify the splitting of slave families. Although slavery has been abolished for over a hundred years, its myths and attitudes have not been completely eradicated. This is why twentieth-century black women writers continue to broach this topic and seek to prove that their female protagonists do indeed have maternal feelings as well as a feminine perspective before questioning what is meant by such a perspective.

1

The Breeding Ground
The Degendering of Female Slaves

In the following chapter, I intend to lay the theoretical ground for my later readings of black women's fiction. In the course of my reading, I noticed that slavery was a recurring theme or reference in many texts, but even more interestingly, that slavery and motherhood often seemed related. The nexus of the slave mother appears to be a fruitful departure point for discussions of gender in that she forces one to question what it means to mother as well as what it means to be a mother. I argue that the historic instance of American slavery provides at least one example of maternity being experienced differently by two different groups of women, white women and female slaves. Their masters regarded female slaves as breeders, rather than mothers; however, female slaves continued to view themselves as mothers, but mothering took on different meanings. While analyzing American antebellum gender codes

1

and precolonial African gender codes, I assert that female slaves could fit neither society's definition of woman and thus developed different gender ideals.

Before addressing the specifics of slave mothering, I would like to briefly address the significance of mothering in reference to gender identity. Drucilla Cornell has noted the feminist desire to turn toward:

> maternity as the maternal role, to the maternal body as the evocation of a subject not united in itself against the Other, and to reproductive capacity more generally to uncover the irreducibility of the feminine as a basis for a shared female identity and also for an expression of the potential within womanliness as it is lived, for a different and better way of being human.[1]

This concern with the maternal in part represents the desire to identify something essential that all females share that can then be used as the basis for feminist discourse. While studies of motherhood and the mother figure might be enlightening on a variety of levels, I agree with Jane Gallup's speculation that the glorification of the mother is in part a response to the "pressure to cover over differences between feminists."[2] Certainly this is not the only purpose that feminist explorations of the maternal serve, but it does appear to be part of the tradition of feminist theory to create a monolithic femininity. Object relations psychoanalytic theory and Lacanian and Freudian psychoanalysis are now among the most influential approaches to the maternal. Feminists have utilized both methods in their analyses of maternity. Despite the feminist perspective of their work, however, they are susceptible to eliding the numerous differences among women in an attempt to identify the essence of female identity. The problem is not so much that maternity is used to find a common bond, but that mothering is conceived of as a static shared experience. This limited view of maternity is further problematized when the maternal relationship is used to identify an essential characteristic shared by all women. By assuming all women share the same relation to the maternal, these discourses omit those who are not mothers and assume that all mothers are the same. One means of avoiding this harmful slippage is to take a historical approach in the analysis of motherhood, so that mothering may be placed within the context of the numerous events and issues that effect how and why one mothers or does not mother.

However, object relations theorist Nancy Chodorow appears to take the opposite approach in her text *The Reproduction of Mothering,* in which she assumes that all women have the same relation to the maternal as she analyzes women's mothering and the way mothering is reproduced. She argues that the reproduction of mothering is central to social organization and gender development and is implicated in the reproduction of male dominance. Chodorow's text has been quite influential in the field of feminist theory and has inspired numerous feminist studies of mother-daughter and woman-woman relationships in literature, film, and culture. Although many scholars have critiqued and superseded Chodorow's work, *The Reproduction of Mothering* is a seminal text and its flaws often reappear in the works that seek to critique it.

Central to Chodorow's argument is the different relationship between girls and boys and their mothers. She argues that since mothers and daughters share the same sex, girls are seen as an extension of the mother, while boys are seen as other.[3] From this she concludes that females tend to form their identity in relation to others while males form their identity in opposition to others.[4] Because of the sameness of daughters and mothers, daughters develop the capacity to mother and nurture. In other words, mothers reproduce their daughters as themselves. However, mothers' difference from their sons limits boys' ability to develop the sense of continuity and connectedness that daughters have.

Chodorow formulates this theory without addressing such factors of identity as race and class. Is the daughter's sense of continuity and connectedness affected by her place in society? Would a poor black girl feel the same level of connection as a rich white girl who has the advantages of race and class? Despite the fact that she acknowledges that "[t]he development of the self is relational,"[5] she does not consider other aspects that might affect gender development. Chodorow acknowledges that "mothering does not exist in isolation,"[6] but she continues to assume that all mothering is the same and results in the same kind of gender identity.

However, Elizabeth Spelman argues that an "investigation of ethnicity and class and race within that social structure might make us consider the possibility that what one learns when one learns one's gender identity is the gender identity appropriate to one's ethnic, class, national, and racial identity."[7] What is considered feminine in America may not be feminine in another country. For example, in *The Woman Warrior* Maxine Hong Kingston notes the difference between Chinese feminine and American feminine as she attempts to negotiate a Chinese American concept of femininity.[8] If concepts of femininity fluctuate from nation to nation, is it not possible to have variations within the same country? Spelman's realization that gender identity might be affected by various societal factors leads her to question whether all women have the same gender. Her answer is "no: not if gender is a social construction and females become not simply women but particular kinds of women."[9] Clearly if gender is not biological, but constructed, then one's gender construction cannot be isolated from other aspects of one's personhood. Thus for Spelman there is not an essential woman.

Spelman's position that there is not "an essential woman" underscores Judith Butler's point in *Gender Trouble* that the "very subject of women is no longer understood in stable or abiding terms. . . . [T]here is very little agreement after all on what it is that constitutes, or ought to constitute, the category of women."[10] Butler argues that:

> If one "is" a woman, that is surely not all one is; the term fails to be exhaustive. . . . because gender is not always constituted coherently or consistently in different historical contexts, and because gender intersects with racial, class, ethnic, sexual, and regional modalities of discursively constituted identities.[11]

In other words, gender is not the same as sex; females may share the same sex, but not necessarily the same gender. By making a distinction between sex and gender, one may address the multiplicity of women's experiences. According to Butler, "the distinction between sex and gender serves the argument that whatever biological intractability sex appears to have, gender is culturally constructed: hence gender is neither the causal result of sex nor as seemingly fixed as sex."[12] It is this distinction between sex and gender, which seems to be missing in Chodorow's theory. Her theory of identity formation is tied to the child's sex, which then leads to a masculine or feminine gender. Spelman, on the other hand, tries to avoid essentializing women by focusing on gender as a construct.

This desire to avoid essentialism is seen as well in Julia Kristeva's "Stabat Mater," which begins by acknowledging Kristeva's concern about essentialism. She recognizes that speaking of "women" risks eliding differences, but she wonders, "If it is not possible to say of a *woman* what she *is* . . . , would it perhaps be different concerning the *mother,* since that is the only function of the 'other sex' to which we can definitely attribute existence?"[13] It is clear that Kristeva is attempting to tease out the complexities of these configurations; however, her formulations are still questionable. In her analysis of mothers, she assumes a shared experience of motherhood despite possible differences in race, class, or culture. Kristeva's argument is based on her belief that Christian civilizations in particular absorb the feminine into the maternal, which is itself merely a fantasy that overwhelms the "real experience" of motherhood. While this may be true, her conception of a singular experience of motherhood is just as problematic. "Stabat Mater" explores the cult of the Virgin Mary and its relation to the maternity and femininity. It is her belief that the demise of religion and particularly the cult of the Virgin Mary have impoverished motherhood discourse. Thus, she proposes a new discourse, a " 'herethics' encompassing both reproduction and death."[14] This "herethics," however, is only available to women who reproduce. For Kristeva, "[w]omen's reproductive capacity carries within it the potential to overcome, at least to some degree, the 'effects' of the castration that both genders suffer in their separation from the phallic mother."[15] I would argue, however, that if she has not created an essential woman, she has at least created an essential mother. If, however, as Spelman posited earlier, there is no essential woman, can there be an essential mother? Kristeva's essential mother pertains to only a certain kind of mother.

Cornell points out that "Stabat Mater" emphasizes "a certain kind of woman's participation in 'herethics,' 'a woman who seeks to reproduce,' and who, therefore seeks stability."[16] What do we do then with the woman who does not seek to reproduce or reproduces against her wishes? Does reproduction necessarily signify stability? In the American slave economy, maternity was quite unstable as Harriet Jacob's slave narrative, *Incidents in the Life of a Slave Girl* illustrates. Linda notes that "[t]he mother of slaves is very watchful. She knows there is no security for her children."[17] Linda's story does not seem to fit Kristeva's vision of "herethics." Cornell notes that

> although Kristeva constantly reminds us that she is aware of the cultural specificity of her own writing as a European woman ... she also continues to locate the universal, in the sense of what women share, in their capacity to mother and in their maternal role.[18]

The fact that not all women are mothers or able to conceive suggests the limitation of a definition of womanhood that is linked to motherhood, but even among all mothers there is not a universal approach or attitude toward mothering. The maternal role is not fixed and static, but fluctuating and dynamic. This is particularly evident when one thinks about the maternal roles available to aunts, neighbors, and the like, who may not be mothers. Thus the search for the essential woman/mother is futile.

It is this search for the essential woman in the mother figure that Hortense Spillers explodes in "Mama's Baby, Papa's Maybe: An American Grammar Book," when one considers racial difference and American femininities. Spillers' essay critiques the notion of a shared womanhood or motherhood based merely on shared biology. Her exploration of slavery in America suggests that although female slaves gave birth, they did not share the same relation to the maternal as the plantation mistress. Spillers' analysis of the maternal is connected to an analysis of gender. Although she tends to conflate the terms "sex" and "gender," Spillers' argument turns on her belief that the biological function of giving birth cannot be used to determine a socially constructed gender. She critiques Anglo-American feminism's account of gender transmission as not applicable to female slaves. Spillers uses the history of slavery to suggest that slaves and their African-American descendants had a different kind of gender than their white mistresses and their descendants.

Spillers proposes that African slaves in America were robbed of their gender. She is in agreement with Angela Davis, who argues, "The slave system defined Black people as chattel. Since women, no less than men, were viewed as profitable labor-units, they might as well have been genderless as far as the slaveholders were concerned."[19] This point is echoed in Spillers' account of the slave ship's cargo in which slaves are viewed and accounted for as quantitites, not as male and female subjects.[20] Slaves were not seen as men and women, but as merchandise.

Although female slaves might be valued as breeders, "[w]here work was concerned, strength and productivity under the threat of the whip outweighed considerations of sex."[21] Even though there were variations regarding the division of labor between male and female slaves, it was not uncommon for female slaves to perform the same work as men. As Dorothy Sterling notes, "[w]oman's work was scarcely distinguishable from man's."[22] Her collection of oral history, letters, diaries, autobiographies, and newspaper accounts include anecdotes about the work of female slaves:

> I had to do everythin' dey was to do on de outside. Work in de field, chop wood, hoe corn, till sometime I feels like my back surely break. . . . I have done every thing on a farm what a man done 'cept cut wheat. I split rails like man. I used a iron wedge drove into the wood with a maul.[23]

Clearly Sterling's informants recognize sex differences by acknowledging that they worked like men, but sex distinction does not impact labor expectations. According to Moses Grandy, a former slave, a pregnant woman was still expected to work and was often beaten if she did not perform well:

> A woman who gives offense in the field, and is large in a family way, is compelled to lie down over a hole made to receive her corpulency, and is flogged with the whip or beat with a paddle, which has holes in it; at every stroke comes a blister. One of my sisters was so severely punished in this way, that labor was brought on, and the child was born in the field. This very overseer, Mr. Brooks, killed in this manner a girl named Mary.[24]

Grandy's account is substantiated by one of Sterling's informants: "When women was with child they'd dig a hole in the groun' and put their stomach in the hole, and then beat'em. They'd allus whop us."[25] In *Labor of Love, Labor of Sorrow: Black Women, Work, and the Family from Slavery to Present*, Jacqueline Jones comments that the uniformity of this process for whipping the pregnant slave suggests that the practice was not uncommon.[26] This hole serves as an interesting symbol in that it both names and seeks to efface the difference of female maternity. This concession to the female's corpulency is a sex or biological concession, while the beating signifies the refusal of gender concessions. These anecdotes illustrate that female slaves did not necessarily receive preferential treatment due to either their femininity or their maternity.

Elizabeth Fox-Genovese notes that

> the law of slavery had no cause to differentiate between women and men. Its gender blindness, which acknowledged women only as the transmitters of the condition of slavery—and which did not recognize the rape of slave women as a crime—stolidly proclaimed that, in all formal respects, a slave was a slave was a slave.[27]

According to the ideology of the period, all slaves were merely slaves, not men and women, however, the acknowledgment of females as the transmitters of slavery creates a difference. This difference, though, is not a gender difference, but a sex difference based on the female's ability to give birth. When convenient, sex difference was recognized, but not gender difference. The degendering of slaves is a concept that goes back at least as far as Aristotle's *Politics*, according to Spelman: "Aristotle does not allow for the possibility of slaves who are women, but only for slaves who are female—for he draws a distinction between woman and slave in such a way that 'woman' can only mean free woman, not slave woman."[28]

Spelman acknowledges the presence of female slaves by differentiating between sex and gender. However, Spillers inadvertently equates the two by using sex terms (female and male) to discuss gender issues. For example, in describing the slaves as cargo, she states that the slaves are neither male nor female, but quantities. By using the terms "female" and "male," rather than "woman" and "man," Spillers suggests that the slaves were not sexed when they were actually seen as degendered, not unsexed. The fact that gender, not sex, is the central issue is apparent when Spillers recounts the "Brookes Plan," which recommends that five females be counted as four males in terms of the amount of space allotted for them in the cargo hold. She states that some would consider this a gender rule, but she does not because gender is established in the domestic realm and she does not consider the cargo hold a domestic space. Spillers assumes that gendering necessarily takes place within the domestic realm, but this need not be true. The gendering process is a social construction that is affected by one's particular environment, but not limited specifically to the domestic sphere. I would, however, agree that her example is not a gender rule, but for a different reason. The determination of space is based on sex differences, not gender differences. Captain Perry and James Jones made their recommendations about space allotment based on their assumption that females require less space than males. Spillers' argument is based on the view that gendering is a process, yet this process need not ignore the anatomical differences of slave bodies. In other words, the gendering process does not necessarily exclude the possibility of a sexed body. It seems that conceding that the slaves were sexed, but not seen as gendered would strengthen Spillers' argument. After all, slaves were considered livestock and animals are said to be sexed, but not gendered.

Like Spillers, Davis conflates sex and gender. Her argument turns on the fact that slave women were alternately gendered or degendered depending on what suited the owner: "[W]hen it was profitable to exploit them as if they were men, they were regarded, in effect, as genderless, but when they could be exploited, punished and repressed in ways suited only for women, they were locked into their exclusively female roles."[29] I would argue that sex differences account both for slave women being raped and valued for reproduction. It is not that sometimes they had gender and sometimes they did not—in the eyes of the slaveowners, female slaves were always females; they just were not women. According to bell hooks, slaveholders justified working female slaves as hard as males by claiming that they "were not 'real' women but were masculinized sub-human creatures."[30] This may sound like the masculinization of female slaves, as opposed to degendering, but if one looks at their masculinization alongside the feminization of male slaves, the two processes suggest not merely a different gendering, but a degendering of the entire slave population. It is not that slaveholders treated female slaves like men and male slaves like women, rather they treated all slaves as degendered beings. Gender is an aspect of personhood; but since the slaves were not regarded as people, they could not have gender. By not acknowledging the slaves as gendered, slaveholders could more easily think of slaves as chattel, rather than as fellow humans.

Spillers illustrates the degendering of the slaves through the metaphor of "flesh" and "body." The slave trade "marked a theft of the body—a willful and violent . . . severing of the captive body from its motive will, its active desire. Under these conditions, we lose at least gender difference in the outcome."[31] If one reads "flesh" as "sex" and "body" as "gender," then the slave trade turned bodies into degendered but still sexed "flesh." Spillers makes the distinction between "flesh" and "body" the central distinction between the captive slave and the free person. The slave is relegated to mere "flesh," while the free subject maintains a "body." The "flesh," a precursor of the body, represents the presocial. While the raw "flesh" has mass, it is not yet a coherent body, which must also be gendered.

Spillers makes the distinction between "flesh" and "body" vividly come to life as she describes the brutal wounding of slaves. However, the lacerations from the whip are not merely scars, but text. This concept of the scars as text is also seen in Kaja Silverman's discussion of *Histoire d'O*. In her analysis of this Sadean text, Silverman notes the way in which the female body is structured by its wounding: "That body is charted, zoned and made to bear meaning, a meaning which is always subsequently apprehended both by the female subject and her 'commentators' as an internal condition or essence."[32] In other words, the treatment of the female's exterior leads to the constitution of her interior. Silverman limits her discussion to female bodies because they do not have the same access as men to an active discourse.[33] I would like to extend Silverman's discussion of the body to include female and male slave bodies, since both were excluded from active discourse.

Silverman describes the way O's body is formed by the whippings and penetrations. In effect O's body is unmade—she is degendered and then regendered through the wounding of her body. I would argue that the American slave's body was constituted in a similar fashion. Silverman notes that "the whip-lashes which crisscross her [O's] body construct her as an object to be maltreated."[34] The lash marks on the slave body similarly marked the person as a slave. For example, in Sherley Anne Williams' *Dessa Rose,* Dessa is inscribed with whip marks across her hips and branded with an "R" on the thigh. The fact that she is marked as slave in the same area that marks her as woman appears to be a means of depriving Dessa of her femininity.[35] Dessa's shame regarding her scar affects her inner being. As illustrated by her encounters with Harker, Dessa feel less desirable and less feminine as a result of her scarring. The lash not only influenced how she saw herself, but also how others saw her, since the lash inscribed slaves in a manner that could later be read by others. Thus Dessa's scars identified her as a slave. It is interesting to note that it was common practice at abolition meetings to have escaped slaves reveal their bare backs so that the audience might read the text of slavery.

Spillers uses the slave mother to illustrate the disjunction between biology and gender, between the flesh of female slaves and the bodies of white gendered females. According to Spillers, the degendering of the female slave affected her relation to motherhood and thus her relation to gender. She argues that mothering within slavery lacks the benefits accrued by patriarchalized femininity. In fact, under this system patriarchalized femininity is the only female gender.[36] Patriarchal law has a different meaning within the slave economy because the Father's name designates property, not gender.[37] This change in the Father's law is possible because slavery eliminated the African American male's ability to replicate the Father's law as established in dominant society.[38] Spillers notes that children followed the condition of the mother, thereby displacing the usual role for the father assumed by psychoanalytic theory.

This displacement of the male slave was just one means of degendering him. As Davis notes, "if Black women were hardly 'women' in the accepted sense, the slave system also discouraged male supremacy in Black men."[39] The demands of slavery required that male and female slaves be equally submissive to the will of the master. The slave economy placed the slaves in a peculiar situation in which they were supposed to be like, but not quite like, their masters. Familial bonds and gender relations were disregarded, yet slaves were expected to somewhat replicate the values and traditions of their masters. In *The Peculiar Institution,* Kenneth Stampp observes that slaves were usually encouraged to live as families and to follow white moral values, but "slavery inevitably made much of the white caste's family pattern meaningless and unintelligible—and in some ways impossible—for the average bondsman."[40] The impossibility of this replication is built into the slave economy. How are slaves to create families in an environment in which their children do not belong to them and are seen merely as an increase to the master's wealth?

Mothering in the slave community is disrupted so that the child does not belong to the mother, but is owned by the slave master who may or may not be related to it. This is part of the larger kinlessness of slavery, in which family members were often separated without regard to familial ties. Spillers asserts that kinlessness is mandated by slavery because kinship would undermine property relations by allowing children to belong to their mother and father, rather than their owner.[41] In other words, kinship would allow the father's name to establish gender rather than property. Thus kinship must be disrupted to maintain property values. The offspring would lack value if they could belong to slaves rather than their master. Spillers, in fact, separates the concept of "mothering" from birthing. Birth within an enslaved community may not be read as the reproduction of mothering because the female slave is denied parental rights. Thus Spillers argues that birthing is not necessarily mothering, nor is birthing somehow connected to femininity. Davis also distinguishes between motherhood and birthing: "Ideological exaltation of motherhood—as popular as it was during the nineteenth century—did not extend to slaves. In fact, in the eyes of slaveholders, slave women were not mothers at all. . . . They were 'breeders'—animals."[42] Female slaves were not recognized as women and mothers; they were merely sexed property. Davis and Spillers appear to challenge feminists such as Chodorow who essentialize the mothering process.

Female slaves were quite aware of their status as property and the way in which this status affected their ability to mother. This is profoundly depicted in Toni Morrison's *Beloved*. Sethe attempts to kill her children rather than see them taken back into slavery. Cornell notes that in Morrison's retelling of the Medea myth, "the 'meaning,' the deep significance of killing one's children, is problematized, by the slave 'reality' in which the mother is allowed to bear the children but not to 'raise' them."[43] *Beloved* depicts the female slave's very different relation to motherhood. Sociologist Patricia Hill Collins has stated that: "Racial domination and economic exploitation profoundly shape the mothering context."[44] This fact is particularly evident within the slave economy as "even one's own body is not one's property, the white masters can rob Sethe of everything, including her mother's milk. Her maternal labor is supposed to be theirs, not hers or her children's. . . ."[45] In fact, by trying to kill her children, Sethe is asserting her right to her children. In the face of her impotence as a mother, Sethe believes killing her children is the only way that she can protect them. While one might argue that fiction cannot serve as evidence of the female slave's perspective, Morrison's novel is based on the actual event of Margaret Garner's act of infanticide. On January 26, 1856, after a failed escape attempt, Garner slit the throat of her three-year-old girl and wounded her other three children to prevent their master from remanding them to slavery.[46] Morrison's depiction of Sethe's sentiments are also substantiated by Jacobs' slave narrative. The desire to protect one's child from slavery is seen in Linda Brent's narration of her repeated desire to free her children: "I knew the doom that awaited my fair baby in slavery, and I determined to save her from it, or perish in the attempt" (416). Although Linda does not kill her children, she often wishes for their death that they might be spared the horrors of slavery. Thus female as well as male slaves had no parental rights; they were breeders, not parents.

The distinction between parenting and breeding is clearly a valid one. Spillers has already argued that female slaves did not have gender, and thus could not possibly be mothers. The only mothers, according to Spillers, are the white plantation mistresses, who are also the only females with gender. This highlights the difference between sex and gender. As sexed females, slaves may give birth, but only gendered women may mother. Female slaves did not have the option to mother because they were not gendered in the eyes of the slaveholding class. That the female slaves were sexed, however, is evidenced by the fact that female slaves were valued at least in part for their breeding capacity.[47]

Although slaveholders resented the accusation of slave breeding, Frederick Law Olmsted reported, "a slave woman is commonly esteemed least for her laboring qualities, most for those qualities which give value to a broodmare."[48] The value placed on slaves' breeding capacity was in direct proportion to the value of potential offspring: "Every child born to a slave woman became the master's property, and usually the child's ultimate capital value far exceeded the cost of raising him."[49] As breeders, female slaves added to their owner's property because their children followed the condition of the mother. Spillers, however, opens up this legacy by asking whether this refers merely to enslavement or if the mother might not mark the child in some other way.[50]

With this question, Spillers is suggesting that slave mothers pass on more than the condition of slavery—they also continue a maternal line of descent that is in opposition to the American tradition of patrilineage. What makes this situation threatening is that it does not follow the patriarchal norm. According to Abel, Spillers imagines a maternal line of descent that despite the denial of parental rights is not completely destroyed.[51] Although female slaves were breeders, not mothers, they passed on part of themselves; they determined identity by determining the child's "condition." This determination of the child's condition fosters a relationship between African-American males and their mothers that is not replicated in white families, according to Spillers.[52] This maternal contact not only survives the conditions of slavery, but also is in fact a result of enslavement.

This maternal contact becomes a source of strength for Spillers. The female slave's position in slavery created a great difference between her and other females in that her motherhood was at once denied and allowed to create a female line of descent. Spillers argues that this paradoxical position creates a different relation to gender for African-American females, which can be radically empowering. Spillers suggests that since black females have been termed matriarchs, they should actually become matriarchs by reclaiming a maternal genealogy. Abel notes that this would open up the possibility of a new social subject, one determined by neither the phallus/castration dichotomy of Lacanian feminism nor the domestic conventions believed to produce Anglo-American femininity.[53] According to Spillers, African-American women have been gendered differently because of a history of slavery and degendering, but they should not become like Anglo-American women; rather, they should embrace their different gender as a strength. Elsewhere, Spillers comments on the power of these types of feminist revisions to "at once define a new position of attack and lay claim to a site of ancestral imperative."[54]

Although Spillers makes an excellent case regarding the degendering of slaves, she does not emphasize that such degendering is from the viewpoint of the slaveowners. The slaves probably considered themselves gendered. For example, *Incidents in the Life of a Slave Girl* illustrates the disjunction between the female slave's interpretation of her womanhood and the slaveowner's. Throughout the text, Linda appeals to the white woman reader and the feminine values and sense of motherhood that she shares with them. Linda observes that the slave mother "may be an ignorant creature, degraded by the system that has brutalized her from childhood; but she has a mother's instincts, and is capable of feeling a mother's agonies" (350). These are not the words of a female who sees herself and other slaves as mere degendered breeders. Jacobs purposely makes use of elements of sentimental fiction, which is regarded as a feminine genre, and identifies a female audience as part of her attempt to engender herself in their eyes. She realizes that she does not fit within their construct of femininity, yet she seeks to include herself within the feminine realm. This suggests that Jacobs realized she was not seen as a woman, but did see herself as one. Jacobs and other slaves surely experienced great confusion when they were removed from their homeland and reconfigured as mere "flesh," as opposed to gendered bodies.

In order to better appreciate the confusion experienced by slaves entering the United States, it is necessary to look at their homelands.

American slaves were brought from various areas of Africa, but scholars such as Sterling Stuckey, Philip Curtin, and James H. Rawley agree that the majority of the slaves came from the central and western regions of Africa: Congo-Angola, Nigeria, Dahomey, Togo, the Gold Coast, and Sierra Leone.[55] With such divergent backgrounds, it is difficult to reconstruct a common heritage, but some similarities can be found. For example, Kamene Okonjo notes that several West African traditional societies had "dual-sex" political systems in which "each sex manages its own affairs, and women's interests are represented at all levels."[56] According to Okonjo, "the dual nature of the system aimed at harmonious and effective division of labor by which both sexes would receive adequate attention to their needs."[57] Thus a division of labor based on sex difference does not necessarily lead to a hierarchical arrangement with one gender becoming the dominant one.

The division of labor was also practiced in antebellum America, but with different connotations—white plantation women were confined to the private sphere, while white men dominated the public arena. However in West Africa, according to Niara Sudarkasa, " 'the public domain' was not conceptualized as *the world of men*," as both sexes played important roles in the public domain.[58] Sudarkasa also stipulates that she is unaware of an indigenous African society in which men and women's labor was valued or rewarded differently.[59] This point is substantiated by Annie Lebeuf, who states that although separate tasks are assigned to men and women, the separation stresses the complementary nature of the tasks, nor does the division imply superiority of one over the other.[60] Gender relations have changed in Africa since colonization, but the observations made by these historians illustrate the experience of many Africans prior to their enslavement.

The fact that the division of labor in several West African societies was not hierarchical in nature may be attributed to a general de-emphasis of gender. Sudarkasa points to the existence of woman to woman marriage in Africa as an example of an emphasis on seniority and social standing, rather than an emphasis on gender.[61] Sudarkasa notes that the absence of gender in the pronouns of many African languages and the interchangeability of first names among men and women may be related to this de-emphasis of gender. She observes that many cultural traditions such as dress and adornment, religious ceremonies, and intragender socialization patterns suggest that Africans privilege seniority and other signs of status while de-emphasizing gender.[62] She also argues that the presence of woman to woman marriage "signifies most of all that gender is not the sole basis for recruitment to the 'husband' role in Africa; hence, the authority that attaches to that role is not gender-specific."[63] If one complicates Sudarkasa's argument by distinguishing between sex and gender, one might argue that woman to woman marriage merely implies the insignificance of sex, not gender. A husband may be male or female, but still retains certain gendered qualities; however, Sudarkasa's emphasis on seniority and status suggests that these issues take the place of gender in these societies. Thus the husband role is not based on gender, but status, which is equally available to males and females. The work of Okonjo and Sudarkasa suggests that West African societies did have specific sex roles—different things were expected of males and females—but these sex roles did not carry the same connotations as they did in antebellum America.

It is clear from the research of these scholars that gender was manifested differently in Africa; however, the significance of this difference continues to be debated. While the work of Sudarkasa, Okonjo, and Lebeuf suggests that there was perhaps a more egalitarian relationship between the sexes because they were both involved in the public domain, other scholars argue that this difference does not translate to egalitarian relations. In her discussion of dual sex systems, Christie Farnham argues that separate is not equal; the systems were complementary, not parallel. She states, "That this work was organized and regulated by the women themselves does not erase the subordinate character of the enterprise."[64] Farnham's study of slave families traces family structures within African societies and despite the variations, she asserts that traditional African women were often able to be self-reliant due to separate property and income, decision-making power, as well as the power of women's organizations and allies in natal villages. However, she warns against confusing self-reliance with equality.[65] Although Farnham's warning has merit, her view seems clouded by her investment in proving that female slaves were not matriarchs.

She asserts that the female slave's work in the home and the field or the private and public spheres should not be seen as equality. Farnham describes their agricultural labor as "double duty, not power parity" because the public sphere did not provide access to wealth or power.[66] I am in agreement with her assessment of the over worked female slave and the inaccuracy of labeling them matriarchs, however, I believe she goes too far in her dismissal of the authority of African women prior to their removal to America.

Scholars continue to debate the degree of this authority, but it is clear that gender relations were different in precolonial Africa. Claire Robertson argues against any matriarchal society equivalent to a patriarchal society, but she does allow for the validity of matrifocal African societies. Matrifocality describes a society in which females *"in their role as mothers* are the focus of familial relationships." This, however, does not mean that fathers are absent, but that mothers are the focus. In matrifocal societies, the mother-child bond is the most important relationship.[67] However, Robertson insists that while many precolonial West African societies were partially matrifocal in that women actively provided for the family's maintenance, men normally made decisions. But in spite of this concession to men's tendency to make decisions, Robertson also alleges that there are African societies in which women had and have more autonomy and political power than European women have ever had and thus it is possible to suggest that African cultural forms may have encouraged more authoritative roles for women but this did not translate to African-American matriarchs.[68] The controversy about African-American matriarchs will be discussed at greater length later in this chapter, but I would like to draw attention to the way in which this debate colors the study of gender in precolonial Africa. This is a murky area in which consensus may never be reached and the pendulum swings between romanticizing African women's power and the imposition of Western gender traditions upon African societies. My intention is to place myself somewhere in between these polarities. My research suggests that African societies maintained different gender relations that allowed African women more access to power. Perhaps they were still dominated in some respects by men; however, when African women were brought to America and exercised traditional

African gender relations, their actions carried a different meaning on American soil.

Upon their arrival in North America, an attempt was made to strip slaves of their cultural traditions and sex roles. As mentioned earlier, female slaves often worked alongside males. In "African Women in the Atlantic Slave Trade," Herbert S. Klein notes that several studies confirm that planters showed little to no sexual preferences in regards to labor use: "Women in most American plantations were, in fact, overrepresented in all the brute force fieldhand labor occupations, and in mature plantation areas they tended to be the majority of actual fieldgang plantation workers."[69] Although fieldwork may have fit with African traditions, Fox-Genovese notes that it departed from Euro-American views of women's gender roles.[70] Historian, Jacqueline Jones, observes that although frontier women probably cleared, plowed, and harvested land, white upper- and middle-class women confined themselves to the house. White female indentured servants might be sent to work the fields on occasion, but this was not their ordinary duty. Regardless of class, white women were not regular field workers.[71] According to the dominant culture's perspective, female slaves often performed men's work.[72] The demands of slavery influenced the slaveowners' decision to relax their strict view of gender roles. Thus, unlike white women, female slaves were not limited by gender roles because it was more economical to disregard gender difference and work female slaves as hard as the males.

Davis suggests that American industrialization led to a division between the home and the public economy and thereby more firmly established female inferiority; however, the "economical arrangements of slavery contradicted the hierarchical sexual roles incorporated in the new ideology."[73] This contradiction was then accounted for through the myth that female slaves were not really women, but "masculinized sub-human creatures."[74] This myth, however, only accounts for part of the situation. By masculinizing the female slaves, slaveowners account for their ability to cope with what were considered to be male roles, but this did not account for the female slave's ability to perform "feminine" tasks, such as cooking, housekeeping, and child rearing. The ability to perform these tasks allowed female slaves to live up to the expectation that women be domestic. However, slavery would not have survived if female slaves were seen as women, not chattel. Therefore, female slaves were excluded from womanhood based on their lack of "purity." Female slaves were described as promiscuous, whether their masters forced them into the role of concubine or they freely chose to enter into premarital sexual relations.

The supposed promiscuity of female slaves went against the societal definition of true womanhood, which was based on a woman's chastity. According to Judith Van Allen, "The ideal of Victorian womanhood . . . was of a sensitive, morally superior being who was the hearthside guardian of Christian virtues and sentiments absent in the outside world."[76] However, this ideal of womanhood was not available to female slaves, who were constantly reminded that they were not true women. True womanhood, as defined by Barbara Welter, consisted of the four cardinal virtues of piety, purity, submissiveness, and domesticity. The loss of purity was associated with madness or death, since "purity was as essential as piety to a young woman, its absence as unnatural and unfeminine."[76] Obviously a womanhood based on purity or chastity would not be available to the vast majority of female slaves, who were frequently raped and otherwise immodestly treated. In *Sex and Racism in America,* Calvin Hernton argues that:

> When any group of women has to submit to such atrocities, when they are denied the smallest privacy of body, when they have to stand in public before men and women naked on an auction block and be fingered in the most intimate places, it is absurd to ask them to esteem themselves as restrained ladies and conduct their sexual activities along the lines of female refinery.[77]

Thus, the institution of slavery necessarily eradicated the possibility of female slaves fitting the definition of true womanhood.

The portrayal of female slaves as promiscuous may be attributed to two different developments. The stereotype of promiscuous slaves helped to substantiate slavery because it could be argued that the slaves were heathen, who should be enslaved. The promiscuity may also be accounted for based on cultural differences. Denise Paulme notes that despite the various modes of life among African females, certain features are common, including a great deal of premarital sexual freedom and the importance of motherhood.[78] The premarital sexual freedom provided to young African females was foreign to their Christian counterparts. In *Roll, Jordan, Roll,* Eugene Genovese notes that seventeenth- and eighteenth-century Europeans were shocked by West African sexual mores: "—in a word, the different standards of behavior—convinced Europeans that Africans had no standards, no morals, no restraints."[79] Slaves, particularly female slaves, were described as promiscuous. Michele Wallace argues that although a female slave might live with a series of males, once she chose a mate, she was usually faithful. Premarital sex was not disapproved of within the slave community, but adultery was. Slave owners viewed premarital sex as evidence of sexual promiscuity, but Wallace argues that these actions were part of an African heritage, in which this was common behavior.[80] John W. Blassingame's *The Slave Community* supports Wallace's argument. He observes that the sexual mores of traditional African societies were quite different from those of Europe and antebellum America. He notes that although some African societies required premarital virginity, many accepted and others institutionalized premarital sex as part of the courtship process. In fact, some African societies include the defloration of young girls as part of their puberty rites.[81] The acceptance of premarital sex, however, did not extend to promiscuity. According to Blassingame, "While providing socially sanctioned forms for engaging in pre-marital sex, African societies generally forbade extramarital sex, punishing adulterers with heavy fines, divorce, slavery, and sometimes death."[82] Herbert Gutman also notes that "prenuptial intercourse and bridal pregnancy are not peculiar to slave populations; the decline of these phenomena is often associated with the early stages of 'modernization.' "[83] In other words, the slaves were not amoral or immoral, but merely had a different set of morals and values.

Africans' different attitude toward sex is connected to their religious views and high regard for motherhood. According to Blassingame, "Africans viewed sex as fundamental to procreation, and procreation as a religious duty to ensure the continuation of the family line established by one's ancestors. Barrenness was a

calamity in Africa."[84] Barbara Christian's analysis of motherhood
in Africa finds that throughout the African continent, motherhood
has been central to many religions, philosophies, and ways of life.[85]
Christian points out that although the high regard for mothers did
not lead to matriarchies, the societies were very much mother-
centered.[86] Christian's findings are reinforced by Monique Gessain's
description of Coniaqui women, of whom she observes that the
"essential value of a woman lies in her fecundity."[87] All of these
comments illustrate the importance of procreation and motherhood.
How were first-generation female slaves to respond to the cruel
change from performing the mother role to merely being breeders?
Fox-Genovese argues that West African societies:

> endowed femininity in general and motherhood in particular
> with a sacred character. Slavery negated the sacredness—in
> effect negated womanhood as an ideological category. In the
> absence of an ideology of womanhood— ideology of gender
> difference—female slaves lost a vital part of the basis for gender
> solidarity and identification.[88]

Fox-Genovese, like Davis, seems to suggest that slavery degendered
female slaves, but I would argue that the degendering process was
not successful—female slaves did not view themselves as degendered.
While female slaves like Harriet Jacobs borrowed the language of
true womanhood, they did not merely emulate their upper- and
middle-class Anglo counterparts' concept of true womanhood, but
developed a different expression of gender.

The new environment created by slavery meant that the trans-
planted Africans would have to create a different culture, including
different gender expectations. It is not that the Africans were without culture, but they could not maintain all aspects of their culture
in the new world. According to Stampp, "In Africa the Negroes had
been accustomed to a strictly regulated family life and a rigidly
enforced moral code. But in America the disintegration of their
social organization removed the traditional sanctions which had
encouraged them to respect their old customs."[90] The removal of
these traditional sanctions created a vacuum, which was filled with
new traditions. These new traditions, however, were not always

radically different from their predecessors—enslavement did not completely strip the Africans of their culture. Fox-Genovese supports this contention:

> Transplantation to the New World, however violent and disorienting, never eradicated African conventions but did divorce them from the material and institutional conditions in which they had flourished; and it exposed the slaves to the power of masters with views and attitudes different from their own.[90]

Thus the slaves created a new culture, "a way of seeing and dealing with life, that was based upon the amalgamation of their African past and the forced realities of their American experience—in other words, an African-American culture."[91]

To some extent slaves were encouraged to follow Anglo-American role models because they were judged by the same standards, but slavery restricted their ability to follow these examples. For example, middle-class Anglo women were expected to be homemakers, but this was rarely expected of female slaves. According to Stampp:

> The slave woman was first a full-time worker for her owner, and only incidentally a wife, mother, and home-maker. She spent a small fraction of her time in the house; she often did no cooking or clothes making; and she was not usually nurse to her husband or children during illness.[92]

Fox-Genovese supports Stampp's observation, but she also comments on the different way gender roles developed within the slave community. She notes that female slaves

> did not primarily devote themselves to the care of their own children and houses, and their gender roles did not necessarily emanate directly from their relations with black men or from African traditions. Within the big house, they performed the labor deemed appropriate to the gender roles of white women, but they worked as servants—the opposite of mistress.[93]

Fox-Genovese argues that although female slaves might cook and sew for their own families, their roles as mothers, wives, and daughters depended upon the will of a master who could separate the family at any time. Due to these circumstances, Fox-Genovese believes that the female slave's sense of gender identity remained separate from gender relations and roles.[94] Thus, the domestic activities that might form the mistress' gender did not form the female slave's in the same way because the mistress was interacting with her family, while the slave was responding to a power outside of her immediate family.

The effect that slavery has had on gender formation has spawned heated debate. In *The Negro Family in the United States*, E. Franklin Frazier argues that:

> As a rule, the Negro woman as wife or mother was the mistress of her cabin, and, save for the interference of master and overseer, her wishes in regard to mating and family matters were paramount. Neither economic necessity nor tradition had instilled in her the spirit of subordination to masculine authority.[95]

Frazier's thesis was later supported by Daniel Patrick Moynihan's 1965 report, which blamed the problems of the black family on a matriarchy that could be traced back to slavery.[96] The criticism that arose from the report led to a reevaluation of slavery and the matriarchy theory was reversed. Robert Fogel and Stanley Engerman's *Time on the Cross: The Economics of American Negro Slavery* finds that men played the dominant role in the slave community:

> It is not true that "the typical slave family was matriarchal in form" and that the "husband was at most his wife's assistant." Nor is it true that the "male slave's only crucial function within the family was that of siring offspring." For better or worse, the dominant role in slave society was played by men, not women. It was men who occupied virtually all of the managerial slots available to slaves. There were very few female overseers or drivers.[97]

This assessment is supported by Genovese's view that "slaves from their own experience had come to value a two-parent, male-centered household no matter how much difficulty they had in realizing the ideal."[98] Deborah White critiques these later interpretations for de-emphasizing the female slave's role. She argues along the same lines as Denise Paulme when she asserts that despite the fact that female slaves did most of the domestic chores, this was not evidence of male dominance.[99] White concludes that chores performed by female slaves and the presence of highly ranked female slave occupations suggest they maintained roles that complemented those held by men. Female slaves were able to obtain a sense of self apart from male slaves and white men.[100] White's conclusions are in line with Davis' contention that domestic life in the slave quarters was one of sexual equality in which the sexual division of domestic labor did not appear hierarchical. Although there was sex differentiation in labor, it was not always rigid and the work performed by males and females was equally necessary.[101] Familial duties, whether performed by males or females, were not paid activities but they were necessary to maintain the family and thus were not differentially rewarded.

Davis also argues that domestic labor in the slave quarter did not have the same stigma as it did in the mistress' household. She notes that "traditionally the labor of females, domestic work is supposed to complement and confirm their inferiority."[102] This, however, was not the case for the female slave. When she performed domestic labor, "she was performing the *only* labor which could not be directly and immediately claimed by the oppressor."[103] When she worked in the field, it was for the master's benefit. Even bearing children was for the master, but when she cared for that child or her husband, the master's benefit was incidental and secondary. The primary benefactors were the slave family and the surrounding community. Domestic labor became a tool for survival.

White also observes that for the female slave, domestic labor was not necessarily limited to the home. So-called "woman's work" often required skills that were highly valued because they could be used to attain higher status in slave society. For example, cooking and sewing were considered "woman's work," but they were also skilled occupations. White notes that sewing, particularly when done for white families, could be seen as a skilled art. Midwifery and doctoring were also female occupations that raised a woman's social standing.[104]

According to White, female slaves did not receive the traditional middle-class benefits of matrimony, such as the provision of food, clothing, and shelter by their husbands. She argues that in most societies in which men control women, that control is based on male ownership and control of property, but since this was not part of slave life, female slaves developed independence from male slaves.[105] In fact, both female and male slaves provided supplementary provisions for the family. For example in *Incidents*, Linda's grandmother was given permission to sell her homemade crackers in order to clothe herself and her children.[106] One of Sterling's informants in *We Are Your Sisters* reports, "My mama could hunt good as any man. Ustuh be a coup'la pedluh men come 'round. My mammy'd a'ways have a pile o'hides tuh trade with 'em fo' calico prints. She'd have coon hides 'n' mink, 'n' beavers, lawd!"[107] This suggests that female slaves provided important services for their families.

Despite the importance of the female slave's role in family life, this did not lead to a matriarchy. Davis argues that the institution of slavery did not foster or recognize a matriarchal family. This could not happen because a matriarchy would entail power that female slaves did not have. Slaveholders could not risk acknowledging any type of slave power whether male or female. White asserts that rather than forming a matriarchal society, the slave community was matrifocal. Thus this matrifocal slave community developed in a manner quite different from the larger patriarchal American society. This different development also led to different gender conventions.

According to Joyce Ladner, "the degradation a woman suffered in slavery had total effects on all aspects of her life—her identity as a woman and as an African, her relationship and roles with regard to her husband and family."[108] As a result of slavery, black females were at times labeled Amazons, Aunt Jemimas, and Sapphires. These negative stereotypes have affected the way black females were (and are) perceived by their own race and themselves.[109] Female slaves' ability to survive the horrors of slavery served to justify the proliferation of negative stereotypes and their continued enslavement—if they were real women, they would never survive. These various stereotypes from Sapphire to Mammy seek to create a slanted view of the black female—she is either too masculine, too sexual, or too asexual to be a real woman, let alone a real person.

Each of these stereotypes attempted to contain the female slave. "Each image represented a caricature of attributes that whites celebrated in themselves. Each emphasized physical attributes over social, as if whites had difficulty depicting their slaves in adult gender roles."[110] These stereotypes also helped to maintain slavery by describing female slaves as something other than ladies. They were not real women because they could perform hard labor—they were masculine and animalistic. They were not individuals, but servants who loved their masters. They were not chaste ladies, but wanton sex machines.[111] These stereotypes sought to degender and dehumanize female slaves. Fox-Genovese notes that these images "captured dominant white views of gender roles among slaves and, not least, white anxieties about their relations with servants whom they had tried to deprive of autonomy in gender roles as in all else."[112] These images sought to define the slaves. For each image there is an opposite image, thereby disallowing any room for a middle ground or individuality.

The institution of slavery did not merely affect the gender identification of female slaves, but also their African American descendants. As Spillers notes, "Their enslavement relegated them to the marketplace of the flesh, an act of commodifying so thoroughgoing that the daughters labor even now under their outcome."[113] The effect of the legacy of slavery is particularly evident in the writing of black women who seek to respond to the cult of true womanhood prevalent during the nineteenth century. A number of black women writers turned to the pen and the power of the word to reconfigure a womanhood that included themselves and their black sisters. It is significant that these writers do not call for an emulation of "true womanhood," but instead argue for multiple reconstructions of feminine gender. They are reclaiming a maternal genealogy by writing texts that call for radically different concepts of femininity.

2

The Cult of True Womanhood and Its Revisions

Before discussing the way in which black women writers sought to include black females within the realm of womanhood, I will analyze the cult of true womanhood, which delineated the ideal feminine virtues of the era as well as the concomitant glorification of motherhood. The period 1820–1860 extolled the cult of true womanhood. Barbara Welter has defined the four cardinal virtues of true womanhood as piety, purity, submissiveness, and domesticity. These virtues defined what it meant to be a mother, daughter, sister, wife—woman. These qualities were not merely goals to strive for, but necessary components of womanhood: "Without them, no matter whether there was fame, achievement or wealth, all was ashes. With them she was promised happiness and power."[1] Although this ideal of womanhood was presented for all women to emulate, only white middle-class women

could hope to embody it. This racial bias is apparent in a comment
by Welter: "the nineteenth-century American woman had to uphold
the pillars of the temple with her frail *white* hand."[2] The connection between whiteness and purity is also evident in the numerous
analogies used to describe virginal women: "delicate as lilies, spot-
less as doves, polished as alabaster, fragile as porcelain—but above
all, pure as the driven snow (with its inherent connotation of coldness)."[3] These associations are part of the reason that great emphasis was placed on women's complexions. Catherine Clinton notes in
The Plantation Mistress that "tanned skin . . . was an unforgivable
and unnatural departure for the southern lady. Not only were there
unfavorable racial connotations associated with darker skin, but
ladies preserved their complexion as testifying to their pampered
status within an agrarian society."[4] Thus the cult of true womanhood was not only geared toward white women, but white women
of means. This ideal of womanhood placed certain white women on
a pedestal.

A proper lady of the period was expected to remain in the home.
There were regional and class differences in the type of work performed in the home, but it was clear that the woman's sphere was
the home. In *The Bonds of Womanhood,* Nancy Cott argues that
women had traditionally worked in the household long before the
concept of separate spheres was developed. However, the end of the
eighteenth and beginning of the nineteenth centuries brought
change:

> The shift of production and exchange away from the house-
> hold, and a general tightening of functional "spheres" (special-
> ization) in the economy and society at large, made it seem
> "separate." But a cultural halo ringing the significance of home
> and family—doubly brilliant because both religious and secu-
> lar energies gave rise to it—reconnected woman's "separate"
> sphere with the well-being of society.[5]

Thus women were expected to "mother" the society by providing
moral values and nurturance.

Together the cult of true womanhood and separate spheres ideology developed into a cult of motherhood. Cott observes, "The canon

of domesticity made motherhood a social and political role that also defined women as a class, and became the prism through which all expectations of and prescriptions for women were refracted."[6] Thus the ideals of motherhood and womanhood were often collapsed into one set of ideals that implied women and mothers were one and the same. This consolidation of women and mothers is what made the removal of maternal rights from female slaves a means of degendering. Because women and mothers were seen as synonymous, disallowing female slaves the rights and privileges of motherhood also denied their status as women and omitted them from the cult of true womanhood.

While the ideals reflected in the cult of true womanhood often limited women's behavior, according to some historians, this cult of domesticity also allowed for some degree of power, as Cott notes:

> Legally and economically the husband/father controlled the family, but rhetorically the vocation of domesticity gave women the domestic sphere for their own, to control and influence. Motherhood was proposed as the control lever with which women could budge the world and, in practice, it offered the best opportunity to women to heighten their domestic power.[7]

Motherhood gained significance because mothers were responsible for raising the young men, who would in turn become the future rulers of society.

Although the separate spheres ideology increased the importance of motherhood, antebellum American society was not described as matriarchal or even matrifocal. What differentiated this cult of motherhood from the African tradition of matrifocality, which later opened the African-American community to criticism for its "matriarchal" qualities? In her discussion of matrifocality, Nancy Tanner distinguishes matrifocality from Anglo-American "mommism." Tanner argues that:

> Among middle-class whites, women create affectively central roles for themselves within the household as a counterbalance to their economic and emotional dependence on their husbands; women can gain considerable power over their offspring,

but this must be seen in the context of their powerlessness in the wider society.[8]

What differentiates "mommism" from matrifocality is that matrifocal or "mother-focused" societies have relatively egalitarian relationships between the sexes and both women and men have significant roles in the economy and rituals.[9] Another important distinction is the duration of the mother's role. The mother's importance in African societies appears to remain strong even as the child moves into adulthood, but this did not appear to be the case in antebellum America. In *Ar'n't I A Woman?* Deborah White observes that "it was above all as mothers that women were credited with social influence as the chief transmitters of religious and moral values."[10] This influence, however important, was limited as children were expected to become self-governing as soon as possible.[11]

Motherhood was seen as a form of self-denial—women were expected to give themselves over to the children. The self-effacing quality of child rearing is particularly evident in the act of breast-feeding, in which the mother is literally giving herself to her child in the form of milk. In *Womanhood in America,* Mary Ryan notes, "Breast-feeding was sanctified as 'one of the most important duties of female life,' 'one of peculiar, inexpressible, felicity,' and the 'sole occupation and pleasure' of a new mother."[12] Breast-feeding took on symbolic significance; it was not merely nourishing the child, but the beginning of the child's socialization, "for a mother's milk and the warmth with which she offered it also conveyed the child's first moral lessons."[13] The eminence of the breast-feeding woman is reinforced by images of the virgin mother, which emphasize nursing, and hence a connection is made between mothers and piety. Consequently, the breast-feeding woman became the icon of motherhood.

Despite the symbolic significance placed on breast-feeding, Clinton observes that nursing was often physically exhausting. By the mid-nineteenth century, many upper-class southern women alleviated their physical distress by utilizing white wet nurses or slaves to nurse their babies.[14] It was often Mammy who would nurse and care for the children. As caretaker, housekeeper, and family advisor, Mammy fit the ideal of womanhood, White observes; adding,

"As the personification of the ideal slave, and the ideal woman, Mammy was an ideal symbol of the patriarchal tradition."[15] The fact that Mammy was a symbol is precisely Clinton's point in *The Plantation Mistress*. Clinton argues that Mammy "is not merely a stereotype, but in fact a figment of the combined romantic imaginations of the contemporary southern ideologue and the modern southern historian." Pre–Civil War records indicate only a few examples of female slaves who occupied the position attributed to Mammy. Clinton notes that it was not until after Emancipation that black females began to hold such positions in white households.[16] However, the image of Mammy was used to illustrate the closeness of the slave to the master and his family. This supposed closeness of master and slave was often more imagined than real.

Mammy is seen as the ideal mother-figure, yet ironically, in breast-feeding the white mistress' children, she is often unable to perform the same duties for her own children, which is what keeps her from attaining the title of "mother" within the rubrics of the cult of true womanhood. In the first chapter, I noted the significance of domestic duties performed for one's family versus the master's family. Mammy's mothering is separated from her own family, so it has a different impact on her gender identity and the way that others view her. Linda's grandmother in *Incidents in the Life of a Slave Girl* provides a good example of Mammy's privileged role in slave society. She is more respected than most slaves because she is not seen as promiscuous, and while she may not be a Christian, she is seen as a godly woman. Mammy appears to meet the qualifications of true womanhood: piety, purity, domesticity, and submissiveness, but she is still not a true woman. I would argue that her continued exclusion is based on the artificialness of her position. Mothering was viewed as "natural," however, Mammy does not mother her "natural" children, but her master's.

This tension between the roles of Mammy and mother is illustrated in Sherley Anne Williams' *Dessa Rose*. When Rufel, a white woman, relates her memories of Mammy, she is interrupted by Dessa's accusation, "You don't even know mammy." Rufel attempts to prove that she does indeed know Mammy, only to have Dessa declare, " 'Mammy' ain't nobody name, not they real one."[17] Once she calms down, Rufel does remember that Mammy's name was

Dorcas. She also acknowledges that Mammy was not a birthday present as she claimed, but a servant for all of the women of the house—at eleven hundred dollars, she was too expensive for a little girl's gift. Rufel's family called Dorcas Mammy to give the illusion that she'd been with the family for a long time, but Rufel was thirteen when Mammy was bought. Rufel's memory of Mammy is countered by Dessa's memory of mammy, Dessa's mother. When Dessa takes issue with Rufel's memory of Mammy, she is not actually thinking about Dorcas, but her own mammy. Rufel and Dessa are actually speaking about two different women, but they offer competing definitions of M(m)ammy.[18] Rufel wants Dorcas to be Mammy, while Dessa wants mammy to be her mother.

Dessa is angered by what she views as Rufel's exploitative use of Mammy to fulfill white needs. In response to Rufel's reference to her Mammy, Dessa says, " 'Your "mammy"'! No *white* girl could ever have taken *her* place in mammy's bosom; no one. 'You ain't got no "mammy," ' she snapped" (125). Dessa responds with anger to Rufel's fond memories of Mammy. What Rufel does not realize is that her memories of Mammy are bought at a cost, literally and figuratively. Not only must Rufel's family pay for Mammy's labor, but also children like Dessa pay emotionally because every time Mammy enters the master's home she leaves her own. In fulfilling the master's needs, Mammy is forced to deprive her own family's needs.

In creating Mammy, slaveholders interfered with the slave family's conception of motherhood. Motherhood is in a sense perverted by removing if from the affective realm and transforming it into a service performed against one's will. This not only places Mammy in an artificial relationship with the master's family, but also diminishes her ability to provide for her own family, including the ability to nurse her own children. In antebellum society, the breast-feeding woman reached mass symbolic proportions, so how were slaves to respond to the removal of nursing females to serve the master's needs? The female slave as Mammy was at once the ideal mother and the antithesis of motherhood. This in turn undermines her ability to be a true woman.

The connection between breast-feeding, motherhood, and womanhood was not lost on the female slaves or on their descendants who return to the scene of the crime in their fiction. This is why Dessa cannot bear to acknowledge that Rufel is the only nursing woman, and in Toni Morrison's *Beloved*, breast-feeding figures as the primary means by which Sethe defines herself as a mother and a woman. When Sethe escapes from slavery, her main concern is getting her milk to the baby girl she sent ahead. Sethe, however, was not able to bring her milk before having it violently taken by the Garner boys. When Sethe tells Paul D about the boys taking her milk and later whipping her for telling Mrs. Garner, Paul D focuses on the fact that they beat Sethe while she was pregnant, but Sethe keeps repeating that they took her milk. Sethe's sense of violation stems more from the theft of her milk than from the beating. This milk theft may be seen as analogous to the use of Mammy as a wet nurse. As *Dessa Rose* and *Beloved* illustrate, Mammy is often reduced to a body to be used. Clinton says of Mammy, "the image reduced black women to an animal like state of exploitation: Mammies were to be milked, warm bodies to serve white needs—an image with its own sexual subtext."[19] Hence, Mammy is ultimately a symbol of exploitation rather than an illustration of cross-racial bonding.

Although Morrison's text is a fictive account, a comment by Moses Grandy suggests that the mistreatment of pregnant slaves was not uncommon: "I have seen the overseer beat them with raw hide, so that the blood and milk flew mingled from their breasts."[20] In this account the beating and milk theft are one and the same. Although slaves might lose their milk through violence, their milk also dried up because of other effects of slavery. In *Uncle Tom's Cabin*, Harriet Beecher Stowe relates the story of Prue. Prue is unable to nurse as the result of a fever she contracted while nursing her mistress, yet Prue's mistress refuses to buy milk for Prue's starving infant. Prue is then forced to lock her baby in a garret so her mistress will not be disturbed by its cries. It eventually starves to death.

In *Dessa Rose*, Dessa is unable to nurse her baby because her milk has dried up. Then, in an interesting reversal of the Mammy myth, Rufel, a white woman, nurses Dessa's child. A white woman nursing a black child would have shocked the sensibilities of the antebellum South, but Williams presents this stunning reversal placidly: "The baby was hungry and she fed him" (98). This was not, however, a simple act. Rufel initially picked up the newborn without thought. Not until she looked down on "the nut-brown face flattened against the pearly paleness of her breast, had she become conscious of what she was doing. A wave of embarrassment had swept over her and she had looked guiltily around the parlor" (105). Seeing his brown skin against her white skin, Rufel realized the impropriety of what she was doing, but she reassured herself that no one would know, and after all, he was a hungry baby.

Carole Boyce Davies observes, "Breast-feeding, as Williams poses it, is an expression of responsibility for raising the children and is not assigned racially in *Dessa Rose*. Dessa and Rufel consistently exchange maternal functions depending on need."[21] This type of "cooperative care-giving," according to Davies, is not available to Morrison's Sethe. Sethe's reaction to her appropriated milk and her reduction to animal status is to attempt to hold on to what she believes is hers.[22] This results in a "thick love," which leads Sethe to kill her child rather than allowing her to return to slavery.

Sethe is an example of what Joanne Braxton refers to as "the outraged mother." According to Braxton's definition, "The arche-typal outraged mother travels alone through the darkness to im-part a sense of identity and 'belongingness' to her child. . . . Implied in all her actions and fueling her heroic ones is abuse of her people and her person."[23] Braxton refers to Harriet Jacobs' Linda Brent as an outraged mother because she refused to escape with-out ensuring the safety of her children.[24] Throughout *Incidents*, Linda is motivated by freedom for her children. Although Linda does not carry out her thoughts of infanticide, she too considers death a means of releasing her children from slavery. Linda's desire for death is similar to Prue's death wish after the death of her child. Linda and Prue alternately desire death for themselves and their children, but Sethe actually acts out her desire. Davies argues that *Beloved* "simultaneously critiques exclusive mother-love as it asserts the necessity for Black women to claim some-thing as theirs."[25] Thus infanticide is both an expression of love and ownership.

Sethe, however, is not alone in her "thick love"; Stowe's Cassy also takes her child's life. Gillian Brown describes Cassy's actions as an example of "outraged domesticity." Brown argues:

> Cassy's life is a textbook on domestic violation: she has lost
> her children to the slave trade and her sexual integrity to her
> various masters. She has even murdered her last child in
> order to prevent another separation and loss. . . . Cassy repre-
> sents outraged domesticity; violated by slavery, she protects
> her child from slavery by her own violence.[26]

Cassy killed her third child with laudanum after her first two were
sold away from her. Although Cassy, like Sethe, takes her child's
life, she does not experience the haunting grief that Sethe encounters. Cassy does not regret her actions: "'It's one of the few things
that I'm glad of, now. I am not sorry, to this day; he, at least, is out
of pain.'"[27] Cassy clearly considers her actions to have been in the
best interest of her child. Cassy, Sethe, and Linda illustrate Harryette
Mullen's contention that "although the majority of slave women chose
to give life, even if it meant that their children would be slaves,
Morrison's novel, by stressing the alternative underscores that motherhood was an active choice, as does Jacob's narrative."[28] The same
may be said about Stowe's text. The act of infanticide highlights the
active choice of motherhood and the "maternal imprint," which Spillers argues survives the master's attack. Female slaves not only
determine the status of the child, but first and foremost whether the
child would in fact survive.

This very brief analysis of motherhood in these texts illustrates
a very different discourse of motherhood for these slaves, as com-
pared to their mistresses' experience of motherhood. Slaves were
denied the gendered privileges of motherhood, but this did not
prevent them from having a mother's feelings. According to slave
society, female slaves were numb to any maternal feelings, but
slave accounts contradict this assumption. They were clearly aware
of the cult of true womanhood and the glorification of motherhood,
and in all probability maintained some remembrance of African
traditions, including the high regard for motherhood. All of this
allowed them to feel what they referred to as maternal instincts.
However, the slave mother's feelings and her anguish went unrec-
ognized by slaveholders. In her often quoted speech at the Seneca
Falls Woman's Rights Convention, Sojourner Truth stated, "'I have
borne thirteen chilern and seen 'em mos' all sold off into slavery,

and when I cried out with a mother's grief, none but Jesus heard—and ar'n't I a woman?'"[29] Davies argues that Truth's assertion of her experience of womanhood, which included motherhood as loss, is a critique of the experience of motherhood assumed for white women.[30] This is the same critique Spillers and others make of feminists that desire to make motherhood the site of common ground for all women.

The nineteenth-century black women writers were faced with a similar situation when they sought to find a way around a cult of motherhood and womanhood, which implicitly excluded the experience of black females, yet still presented their definitions of motherhood and womanhood as desires for all women. This is not to say that the definition of womanhood was inclusive for all white women, but rather that its very tenets excluded black females. These early writers, therefore, sought a means of negotiating the cult of true womanhood in such a way that black females could be recognized as mothers, and therefore women. In other words, their writing in many respects was an attempt to engender themselves in the eyes of dominant society. I argue that although black females were never without gender, their gender was not recognized by whites, and thus had to be made recognizable.

One means of making their gender visible was for black women to enter the literary arena. Writing could be a way of combating negative stereotypes by presenting themselves in a positive light. However, in order to address their race and gender concerns, black women writers could not merely plug black women characters into the existing styles and genres. Instead, the writers utilized the traditions before them but also made strategic changes to develop a literary form that could address both race and gender issues. *Uncle Tom's Cabin,* although often disparaged as racist, is a text that addresses both of these issues and therefore is capable of inspiring black women writers with literary possibilities. According to Richard Yarborough, Stowe's novel established "the level of discourse for the majority of fictional treatments of the Afro-American that were to follow" including those written by blacks.[31] Mullen shares this view as she argues that *Uncle Tom's Cabin* is a significant precursor of the African-American novel due to the popularity garnered by its sympathetic black characters.[32] According to Yarborough, this does not mean that black writers used *Uncle Tom's Cabin* as a model, but Stowe's success encouraged them by showing that it might be possible to use their writing as a means to change white attitudes toward blacks.[33]

This does not mean that the writers shared Stowe's views, but they did share her concerns. Elizabeth Ammons argues that a number of black women writers respond to and remodel the maternal argument Stowe offers in *Uncle Tom's Cabin*.[34] In fact, the texts of many black women writers appear to "talk back" to Stowe's novel. This dialogue between Stowe and early black women writers will be discussed in more detail in later chapters, but as a preface to their work, *Uncle Tom's Cabin* will be briefly discussed. Mullen argues that Stowe's text mixed white women's sentimental fiction with the black male slave narrative in such a way that black women writers had to question their place in these two models.[35] White women writers to address gender issues often used sentimental fiction, but these texts conceived of womanhood in such a way that the experiences of black women did not seem pertinent. Black women could and did write slave narratives, but male writers and masculine perspectives dominated the genre. Thus neither of these models were sufficient for the expression of a black woman's perspective.

Before exploring the way in which black women writers reconfigured these models or responded to Stowe's own merging of genres, the sentimental novel and slave narrative traditions will be discussed. The belief in mankind's inherent goodness is essential to the sentimental formula. This formula foregrounds moral purpose while subordinating all other elements. The typical ending of the sentimental novel entails punishments, which fit the crime, and rewards, which are well deserved.[36] For many of these novels, the ultimate reward was a good marriage. According to Philip Fisher, sentimental novels feature

> extended central scenes of dying and deathbeds, mourning and loss, the rhetorical treatment of the central theme of suffering, the creation of the prisoner as the central character, the themes of imprisonment, the violation of selfhood, power relations in the intimate and familiar territory, freedom, the centrality of the family and the definition of the power of literary representation in terms of tears.[37]

Those familiar with *Uncle Tom's Cabin* will recognize these features in Stowe's text. In fact, Jane Tompkins goes as far as to say
that it is "the most dazzling exemplar" of the sentimental novel.[38]

Sentimental novels have been criticized for their overindulgence
in emotion, but Tompkins argues that the sentimental novel should
be viewed "as a political enterprise, halfway between sermon and
social theory, that both codifies and attempts to mold the values of
its time."[39] Barbara Christian remarks that protest novels often
rely on sentimentality, "an excessive display of emotion as well as
prettifying of ugliness, to move the reader, to set him on the right
side of the question."[40] The desire to appeal to the reader's sentiments is often mentioned explicitly by the author. For example, in
her concluding remarks, Stowe states:

> There is one thing that every individual can do,—they can see
> to it *they feel right.* An atmosphere of sympathetic influence
> encircles every human being; and the man or woman who
> *feels* strongly, healthily and justly, on the great interests of
> humanity, is a constant benefactor to the human race. See,
> then, to your sympathies in this matter: Are they in harmony
> with the sympathies of Christ? or are they swayed and per-
> verted by the sophistries of worldly policy? (624)

Writers of sentimental fiction appeal to the reader's emotions by
drawing attention to the suffering experienced by the characters.
For example, in the preface to *Incidents,* Harriet Jacobs states, "I
do earnestly desire to arouse the women of the North to a realizing
sense of the condition of two millions of women at the South, still
in bondage, suffering what I suffered, and most of them far worse."[41]
According to Fisher, suffering is the primary subject matter of
sentimental narrative because suffering elicits compassion, which
is the primary emotional goal of sentimental narration.[42] Stowe
and Jacobs seek compassion as a precursor to political action to
end slavery.

Fisher notes that between 1740 and 1860, sentimentality was a
crucial means of politically radical representation.[43] It is significant
that the use of sentimentality declined after 1860. This decline
may in part be attributable to the beginning of the Civil War in

1861. War is about forcing change through superior strength, while sentiment is about moving people by changing their beliefs. This decline in the use of sentimentality will be evident in the later texts. For example, Frances Harper and Pauline Hopkins are still clearly writing from within the sentimental novel tradition, but their appeals to the reader's sentiments are not nearly as direct as those of Stowe and Jacobs.

The appeal that sentimental fiction makes on the reader's emotions is not too dissimilar from the intended impact of the slave narrative. While *Uncle Tom's Cabin* is the exemplar of the sentimental novel tradition, the most celebrated of the slave narratives is Frederick Douglass' *Narrative of the Life of Frederick Douglass*, which is also seen as the quintessential slave narrative. In *To Tell a Free Story: The First Century of Afro-American Autobiography, 1760–1865*, William Andrews notes the difficulty of defining black autobiography, the genre to which slave narratives belong. He cites the difficulty in tracing a steady progression in the development of the genre: "The tradition of black autobiography is not layered in strata of ground-breaking predecessors anticipating conscious successors. Some stages of development can be marked in rough outline, but the route of the genre's historical evolution is dotted with detours, deadends, half-blazed trails, and roads not taken."[44] This difficulty of definition is reduced slightly when focusing on the subgenre of the slave narrative. In her pioneering text, *The Slave Narrative: Its Place in American History*, Marion Wilson Starling describes slave narratives as "autobiographical or semiautobiographical records of American Negro slaves." She also observes that along with race and slave status, the dominant characteristic of slave narratives is the sense of adventure.[45] Despite the difficulty of defining a genre that includes many permutations, Charles T. Davis has outlined several conventions of the classic slave narrative that include the following: birth at an undetermined time with an unknown father, early separation from the mother, descriptions of physical and sexual abuse of female slaves, the threat of being sold down South, the denial of education or religious instruction, and the lack of legalized marriage between slaves.[46] Douglass' text opens up with a vague description of his birth at an unknown time. He knows that his father is white, but he is not sure who he is, although it is rumored that his master is also his father. Douglass notes that this vague account of his birth is the standard, not the exception:

> By far the larger part of the slaves know as little of their ages as horses know theirs. . . . My father was a white man. He was admitted to be such by all I ever heard speak of my parentage. The opinion was also whispered that my master was my father. . . . [T]he slaveholder, in cases not a few, sustains to his slaves the double relation of master and father.[47]

By presenting his story within the framework of the lives of other slaves, Douglass is able to construct his history as the history of slaves. Other slave narratives written by men tended to follow the basic plot identified by Davis. For example, William Wells Brown's narrative is quite similar to Douglass' account. Brown, too, is unsure of his exact birth date and, like Douglass, is separated from his mother. However, Brown is a little surer of his parentage; he knows that his white father is a close relation of his master's.[48]

Another important element of the slave narrative convention is the denial of an education. Douglass is at first educated by Mrs. Auld, his mistress, but this comes to a halt when Mr. Auld discovers what she is doing. Mr. Auld warns that not only is it illegal to educate a slave, it is also dangerous: "'[I]f you teach that nigger . . . how to read, there would be no keeping him. It would forever unfit him to be a slave. He would at once become unmanageable, and of no value to his master'" (274). Once Douglass realizes that his master is against his education, he does everything he can to trick white children into teaching him their lessons. Thus Douglass' experience follows the convention Davis describes. Not all slaves, however, were denied an education. For example, in her narrative, *History of Mary Prince, A West Indian Slave*, Mary Prince describes her fortunate learning from the daughter of her mistress, who would have Prince repeat school lessons to her. Although Prince does receive an education of sorts, she does report the difficulty of receiving religious instruction.[49] In her narrative, Elizabeth Keckley does not discuss her schooling, but it is apparent that she knew how to read and write while a slave because she refers to letters she exchanged during her enslavement.[50]

Elizabeth Keckley's *Behind the Scenes. Or, Thirty Years a Slave and Four Years in the White House* is at once a typical and atypical slave narrative. She begins her narrative with the announcement of her birthplace, but she does not provide her birth date. Keckley knows her parents, but her silence in regard to her date of birth suggests that she is unaware of this important piece of information. She reports the abuses of slavery and the separation of families while also lamenting her own family's separation. However, her narrative differs from Douglass and Jacobs' in that the focus of her text is on her experiences as a free woman. Her narrative was also published after slavery's abolishment, so she does not have the same antislavery impetus guiding her text. Keckley, like Jacobs, also borrows from the sentimental novel tradition to tell her story. By crossing generic boundaries, Keckley is better able to express her life experiences.

However, Mary Prince's narrative follows more of the classic conventions, but not all. Unlike Douglass and Brown, she does not suggest any uncertainty about her birth. In fact, her early childhood was quite happy. Prince's description of her early years is quite similar to that described by Jacobs in *Incidents*. Linda seems to know her birthday and she is raised with both parents, her brother and her grandmother. In fact, it is not until she is six that she realizes that she is a slave.

This brief discussion of slave narratives provides some sense of the traditional elements, while noting the variety of individual lives and narrative strategies. Although these narratives frequently do not meet the level of sophistication to be awarded literary merit, they have had a significant impact on the development of American literature. Starling comments on the influence of the slave narratives upon the slave novels of the 1850s in general and *Uncle Tom's Cabin* in particular. She identifies five narratives upon which Stowe based her novel: *(1) Narrative of the Life of Frederick Douglass, an American Slave, Written by Himself*; (2) *Narratives of the Sufferings of Lewis and Milton Clarke, Sons of a Soldier of the Revolution; during a Captivity of More than Twenty Years among the Slaveholders of Kentucky, One of the So-Called Christian States of*

North America; (3) *Narrative of William Wells Brown, a Fugitive Slave, Written by Himself*; (4) *The Fugitive Blacksmith; or, Events in the History of James W. C. Pennington, Pastor of a Presbyterian Church, New York, Formerly a Slave in the State of Maryland, United States*, and *(5) The Life of Josiah Henson, formerly a Slave, Now an Inhabitant of Canada, as Narrated by Himself to Samuel Eliot*.[51]

Although Stowe borrowed the content of slave narratives for her novel, she utilized the narrative techniques of sentimental fiction. This proved to be an ideal approach as the ideology of the period included the perception of women as moral superiors and arbiters of morality. Thus Stowe works within her cultural landscape to admonish the nation about the horrors of slavery. She appealed to her reader's sentiments in order to further her political aim of abolishing slavery. It was her hope that if the reader could sympathize with the sufferings of the characters, he or she would eventually see the injustice of the characters' situation. Stowe used sentimentality to create a common feeling between the reader and the characters. In order to create this common feeling, Stowe imagined a woman reader and appealed to her motherly instincts. Stowe's desire to elicit sympathy from fellow mothers is an aspect of the centralized position of women in her novel. For Stowe, mother is synonymous with woman; all of her adult female characters are also mothers. By appealing to mothers, she is appealing to all women who relate to the cult of true womanhood. She speaks to women that she assumes to be pious, pure, domestic, and submissive. According to Tompkins, "Out of the ideological materials at their disposal, the sentimental novelists elaborated a myth that gave women the central position of power and authority in the culture."[52] The virtues of true womanhood become an access to power. Stowe cultivates this power to critique slavery.

Clearly Stowe had good intentions regarding race and gender disparities; however, scholars have questioned the success of her call for social reform. She definitely garnered a great deal of attention for her cause, but the degree of change that she envisioned has been questioned and challenged. For example, although Stowe attempts to present a woman-centered utopia, there is still much debate among critics about whether or not Stowe wrote a feminist text that used the separate-spheres ideology as a means to attain power. Yarborough concludes, "Ultimately, Stowe's challenge to the racial and gender hierarchies in American society was bounded by the same assumptions that helped support the superstructure she strove to topple."[53] Gillian Brown appears to reach a similar conclusion when she observes that Stowe's matriarchy still uses the methods of masculine power: "Stowe borrows from patriarchal authority the prerogative of dispatching human destinies, the same prerogative exercised by men and slave-masters."[54] In other words, while Stowe may want to use power differently, she is claiming for women the same type of power wielded by white male patriarchs. Although Brown is ultimately critical of Stowe's success, she does stress that Stowe was not merely advocating domesticity, but also reformulating domesticity:

> [T]he domesticity Stowe advocates must be understood as a revision and purification of popular domestic values—domestic values which Stowe regards as complicit with the patriarchal institution of slavery. Stowe's domestic solution to slavery, then, represents not the strength of sentimental values but a utopian rehabilitation of them, necessitated by their fundamental complicity with the market to which they are ostensibly opposed.[55]

Therefore, according to Brown, Stowe is not merely calling for women to stay in the kitchen; rather, Stowe is revitalizing all that the kitchen entails. It seems that Brown would agree with Cott in arguing that Stowe used motherhood and domesticity as a source of power.

If one agrees that for Stowe the domestic realm is a site of power and the mother is the ultimate ideal, one must still question the place of the black mother in Stowe's formula. Does she have the same access to power? What happens when gender and race come together in the form of black females? Angela Davis argues that "because she accepted wholesale nineteenth-century mother worship, Stowe miserably fails to capture the reality and the truth of Black women's resistance to slavery."[56] Davis is critical of Stowe's portrayal of black motherhood, asserting that "Eliza is white motherhood incarnate, but in blackface—or rather, because she is a 'quadroon,' in just-a-little-less-than-whiteface."[57] Davis is critical of Stowe's effacing of the differences between black slave mothers and free white mothers. According to Davis, female slaves sought to defend their children, but their strength did not come from the "mystical power" of motherhood, but their slave experience. Eliza, however, is not concerned with the overall inhumanity of slavery.[58] After all, Eliza is at first content with her life as a slave. She attempts to calm George down by telling him, "'I'm sure we've been very happy, till lately'" (60). Eliza tries to persuade George not to run away, and it is not until her son, Harry, is sold that Eliza decides to make her escape. Stowe appears to suggest that if slave families were left intact, they would be content as slaves. This is not to say that motherhood and separation of families did not effect a slave's desire to flee, but they were not the only reasons to escape slavery.

According to Davis:

> *Uncle Tom's Cabin* is pervaded with assumptions of both Black and female inferiority. Most Black people are docile and domestic, and most women are mothers and little else. As ironic as it may seem, the most popular piece of anti-slavery literature of that time perpetuated the racist ideas which justified slavery and the sexist notions which justified the exclusion of women from the political arena where the battle against slavery would be fought.[59]

Davis appears to be critical not only of Stowe's racism, but also of her adherence to a separate-spheres ideology. Although Brown and Tompkins do not adequately address Stowe's implied racism, they see the use of a separate-spheres ideology as an avenue to power.

Stowe's novel places Rachel Halliday's kitchen at the center of a woman-centered world. Although a number of women are presented to the reader with different degrees of domestic power, Rachel is presented as the ideal. The Halliday home is presented as warm and inviting, and Rachel is clearly the ruler of the roost. The entire family joins in the preparations, but it is Rachel who is described as never looking as "truly and benignly happy as at the head of her table" (223). A number of literary critics confirm Rachel's rulership with Stowe's reference to Simeon Halliday standing "in his shirt-sleeves before a little looking-glass in the corner, engaged in the anti-patriarchal operation of shaving" (223). Stowe would like the reader to see this scene as symbolic of Simeon's abdication of patriarchal rule and as the confirmation of mother rule.

While this scene may establish Rachel's superiority in the home, it does not extend her power beyond the domestic sphere. Brown and Tompkins discuss the domestic sphere as a means to power, but Rachel's power does not appear to reach any further than the kitchen. For example, it is Simeon who brings news of the outside world; he is the one who knows about George's presence. This suggests that Rachel does not have access to the public domain. Even within the home Rachel is not completely in charge. While at the dinner table, even though she is at the head of the table, it is Simeon who admonishes their son. Simeon scolds his son by saying, " 'Thy mother never taught thee so' " (224). This suggests that although Rachel may take the lead in raising the children, Simeon is not completely withdrawn from the patriarchal role of family disciplinarian.

Despite the fact that I disagree with the significance that some feminist critics give to the shaving scene, I would agree that this chapter does make some progressive comments about family relationships. This chapter describes a communal atmosphere. The relationship of Rachel and Simeon seems much more egalitarian than that of other couples in the text. The most significant contribution of the chapter, however, is the fact that the wives presented are given their own names. Except for the female slaves and Marie St. Claire, the reader does not learn the names of the other married women. Mrs. Shelby and Mrs. Bird appear to be so inextricably entwined in their husband's personalities that they do not require their own given names.

While Rachel is presented as the ideal "mother ruler," Mrs. Shelby and Mrs. Bird also aspire to the ranks of domestic rulers. The men are expected to take care of worldly concerns, while the women look after moral concerns.[60] Just as Mrs. Shelby appeals to her husband on moral grounds regarding the sale of Tom and Harry, Mrs. Bird also appeals to her husband in the name of Christianity in reference to the fugitive slave law. Mrs. Shelby and Mrs. Bird occupy the realm of the heart as they seek to convince their husbands to follow Christian principles.

Clearly, it is the women in the novel who represent a private, domestic brand of liberal morality.[61] The women are expected to share their morality with their husbands and thus reform them. This is similar to their duty toward their children, thus the moral influence women have on their husbands is akin to mother love. Myra Jehlen argues that Stowe "did not seek to advance the cause of women's self-rule, in fact, she affirmed their feudal placement."[62] I, like Jehlen, must disagree with Tompkins' belief that Stowe's very conservatism is the source of her revolutionary power. Stowe's conservatism is just that—conservative. Perhaps she desired a matriarchy as Tompkins and Brown contend, but the only woman that can claim the title of matriarch is Marie St. Claire, and she assumes patriarchal prerogatives. Marie is a female patriarch, but there are no matriarchs. She is described as the antithesis of what a woman should be. Tompkins and Brown discuss matriarchy as though it would have a different quality than a patriarchy, but this does not appear to be the case. Stowe is ultimately unsuccessful in creating a world centered on mother love.

Whatever one might think about Stowe's brand of feminism, clearly she is writing within the cult of true womanhood. Although critics disagree about whether Stowe sought to redefine womanhood and whether or not she was successful, it is clear that her writing is influenced by her society's definition of womanhood. At the core of the cult of true womanhood is what Cott defines as "passionlessness." The belief that women lacked carnal passion provided the basis for claims of female moral superiority, which in turn, according to Cott, allowed women to gain greater power within their society.[63] Thus when Stowe attacks slavery from a moral high ground, some would read this critique as also a critique of the patriarchal status quo. Although I do not find Stowe's use of the cult of true womanhood to be particularly powerful, as I have argued here, it is one method of criticism. This technique, however, is not equally accessible to all females. Ann duCille observes:

> For early black women writers, literary passionlessness negated a negative: it endowed virtue to the historically virtue-

less. In black women's novels, then, the trope of sexual purity must be scrutinized not simply as an inscription of middle-class mores but as a critique that held up to scorn the same hegemonic values it, on some level, inscribed.[64]

Thus Stowe's formula could not work the same way for black women writers because they were writing from a different subject position. Since black females were seen differently within society, they could not make the same gender critique. Nor did they make the same critique of slavery and racism as did Stowe. The focus of Stowe's text was not blacks, but the response of white Americans to slavery. In later chapters I will go into more detail regarding the way that later black women writers reconfigure and talk back to Stowe's text. Yet *Uncle Tom's Cabin* in many ways serves as a starting point for the literary creations of these black women writers; however, they seek to go beyond Stowe's initial race and gender critiques.

Slave narratives were also significant precursors for African-American literature; in fact, they are often discussed as a founding genre of African-American literature. However, a male perspective dominated the slave narrative tradition. Black women writers were confronted with a black male-dominated slave narrative tradition and a white female-dominated sentimental novel tradition, which equally, if differently, eclipsed the perspective of black women.

Thus when Jacobs sought to write her narrative, she was faced with two equally dissatisfying models. For example, although Jacobs is clearly aware of the issues that Charles T. Davis highlights in his list of slave narrative conventions, her response does not fit within the conventions that he describes. While Jacobs discusses the separation of slave children from their mothers, as do Douglass and Brown, unlike them, Jacobs is aware of her parentage. Jacobs responds to similar themes as the male narrators, but while they gloss over the sexual abuse and focus on attaining freedom and manhood (which for them are one and the same), she reveals the way slavery interrupted maternity and the way slavery helped to form gender identity and sexuality.

This difference in emphasis has to do with the way in which the writers define freedom. For Douglass, freedom was manhood, but for Linda, freedom was community. I will develop this point in further detail in the following chapter, but suffice it to say that the two writers had different aims. This difference can be seen in their writing styles. Douglass presents himself as the ultimate example of slavery's effects; he desires to impress the reader with his astounding success story. Jacobs, on the other hand, seeks community by drawing on her reader's sympathies. However, while creating a sense of shared community, Jacobs refuses to completely elide differences. Just as the slave woman is in a different position than her mistress, not all slave women have the same experience. This point is particularly well made when Linda compares her lot with that of Fanny. Fanny agrees that they share a similar pain due to the separation from their children, but she quickly observes that Linda will see hers again, while she will not. This very brief comparison of male- and female-authored slave narratives suggests that black female writers have different critiques of race relations than black men because their experience of racism is always filtered through the lens of gender bias as well.

It might appear that Jacobs' slave narrative would adequately address the issues of racial and sexual discrimination; however, her ability to address both issues is directly proportional to her departure from the conventions of the slave narrative. Her departure from the traditional narrative style allows Jacobs to incorporate devices of the sentimental novel to address race and gender issues. Just because a woman writes within the same genre as a man does not mean that she will necessarily bring anything different to the genre. Yet by reconfiguring the slave narrative genre, Jacobs is able to address issues, such as motherhood, that are neglected within the traditional format. Keckley, like Jacobs, also borrows from the sentimental novel tradition to tell her story. *Behind the Scenes* at times reads like a sentimental novel, but the story is not fiction. In some ways it is a slave narrative, but in other ways more like an autobiography or a memoir. Keckley's text crosses many generic boundaries in order to best express her life experiences.

Jacobs' text is just one example of the many texts written by black women that manipulate established genres in order to more fully address the concerns of those who are both black and female. According to duCille, the texts of early black women writers "indict

racism *and* sexism as conspiratorial forces in patriarchal domination, often offering sophisticated analysis of the interplay between
racial and sexual ideology."[65] In the following chapters, I will discuss nineteenth-century texts that challenge racism and sexism in
ways that are significantly different from women's sentimental
fiction and male-authored slave narratives. I will argue that the
changes that are made are directly related to the history of slavery
and the subsequent formulations of black female identity based on
the slavery experience as well as slavery myths. In the final chapter, I will turn to the twentieth century in order to point out that
although the writers have moved away from the sentimental novel
tradition, the specter of slavery has not been exorcised. Literary
representations of black women's gender in general and maternity
specifically are clearly responding to the history of slavery and the
degradation of black womanhood and motherhood.

3

Reclaiming True Womanhood

While I will argue that the slave experience shaped the writing of African Americans even after the abolition of slavery, the most direct relationship may be seen in slave narratives themselves. The slave experience prompted many African Americans to document their personal account of slavery. These narratives provided the perspective of the slaves themselves and were often used to further the abolitionist cause. William Andrews notes that women's slave narratives originated with the assistance of the abolitionist movement. By the mid-nineteenth century, a number of fugitive slaves, including William Wells Brown and Frederick Douglass, presented the experiences of the slave, but the voice of the female slave was remarkably absent. Andrews observes that if the history of black autobiography is reconstructed, one notes that from 1760 to 1865, only rarely did escaped female slaves receive the kind of attention and encouragement that prompted them to write or dictate their stories.[1] This reticence on behalf of

53

female slaves is in part due to the gender expectations of that time. Such a sense of a woman's self-importance would go against the tenets of true womanhood, which demanded submissiveness and implied silence for women. And for many female slaves, a truthful documentation of their slavery experiences would often involve the revelation of incidents that would question their purity and chastity and thus unsex them before their readers. Thus it is quite significant when as early as 1831, Mary Prince asserts, "I know what slaves feel I can tell by myself what other slaves feel, and by what they have told me. The man that says slaves be quite happy in slavery—that they don't want to be free is either ignorant or a lying person."[2] With these words, Prince asserts the right to not only speak for herself, but for fellow slaves, male and female. According to Andrews, this "constitutes the first claim in the Afro-American autobiographical tradition for the black woman's authority as a spokesperson for *all* black people, regardless of gender, on the subject of 'what slaves feel' about the morality of slavery."[3] The tradition that Prince inaugurates is reflected in the narratives of Old Elizabeth, Mattie Jackson, and Harriet Jacobs.[4] Later narratives such as Lucy Delaney's *From the Darkness Cometh the Light or Struggles for Freedom* (1891), Kate Drumgoold's *A Slave Girl's Story* (1898), and Annie L. Burton's *Memories of Childhood's Slavery Days* (1909) reveal the continuing significance of the slave narrative within the black female literary tradition.

Despite the importance of the slave narrative tradition within this literary tradition, the slave narrative form was not replicated but reconstructed. The genre as illustrated by Brown and Douglass was not completely amenable to the issues faced by female slaves, thus a refabrication was in order. Jacobs' *Incidents in the Life of a Slave Girl* and Harriet E. Wilson's *Our Nig* provide interesting examples of the reconfiguration of the slave narrative and sentimental novel genres in order to address race and gender issues. The authors use motherhood as the lens to analyze gender and race. Both texts were written during slavery when the humanity of slaves, and blacks in general, was continually denied. Female slaves and even free black females were not regarded as gendered ladies and mothers. Thus Jacobs and Wilson use their texts to claim the titles of woman and mother for black females. However, they do not just ask to be included within the cult of true womanhood, they also question the appropriateness of society's definition of womanhood. The exclusion of black females from the cult of true womanhood is directly related to slavery. The slave experience influenced the way slaves and free blacks were seen by the dominant society. Thus when blacks began to write, they wrote in an atmosphere in which they had to prove their humanity.

For many the solution to this dilemma was not to write within accepted genres, but to reconfigure them. As I noted in the previous chapter, Harriet Beecher Stowe, a white woman, was the first to bring the slave narrative and the sentimental novel genres together and in many ways served as a precursor for black women writers. There is a direct relationship between Stowe and Jacobs since Jacobs initially sought Stowe's aid in producing a dictated text.[5] Stowe, instead, proposed to include Jacobs' story in *A Key to Uncle Tom's Cabin* and forwarded Jacobs' story to Mrs. Willis (the second Mrs. Bruce in the narrative) for verification. In a letter to Amy Post, Jacobs explains that she had never discussed the origin of her children with Mrs. Willis, and that they both thought it was wrong of Stowe to forward Post's letter; however, Mrs. Willis did respond by telling Stowe that although Jacobs wanted her story to be a separate narrative, Jacobs would be willing to supply details for Stowe's forthcoming work. Stowe never responded to the letter or subsequent ones. Jacobs found this sequence of events quite troubling and regarded Stowe's actions as a personal affront.[6] After what she regarded as a betrayal, Jacobs decided to write her own narrative. And in this narrative, she responds to her sense of betrayal by questioning definitions of womanhood and motherhood. Jacobs questions gender expectations by illustrating the interconnection of gender and other aspects of personhood.

Although contemporary readers find Jacob's narrative compelling, literary critics initially questioned the authenticity of her text. In *The Slave Community*, historian John Blassingame dismisses Jacobs' text as inauthentic. According to Hazel Carby, Blassingame rejects Jacobs' narrative "because it does not conform to the guidelines of representativeness."[7] For Blassingame, a narrative is "representative" if it corresponds with other accounts by former slaves. While he does allow room for personal differences amongst narrators, he believes that the bulk of the narrative should be similar to others of the genre. Jacobs' text does not meet his criteria of "representativeness" because her text was unlike other narratives. According to Blassingame:

> In spite of Lydia Maria Child's insistence that she had only revised the manuscript of Harriet Jacobs "mainly for purpose of condensation and orderly arrangement," the work is not credible. In the first place, *Incidents in the Life of a Slave Girl* (1861), is too orderly; too many of the major characters meet providentially after years of separation. Then, too, the story is too melodramatic: miscegenation and cruelty, outraged virtue, unrequited love, and planter licentiousness appear on every page.[8]

Although Blassingame's points of criticism are often the markers of sentimental fiction that in itself does not warrant the text's dismissal as an inauthentic narrative. At issue in Blassingame's criticism is representation versus the "real." Clearly, he expects slave narratives to be "real," yet he acknowledges the inability of writers "to tell the whole truth about themselves."[9] In light of this recognition, could not an author have been aware of the sentimental genre and borrowed from it in order to tell a "truthful" tale? What Blassingame cites as melodrama constitutes very real concerns for female slaves; however, the social codes of the period prevented frank discussions of sex and violation. Perhaps Jacobs deployed the tropes of sentimental fiction as a means of approaching a difficult and painful subject.

Male narrators often made reference to the sexual victimization of female slaves, but then quickly moved on to another subject. Their reticence to openly engage the subject may in part have been a response to its painful nature, but perhaps they also viewed it as a lesser issue in that it did not directly affect them. This is not to say male slaves were not concerned about the treatment of female slaves, but this would be a more significant issue for female slaves who lived with the continual threat of victimization. In *Reconstructing Womanhood*, Carby argues that "the criteria chosen by Blassingame as the basis for his dismissal of the narrative credibility of Jacob's narrative are, ideologically, the indicators of a uniquely female perspective."[10] Carby convincingly argues that Jacobs' text was disregarded because it deviated from the conventions found in male-authored narratives. Rather than follow in the footsteps of traditional male slave narratives, Jacobs uses her text to reformulate the traditions of the sentimental novel and the slave narrative in order to address the issues of sexism and slavery from a black female's point of view.

Thanks to the scholarship of Jean Fagan Yellin, the authenticity of Jacobs' text is no longer a question.[11] Yellin convincingly establishes the veracity of Jacobs' narrative as well as her authorship. Since Yellin's groundbreaking work, Jacobs' text has reached canonical status. I believe this is in part due to the length of her narrative; Jacobs' text is one of the few female-authored narratives of substantial length. Jacobs' narrative is also an appealing text to study because it operates as a bridge between black women's autobiography and fiction. Although autobiographical, by using elements of sentimental fiction Jacobs provides a nice preface to an analysis of black women's fiction.

In chapter 2, I discuss the traits and conventions of sentimental fiction, and while *Incidents* is not nearly as sentimental as *Uncle Tom's Cabin*, death and mourning are present throughout the text as Linda describes the suffering of the slaves. The text is replete with references to jails and other prisons. In fact, it is while Linda in the garret that she is most like the sentimental heroine. The muteness and delirium that Linda experiences align her with the dying sentimental heroine. "Jacobs thus parallels Brent's attic with the private space that usually confines the sentimental heroine: the kitchen, the parlor, the upstairs chamber, the deathbed, and the grave."[12] Besides the confinement that Linda experiences, she is also confronted with other elements, which are often depicted in sentimental fiction. For example, Phillip Fisher points to personal violation and intimate power relations as key features in sentimental fiction. Since these two elements are inherent characteristics of this "peculiar institution" that accepted the rape of female slaves and the fathering of slave children as matters of course, it is not surprising that they would also find their way into Jacobs' text. Other important features of sentimental fiction are freedom and the centrality of the family. These points are translated in Jacobs' text as the desire for freedom and the importance of community, which are at the core of Linda's description of her escape from slavery. Thus *Incidents* includes many of the features of sentimental novels as outlined by Fisher, but they are transfigured to describe the slavery situation.

Jacobs' borrowing from the sentimental tradition is foreseeable, when one considers Jane Tompkins' argument in *Sentimental Designs* that the sentimental novel achieves its political enterprise through a combination of sermon and social theory that codifies and attempts to mold the values of its time.[13] The abolitionist goal behind slave narratives clearly places them within the bounds of political discourse. Jacobs does not try to hide her reformist goals; in fact, she clearly states her goals in her preface: "I do earnestly desire to arouse the women of the North to a realizing sense of the condition of two millions of women at the South, still in bondage, suffering what I suffered, and most of them far worse."[14] Although Jacobs does not identify her northern readers as white, she clearly uses a geographical shorthand, which designates race and class; the northern women are white, while the southern women are black slaves. Jacobs hopes that her tale of suffering will persuade her reader to work toward the emancipation of slaves. The compellingness of Jacobs' text links it to the sentimental novel, which Tompkins defines as "an act of persuasion aimed at defining social reality."[15] Jacobs seeks to mold social reality by attaining her reader's compassion as a precursor to political action to abolish slavery.

Although the sentimental novel tradition is important to Jacobs' text, Linda's confessional account of sexual error and guilt also links *Incidents* to the seduction novel.[16] Tales of seduction portray a helpless, virtuous woman pursued by a man until she gives into his demands and inevitably dies. When describing Linda's interactions with both Flint and Sands, the narration becomes that of the seduction novel. As with the sentimental novel, the seduction novel's focus on the preservation of virtue reveals its relation to the cult of true womanhood through its emphasis on sexual purity.

In the previous chapter, I note that true womanhood was based on four cardinal virtues: piety, purity, submissiveness, and domesticity. Although all four of the virtues were important, purity appears to provide the foundation for all the rest. The loss of purity was associated with madness or death, since its absence was considered "unnatural and unfeminine."[17] Although these virtues defined ideal womanhood, Barbara Welter observes that "real women often felt they did not live up to the ideal of True Womanhood: some of them blamed themselves, some challenged the standard, some tried to keep the virtues and enlarge the scope of womanhood."[18] Jacobs was one of those women who chose to challenge these standards.

Jacobs' *Incidents* appears to challenge this idea of true womanhood because it is not available to female slaves. Linda comments that not only is the female slave not expected to be virtuous, she is denied the possibility of being so: "She is not allowed to have any pride of character. It is deemed a crime in her to wish to be virtuous" (363). According to Mary Helen Washington, it is this denial of womanhood that separates Jacobs from male authors, "who wrote to show that they had the qualities valued and respected by other men—courage, mobility, rationality, and physical strength—Harriet Jacobs wrote to confess that she did not have the qualities valued in white women."[19] By disclosing her sexual experiences, Linda reveals that she does not meet the definition of a true woman, but then she goes on to question this definition as it pertains to black females.

According to Carby, "*Incidents in the Life of a Slave Girl* is the most sophisticated, sustained narrative dissection of the conventions of true womanhood by a black author before emancipation."[20] The key to this dissection is not an outright denial of these ideals, but the expression of an unavoidable tension between Linda's life experiences and these ideals. When she confesses her sexual history to the reader, Linda does it with shame and reluctance, "I come to a period in my unhappy life, which I would gladly forget if I could. The remembrance fills me with sorrow and shame. It pains me to tell you of it" (384). Michele Wallace argues that the guilt Linda expresses is a sign of the degree to which Jacob's narrative reflects the mores of middle-class, white society. Despite Linda's awareness of her untenable situation as a slave, she expresses guilt about having premarital sex and children out of wedlock. Wallace describes Linda's guilt as "unnecessary agony, the agony of measuring herself against a standard which was not designed to fit her circumstances, and which could only work to destroy her image of herself."[21] Although Wallace refers to Linda's guilt as "unnecessary agony," Linda was not alone in the shame she experienced about a situation beyond her control. In Elizabeth Keckley's narrative, *Behind the Scenes. Or, Thirty Years a Slave, and Four Years in the White House*, she reveals her sexual experience in much the same manner: "I do not care to dwell upon this subject, for it is fraught with pain. Suffice it to say, that he persecuted me for four years, and I—I—became a mother."[22] Clearly both women experience guilt, but neither allows herself to become consumed with guilt. Despite her sexual history, Linda never comes to believe that she does not deserve the title of "woman." If she had done this, the degendering process of slavery would have been successful, however, she refuses to accept the denial of her womanhood on the basis of premarital sex.

Despite the shame she feels, Linda realizes that it could not have been otherwise because "the condition of a slave confuses all principles of morality, and, in fact, renders the practice of them impossible" (385). Because of her different circumstances, Linda asserts that female slaves should be judged differently. By revealing "her failure to live up to the codes of True Womanhood," Jacobs "calls upon her reader to use sympathy *unconventionally*, to try to understand the very different way a slave woman experiences the world."[23] She suggests that people should be judged within their contexts and not by rigid expectations and definitions.

This is a powerful move during Jacobs' lifetime, since, as Welter notes, anyone who dared to tamper with the virtues of true womanhood was damned as an enemy of God, civilization, and the republic.[24] Jacobs, however, does not stop at merely questioning the definition of true womanhood, she also implies that a woman's self-esteem is not the same as her virtue. In her introduction, Jean Fagan Yellin notes that Jacobs' attempts to preserve her virginity, while related to her self-esteem, is not equated to her self-respect.[25] While Jacobs may not have been a true woman based on the standards of her day, she questions the justification of those standards and suggests that a woman be judged by more than her sexual purity.

In the process of questioning the applicability of the cult of true womanhood for black females, Jacobs also questions its effect on white women. *Incidents* suggests "that despite the differences between the female slave and her mistress . . . no woman is free in a patriarchal society."[26] As her call to northern women in her preface makes clear, Jacobs is attempting "to establish an American sisterhood and to activate that sisterhood in the public arena."[27] Like Stowe before her, Jacobs intends to draw upon the sympathy of her fellow women. Jacobs' text includes various white women who aid Linda and thus place a higher value on a sense of sisterhood than on race or class solidarity. These women would include the white woman who hid Linda in her home and both of the Mrs. Bruces.

The white women in *Incidents*, however, are not always concerned about the fate of their enslaved sisters. In the process of providing an alternative to the cult of true womanhood, Jacobs challenges readers to question their own ideology and racism.[28] Jacobs' text points out that although all women are subjected to patriarchy in such a way that feelings of solidarity might be formed, when one woman is empowered over another because of race or class privilege, she is equally likely to betray as to support her fellow woman. This breakdown of sisterhood is evident in Linda's description of the relationship of her mother and mistress. She describes the two as foster sisters, since they had been nourished at her grandmother's breast. According to Karen Sánchez-Eppler:

> To call mother and mistress "foster-sisters" is to suggest that a certain parity and relatedness adhere to sharing the same breast. But the story Jacobs tells reveals that rather than produce social equality, sharing the same breast becomes itself a means of imposing the hierarchies of slavery. Weaning the slave in order to provide milk for the mistress denies both sisterhood and the presumed primacy of familial or maternal ties; it subjugates the claims of biological and emotional relations to the economic relations of the plantation.[29]

Thus what Jacobs describes as a sisterly relationship is actually a parasitic one. The female slave must give up her body as well as its products to sustain the master's family. This seems to undermine any claims that slaves and masters form an extended family. By deploying the family metaphor, Jacobs reveals that the slaveholders' claims about happy extended families are mere myths. Although Linda's family is intertwined with that of the Flint's, Linda is in an adversarial position, rather than a familial one, both in her relationship with Dr. Flint and Mrs. Flint, who should be seen as an aunt according to the foster-sister rubric.

In fact, the possibility of sisterly betrayal is particularly evident in Jacobs' depiction of Mrs. Flint, her mother's foster-sister. Jacobs' text appears to offer a veiled critique of the antislavery feminist movement, which was based on a sense of sisterhood between female slaves and white women. In *Women and Sisters*, Yellin discusses the movement and its use of the emblem of the kneeling female slave. While Yellin presents an interesting analysis of the dominant culture's reappropriation of the antislavery feminist discourse, she does not adequately critique the movement's own appropriation of the female slave's discourse. Jacobs, however, seems to point to the dangers of sympathetic appropriation. Throughout her text, Jacobs' points to the bonds between women, but she is also careful not to completely elide the differences. Although Jacobs desires to build a community of women speaking together, she does not want one group of women to speak for another and erase their individuality. This point appears to be particularly clear in her rather ambivalent response to her purchase by the second Mrs. Bruce. Sisterly solidarity is not easily achieved whether one has good intentions like Mrs. Bruce or malicious intents like Mrs. Flint.

Mrs. Flint, like Stowe's Marie St. Claire, is presented as an antiwoman. Rather than forging a sisterly bond with her slave, Mrs. Flint views Linda with antagonism and antipathy. Despite Mrs. Flint's coldness toward her, Linda seeks a more sympathetic relationship with her. Linda confides in Mrs. Flint in hopes of obtaining protection from Dr. Flint. Mrs. Flint is clearly moved by Linda's account and Linda is touched by Mrs. Flint's pain, but Linda soon realizes that Mrs. Flint's strong emotions contained no sympathy for her slave. While Linda is able to sympathize with her fellow woman's suffering, Mrs. Flint is unable to see beyond her own pain. This is an example of failed sisterhood because Mrs. Flint does not recognize Linda as a sister, but as a competitor. This example of failed sisterhood may be read as a veiled critique of Stowe's world of mother saviors. According to Stowe's ideals, Mrs.

Flint should not only be a maternal figure for the young Jacobs, but also a protectress. She should seek to show her husband the error of his ways, since as a woman she should be his moral superior. However, Mrs. Flint is not only powerless before her husband, she does not even realize that she and Linda are both victims of Flint's patriarchal power.

According to planter mythology, Dr. Flint as Linda's master should be a father figure who provides paternal protection, but instead he plays the sexual predator. Although innumerable female slaves fell victim to sexual exploitation by their masters, both Jacobs' *Incidents* and Stowe's *Uncle Tom's Cabin* focus on the female slave's ability to restrain sexually aggressive masters. A connection can be made between Linda, who is pursued by Dr. Flint, and Stowe's Cassy, who becomes Simon Legree's mistress. Like Linda, Cassy is sassy. For instance, when she says something to Legree in French, "his face became perfectly demonical in its expression . . . he half raised his hand, as if to strike,—a gesture which she regarded with fierce disdain, as she turned and walked away."[30] Despite the fact that Legree is her master, Cassy refuses to cower before him; instead, she makes her contempt known. This is similar to Linda's response to Dr. Flint. Although Dr. Flint owns her, Linda resists complete possession by making her feelings known. At one point, Linda tells Dr. Flint that she despises him, and he responds by warning her that he could kill her if he wished. This threat, however, does not subdue Linda; she replies with contempt: " 'You have tried to kill me, and I wish you had; but you have no right to do as you like with me' " (Jacobs 371). Both Linda and Cassy challenge the domination of their masters, and more importantly, they get away with it.

What is it about their relationships that allows these female slaves to wield this type of power? Linda and Cassy have somehow managed to enter their masters' hearts and minds in such a way that they emasculate their patriarchal owners. Each threat by Flint or Legree becomes a futile attempt to assert their manhood. Linda and Cassy appear to have turned the Jezebel myth around for their own uses. The Jezebel stereotype allows Flint and Legree to view Linda and Cassy as wanton wenches who are both willing and able to satisfy their sexual desires; however, the other aspect of this stereotype is Jezebel's castrating sexual power. Because Linda and Cassy are viewed as wielding great sexual powers, they are able to use this power to manipulate their masters.

Flint and Legree may hold the keys to freedom, but Linda and Cassy possess the keys to their masters' souls. Both men have an uncontrollable passion for their slaves. This passion, however, is more than pure sexual desire, since both men could easily force their slaves to obey their wishes. There appears to be more to the bond between master and slave than mere sexual desire. For example, Cassy can make Legree quite uneasy; she "had an influence over him from which he could not free himself" (Stowe 526). Stowe's narrator comments that Legree realized that Cassy was completely at his mercy, yet he could not avoid being controlled by her: "[S]he had become in a measure his mistress, and he alternately tyrannized over and dreaded her" (567). Linda's power over Flint is not as clearly stated in the text, but her power can be surmised by analyzing Flint's actions. He appears to be consumed with the desire to have Linda willingly give herself to him. At several points, he offers to make a lady of her and eventually free her, if she agrees to be his mistress. He also becomes the most enraged with her when he realizes that she is receiving another's attentions. Upon learning of Linda's second pregnancy, Flint is overcome with anger. Flint heaped epithets upon Linda and referred to her pregnancy as a "crime against *him*" (Jacobs 405). Flint is clearly suffering from sexual jealousy.

Although Flint plagues Linda, she is also able to eventually use his jealously to outwit him when she escapes. This is similar to the way in which Cassy manipulates Legree's fear in order for her and Emmeline to escape. Despite their different circumstances (one is a character in an 1852 abolitionist novel and one is a real runaway slave writing in 1861), Cassy and Linda both rely on wit and cleverness to escape. Cassy's narrative experience and Jacob's autobiographical experience differ from the events that Frederick Douglass foregrounds in his narrative. While Stowe and Jacobs highlight Cassy and Linda's cleverness, Douglass focuses on his ability to read, work hard, and defend himself physically. By stressing these particular aspects, Douglass constructs his escape to freedom as a maturation into manhood. Although both slave narratives focus on the power relations between master and slave, Douglass describes them in terms of physical power, while Jacobs describes a battle of wits. The difference in the representation of power relations appears to be at least in part attributable to gender differences. If one compares the parallel scenes of Douglass' battle with Covey and Linda's verbal sparring with Flint, one notes that the narrators are operating under different auspices. Douglass seeks to assert his manhood by resorting to brute strength, while Linda attempts to deflect sexual harassment with sass and thus preserve her womanhood. Thus it is not just that they use different methods to resist their masters' power, but that there are different issues at stake as well. Both slave narrators are seeking the right of self-definition, but it is a gendered definition. In response to a slave economy that degenders slaves and relegates them to the condition of chattel, Douglass asserts his manhood and Linda her womanhood.

Jacobs depicts a war of words between Linda and Flint that is predicated on the female slave's right of self-definition. Although she is a slave, Linda refuses to acknowledge that Flint has absolute power over her. When Flint asks whether or not she realizes that he has the power to kill her, Linda responds by stating that he does not have the right to do what he would like with her. This exchange is just one of many in which Flint asks her to acknowledge his dominion and Linda refuses. Dana Nelson argues that Flint's "own identity depends on her recognition of it. He apparently cannot feel his mastery until she reflects it to him."[31] Rather than recognize Flint's power over her, Linda continually talks back. According to Joanne Braxton, Linda's backtalk, or sass, is a form of self-defense: "Women resort to wit, cunning, and verbal warfare as forms of rebellion; in *Incidents in the Life of a Slave Girl*, Linda employs verbal warfare and defensive verbal postures as tools of liberation. Quick thinking and invective play vital roles, and Linda becomes a veritable trickster."[32] It is Linda's cunning that empowers her and separates her from the passive heroines of sentimental fiction. Unlike Stowe's Eva, Linda does not hope to effect change by merely inspiring others with her spiritual nature; instead, Linda takes action.

For example, rather than merely collapsing in the face of Flint's attacks, Linda plots a cunning counterattack in the form of an affair with Sands. She introduces Sands to the reader by describing how flattered she feels to receive attention from an unmarried man who is not her master, although she "saw whither all this was tending" (385). It is important to note that Jacobs describes herself as knowing rather than naive. Thus she foreshadows the fact that what is to come is not the traditional seduction of a naive young girl. Although she uses the language of seduction when she refers to giving one's self, in many ways she becomes the pursuer rather than the prey. This suggestion of switched roles is implied by the way in which she appears to set up her own seduction. Sands becomes her tool to enrage Flint.

However, Jacobs realizes that this goes against what is expected from "true" women, so she must justify her actions by acknowledging the impracticability of a slave exercising moral principles. This acknowledgment reiterates the fact that the cult of true womanhood is not available to female slaves. The exclusion of female slaves from the cult of true womanhood is in part due to the fact that true womanhood is constructed in relation to its opposite. Thus "true" women are everything that female slaves are not. Nelson observes that this dichotomy is based on the way the two groups of women are valued differently by white men: " 'white ladies' are valued (by 'white' men) for their sexual chastity; 'black ladies' are valued (by 'white' men) for their sexual permissiveness."[33] This point may be further developed by realizing that it is not merely that black and white females were viewed differently by white males, but that each construction creates the other. In other words, the black female is promiscuous because the white woman is chaste and vice versa. In both instances, however, the females are property. Wallace asserts that "the white woman's purity, like the black female's promiscuity, was based upon her status as property."[34] The pure white woman is as much the property of the white man, who defines her as pure, as is the promiscuous black female, who is defined as sexual property by white men. The most insidious aspect of the cult of true womanhood is not so much the definition, but who does the defining. This ideal of womanhood was based on the assumption that men defined women's roles. Although the cult of true womanhood allowed some white women to be placed upon a pedestal to be admired, the pedestal was merely a gilded cage. The ideal of true womanhood imprisoned both those it excluded and those it included.

Jacobs' critique of true womanhood acknowledges this all-encompassing imprisonment of women within male-defined social codes. While Jacobs overtly attacks the definition of womanhood substantiated by the cult of true womanhood, the way in which she attacks it implies that each woman, not man, should define her womanhood. Linda questions the values of true womanhood when she suggests that female slaves should be judged by different standards. At first glance, this may seem like merely a call for two different standards—one for free women and one for slaves, but Jacobs appears to have more in mind. She implies that morals should be considered in context rather than based on set expectations. This call for a contextual reading of character suggests that there might be as many different definitions of true womanhood as there are women. This implication brings one back to the issue of essentialism which opened the first chapter. Jacobs is not arguing for a different definition of "woman," but instead noting that women are mutually constructed by various aspects of their life experience and thus there cannot be one single definition of womanhood (or motherhood).

Linda has called attention to the fact that she does not meet the definition of true womanhood, but she asks the reader's indulgence while she explains her stratagem. Although the taking of a lover is a clever move by Linda, Nelson notes that her choice must be a strategic one: "A fellow white—a fellow white *slaveholding* male— is the one category of humanity whom Flint cannot hope to command to submission in this social system. Sands—the anonymous white lover—checks Flint's domination of Linda. Linda herself has maneuvered the pieces into position, playing master against master, king against king."[35] Although some critics note that in the end, both men exploit Linda, one should not ignore the agency she commands. Rather than passively avoid Flint, Linda takes the offensive by taking a lover and asserting control of her sexuality. By revealing and justifying her sexual relations, Linda is violating one of the cardinal rules of the cult of true womanhood—purity. The ideal woman was passionless, yet Linda has not only engaged in sexual relations, but also encouraged and perhaps even initiated them.

Linda's willing entrance into sexual relations may be seen as a quest for personal autonomy. Rather than give into Flint's demands, Linda chooses her own partner. This personal autonomy that Linda gains from her actions seems to outweigh Sands' later betrayal. Unlike the traditional seduced maiden, Linda does not have uncontrollable passion for Sands.[36] When Flint asks if she loves the father of her child, she simply responds that at least she does not despise him. Linda's affair with Sands is clearly one of utility, not a love affair gone bad. This is an important distinction to make since usually the female mistress is used by the male lover, but in this case Linda is using Sands at least as much as he is using her.

Taking Sands for a lover is just one example of Linda's cleverness. While hiding in her grandmother's garret, Linda again proves to be quite resourceful. Linda is described as the ideal sentimental heroine when she is in the garret, but this passivity does not last. Linda reverses the role of passive victim for that of the active opponent. While in the garret, she manages to send Flint on wild goose chases by sending letters from herself to him, but dated from New York. Although she is in hiding, she is still able to manipulate her own destiny. She refuses to merely lie still and wait for others to act.

Although Linda is at times able to outwit Flint, it is important that one does not read too much into these acts of rebellion. Carla Kaplan observes that various critics focus on three strategic subversions, which assert Linda's agency: her affair with Sands, her retreat to the garret, and her letters supposedly sent from New York. Kaplan, however, is uncomfortable with interpretations that suggest power is easily subverted and reversed. She argues that "by identifying Brent's agency solely with the rebelliousness of these acts the critic assumes that their liberatory meanings override their self-defeating or submissive ones."[37] According to Kaplan, such readings "risk occluding the very impasse this narrative represents." Throughout the narrative, Jacobs seeks to illustrate Linda's inability to completely escape her master's clutches.[38] While Kaplan's point is well taken, it is also important to note that throughout the text, Jacobs refuses to describe Linda as a completely passive victim because she resists as much as she can. Although one would not want to overstate Linda's agency, it cannot be completely denied. Kaplan, however, would like to find agency not so much in

Linda's actions, but in her refusal to act. She argues that by focusing on Linda's rebellious acts, critics miss the agency of Linda's "refusal of consent and self-justification."[39] An example of Linda's refusal of consent would be her refusal to give herself willingly to Flint. Although some critics question Linda's ability to rebuff Flints' advances, what is more important for our purposes is Linda's refusal to be a willing concubine.[40] An example of her self-justification would be the explanation that she offers for her affair with Sands. As a slave, Linda refuses to be held accountable to conventions established by a free society without regard for those they enslave. Thus Linda's agency comes not just from rebelling, but from her refusal to be co-opted by a system that so clearly excludes her. Thus although she borrows the elements of sentimental fiction, she refuses to be the traditional sentimental heroine.

Just as Jacobs is able to reconfigure the sentimental heroine, she is also able to reformulate the use of sentimentality. Like many before her, Jacobs uses sentimentality to draw attention to the cruelty of slavery. Although Jacobs intends to work on her reader's feelings, she also intends to present a realistic depiction of slavery, not merely a tear-provoking narrative. Part of the slave narrative tradition involves the assertion of the narrative's veracity. For example, Frederick Douglass' narrative is prefaced with a letter from William Lloyd Garrison in which he asserts that the following narrative "is essentially true in all its statements; that nothing has been set down in malice, nothing exaggerated, nothing drawn from the imagination; that it comes short of the reality, rather than overstates a single fact in regard to SLAVERY AS IT IS."[41] These sentiments are echoed in Jacobs' preface: "Reader be assured this narrative is no fiction. I am aware that some of my adventures may seem incredible; but they are, nevertheless, strictly true. I have not exaggerated the wrongs inflicted by Slavery; on the contrary, my descriptions fall short of the facts" (335). Thus both writers not only assert the veracity of their texts, but also their inability to completely describe the horrors of slavery. This inability to tell all is part of their assertion of the absolute inhumanity of slavery. The horrors are too great to contain with mere words.

Although Jacobs acknowledges her inability to provide a complete description, she does her best to describe her experience in a way that will gain her reader's sympathy. Jacobs states this intention directly: "Reader, it is not to awaken sympathy for myself that I am telling you truthfully what I suffered in slavery. I do it to kindle a flame of compassion in your hearts for my sisters who are still in bondage, suffering as I once suffered" (363). She then follows this appeal with the story of two half-sisters—one white and one slave. The fair child is described entering womanhood with a fair path of blooming flowers, while her slave sister and childhood playmate, while also very beautiful, was forced to live a life of sin, shame, and misery. This comparison is similar to Stowe's comparison of Eva and Topsy, but the comparison is of a different nature. While Stowe uses Eva and Topsy as representatives of their respective races, Jacobs presents different histories that are related to race, but not necessarily emblematic of racial characteristics. Stowe describes the girls as "representatives of the two extremes of society. . . . They stood the representatives of their races. The Saxon, born of ages of cultivation, command, education, physical and moral eminence; the Afric, born of ages of oppression, submission, ignorance, toil and vice!" (Stowe 361–62). This implies that Eva and Topsy's characters are in some way predetermined by their racial heritage. Jacobs, however, avoids such biological determinism in her comparison. It is merely a twist of fate that separates the destinies of the sisters. Surely, this fact was not lost on Jacobs' readers as they contemplated the precariousness of their own positions.

The fate of the half-sisters is not determined by their race, but their status as free woman and slave. This view is later reinforced when Linda states, "I admit that the black man *is* inferior. But what is it that makes him so? It is the ignorance in which white men compel him to live" (Jacobs 375). Thus Jacobs is arguing against the South's contention that blacks were inherently inferior and thereby should be enslaved. After describing the very different lives that await these sisters, Linda condemns the silence of the North in face of the evils of slavery. Notice that Linda does not address herself to a white audience, but a free audience. It is the lack of freedom that makes all the difference, not one's racial heritage. She is appealing to a sacred American value—freedom.

Linda also appeals to the woman reader's sense of motherhood by comparing her situation with that of female slaves. Linda's depiction of motherhood within slavery supports the argument of Spillers and Davis; female slaves were seen as breeders, not mothers. Female slaves were not allowed to raise their children. In order to distinguish the female slave's predicament from that of free mothers, Linda describes the New Year's Day festivities. For free women, New Year's Day is a happy occasion because they do not worry that the next morning might bring the sale of their children. Yet this is not the case for the female slave on New Year's Day who fears that one or more of her children might be taken the next morning. After contrasting the different experience of female slaves and free women, Jacobs refuses to allow the reader to assume that the female slave was indifferent to her situation. Although the female slave is unable to play the same maternal role as free women, Jacobs insists that female slaves do still have a mother's instincts. By appealing to shared motherly instincts, Jacobs seeks to create a sense of sisterhood between free white mothers and female slaves. Thus *Incidents,* like other sentimental texts, "creates the extension of feeling on which the restitution of humanity is based by means of equations between the deep common feelings of the reader and the exotic but analogous situations of the characters."[42] Jacobs seeks to find a common ground between slaves and the reader in order to create a sympathetic identification between them.

Not only does Jacobs wish for the reader to sympathize with the slaves, but also with the slaveowners who are corrupted by the institution—slaves are not the only ones who suffer under slavery. In the chapter entitled, "Sketches of Neighboring Slaveholders," Jacobs describes the negative effects slavery has on the master. As evidence of her contention, Jacobs refers to the cruelty of several slavemasters and the sexual improprieties of slaveholding men and women. It is rare to discuss the sexual relations between white women and slaves; however, Jacobs not only mentions the relationships, but also comments on the double standard that brings shame to white mothers, but not white fathers of racially mixed offspring.[43] Although Jacobs only discusses the sexual relations of white women in passing, her remarks do offer a significant critique of slaveholding and sexism. Wallace comments that slavery was based on an intricate balancing of extremes: "That white was powerful meant that black had to be powerless. That white men were omnipotent meant that white women had to be impotent."[44] This system was also predicated on the belief that since white women were chaste, black females were promiscuous, but what happens when slavery begins to sully the white woman's purity? Although Jacobs does not devote much attention to this aspect of slavery, the importance of white women's purity is evident in the postbellum lynching phenomenon, which was frequently justified by the accusations of rape or attempted rape of white women. Jacobs implies that slavery not only excludes female slaves from the cult of true womanhood, but also threatens the purity of white women. Jacobs does not discuss sexual relations in order to incite her reader, but to elicit sympathy. This sympathy is not only for slaves who are victimized by their masters, but also for the masters who are corrupted by their own cruelty and licentiousness.

Another tactic that Jacobs uses to gain sympathy from the white reader is to question the racial distinction between the reader and the slaves. Jacobs, whose grandfather is white, is of mixed heritage. The mixing of the races is referred to throughout the text as Jacobs questions racial designations. The African slaves are said to have been created by God to be slaves, but she asks, "then who *are* Africans? Who can measure the amount of Anglo-Saxon blood coursing in the veins of American slaves?" (376). By stressing the race mixing and the fair skin of slaves who could pass, Jacobs reveals that there is not really that much separating the free from the slave.[45]

Despite the intermixing of white and black and the increasing difficulty of distinguishing white from black, attempts were made to reify the racial categories. The most salient attempt to retain the categories of white/free and black/slave was the determination that the child would follow the condition of the mother. Therefore a near white slave who bears a white man's child gives birth to a slave. What separates the half-sisters whom Linda refers to is not so much their heritage, but their maternal legacies—the maternal mark to which Spillers refers.[46] A child of mixed blood born to a free white woman would not face the same repercussions as the child born to an enslaved black female.[47] This reveals not only the capricious nature of slavery and racial designations, but it also reveals the power of patriarchal authority. White male slaveholders created a structure that allowed them to increase their stock without social stigma as well as control the sexuality of the women in the community.

Thus Jacobs utilizes sentimentality not only to create sympathy, but also to offer veiled critiques of society. Nina Baym observes that "*sentimentalism*, though it denotes private, excessive, undisciplined, self-centered emotionality, also denotes public sympathi and benevolent fellow feeling."[48] It is this benevolence that Jacobs seeks to harness for the antislavery cause.

In order to harness this sympathy, Jacobs is very particular about her use of sentimentality. Nelson observes:

> Many have commented on how *Incidents* draws its structure from popular sympathetic or domestic fiction, producing an appeal to Northern women to identify with the act on behalf of their enslaved "sisters." But while it enlists the productive energy of that genre, it carefully interrogates the power structure implicit in popular configurations of sympathy.[49]

The earlier examples of the use of sympathy capitalize on the comparative nature of the incidents, but Jacobs does not wish to elide all difference in order to create sympathy. According to Nelson, "Sympathy ideally should *bridge* the gap of difference between sisters. Yet it neither can nor should *collapse* the differences that it bridges."[50] Thus although female slaves may feel as free mothers do about their children, there are differences that cannot be ignored. This is also true when one compares the situations of different slaves; although there were similarities among the slaves, slave experiences were not the same for all. Thus when Fanny and Linda commiserate about being separated from their children, Fanny notes the difference between their situations by reminding Linda that she will see her children, while Fanny has no such guarantee. Nelson notes that this exchange illustrates "the important differences in women's experiences that should not be overlooked in the moment of sympathy."[51] Jacobs appears to be aware of the dangers of sympathy, which Yellin discusses in *Women and Sisters*.[52] Although Jacobs' text seeks to create a community of women who oppose slavery, the feminist appropriation of antislavery discourse served to mask the very real differences between the oppression of female slaves and free white women.

This concern about feminist appropriation is evident in the conclusion of *Incidents*:

> Reader, my story ends with freedom; not in the usual way, with marriage. I and my children are free! . . . The dream of my life is not yet realized. I do not sit with my children in a home of my own. . . . But God so orders circumstances as to keep me with my friend Mrs. Bruce. Love, duty, gratitude, also bind me to her side. It is a privilege to serve her who pities my oppressed people, and who has bestowed the inestimable boon of freedom on me and my children. (513)

Mrs. Bruce's sympathy leads her to purchase Linda and set her free, but this type of sympathy does not create an egalitarian relationship. Throughout the text, Linda describes herself as a woman moving beyond the restrictions placed upon the sentimental heroine, but in the end Mrs. Bruce interferes with her pursuit of personal liberation. Linda makes it clear to Mrs. Bruce that she does not wish to be bought because she already considers herself free and such an act on Mrs. Bruce's part would create a tremendous obligation that could not be easily repaid. By not respecting Linda's wishes, Mrs. Bruce violated Linda's personal autonomy. Thus according to Yellin, "the discourse of antislavery feminism became not liberating but confining when it colored the self-liberated Woman and Sister white and reassigned the role of the passive victim, which the patriarchy traditionally had reserved for white women, to women who were black."[53] Linda has already liberated herself by fleeing slavery, but by purchasing Linda's freedom, Mrs. Bruce places Linda in the position of victim and herself in the role of liberator. Linda's ambivalence about her newly purchased freedom is even more apparent in an excerpt Amy Post takes from one of Jacob's letters:

> "I thank you for your kind expression in regard to my freedom; but the freedom I had before the money was paid was

dearer to me. God gave me *that* freedom; but man put God's image in the scales with the paltry sum of three hundred dollars. . . . I was robbed of my victory; I was obliged to resign my crown, to rid myself of a tyrant." (515)

Thus Linda's text not only does not end in marriage, it also does not end in true freedom because she can never repay her debt to Mrs. Bruce.

Although Linda cannot completely escape the bonds of the sentimental heroine, Jacobs, the author, can escape the confines of the sentimental novel in order to write a narrative about a female slave who may not meet the requirements of true womanhood, but is yet a sister and a woman. The end of the text confronts the reader with a woman who bore two children without the benefit of marriage, but who is not apologetic about it.[54] Unembarrassed by her single motherhood, Linda laments a society that will not allow her to attain her dream of a home of her own. It is significant that Linda does not desire a home and husband, but merely a home. The fact that Linda does not foresee nor desire a male provider implies a critique of traditional gender expectations.

Linda's tale of single motherhood is similar to that of Frado in Harriet E. Wilson's *Our Nig; or, Sketches from the Life of a Free Black*. While Linda never marries, Frado is abandoned and later widowed. Clearly the single motherhood of these two women is brought upon by very different circumstances, but the authors of both texts use these circumstances to critique certain patriarchal constructions of family and motherhood. Like Jacobs' text, *Our Nig* contradicts the traditional ending of women's sentimental fiction by not ending in marriage. Instead of ending their texts romantically and conclusively, Jacobs and Wilson both utilize open-ended conclusions. This openness is not due to a lack of husbands, but an inability to provide for their families in a society that expects women to both have and want husbands. While some might argue that the endings of these texts is merely a reflection of the author's circumstances, I would argue that both texts consciously highlight the protagonist's diversion from the norm and suggest that marriage should not be expected by society. Both authors appear to imply that society should have room for independent women and mothers, rather than assert the necessity of a husband and father. According to P. Gabrielle Foreman, "Both authors accept the ideology of home and motherhood, but they demand their own power of definition, and of self-dependency, by insisting on the right to support their children and themselves within their own domestic and woman-centered economy."[55] Jacobs and Wilson both imply that marriage is not a woman's sole reason for living. In fact their treatment of marriage even suggests a critique of compulsory heterosexuality—a woman does not need a man. The fact that both women leave the domestic realm to seek work, rather than rely on a man to provide for their needs suggests a very different view of domesticity and the mother's role. In fact their views appear to be the antithesis of true womanhood, but despite this difference both authors claim true womanhood for their protagonists. This version of true womanhood is one that comes from within rather than without as women, not men, are doing the defining.

Although Jacobs and Wilson offer similar critiques, the authors utilize different genres. While Jacobs ostensibly wrote a slave narrative that borrows from the woman's sentimental novel tradition, Wilson's text is normally referred to as an autobiographical novel.[56] In writing her novel, Wilson, like Jacobs, borrows from the slave narrative genre and the sentimental novel tradition. It is Wilson's borrowings from these traditions that lead Carby to regard *Our Nig* "as an allegory of a slave narrative, a 'slave' narrative set in the 'free' North."[57] One of Carby's justification for such a reading is the subtitle, "Sketches from the Life of a Free Black, in a Two-Story White House, North, Showing That Slavery's Shadows Fall Even There." Carby argues that the two-story white house represents the southern plantation, while Frado is practically a slave. As in the conventional slave narrative, scenes of beatings and brutality exemplify Frado's suffering. Mrs. Bellmont, who is described as a woman with southern principles, controls the household and symbolizes the South's power. Carby notes that as the story unfolds, the house begins to resemble the nation. "In a close resemblance to the position of many abolitionists, Mr. Bellmont and his son offered sympathy and loud protestations but were unwilling to assert the moral superiority of their position by fighting the mistress, the South, and imposing an alternative social order." Thus the two-story house becomes "an allegory for the divided nation in which the object of controversy and subject of oppression was *Our Nig*."[58] Carby's allegorical reading of the text is reinforced by the ironic disjunction between the title and the text. Wilson's *Sketches from the Life of a Free Black* is not too dissimilar from Jacobs' *Incidents in the Life of a Slave Girl*. Frado, technically free, is essentially enslaved in the "free" North. In fact, this is the same position that Linda finds herself in at the end of her story—she is both free and not free.

Wilson's debt to the slave narrative genre is evident in the supporting documents of her text. It was a convention of the genre to preface narratives with letters from distinguished white citizens, which attested to the veracity of the narrative. Although Wilson's text is not prefaced by such documents, three letters follow the text proper. In arguing for the satiric nature of Wilson's text, Elizabeth Breau notes that the letters appended to the text are not as authentic as those that normally accompany nineteenth-century texts by blacks.[59] For example, *Our Nig* is not prefaced with letters from distinguished whites who can attest to the author's veracity. Instead, the text concludes with three letters professing to verify Wilson's tale. Breau argues that this inversion suggests that perhaps Wilson is parodying the slave narrative genre.[60] This inversion is not merely a reversal in the letters placement, but also a change in emphasis. Rather than comment on the writer's character, the letters focus on the text itself. Breau contends that the three letters appended to the end of the text serve to mask the novel's satiric purpose by employing the slave narrative format. In fact, Breau suggests that Wilson's parody might have extended to the point of Wilson actually writing the letters herself. She cites the reversal of the letters' placement and their incomplete signatures, rather than the names of well-known, distinguished white males as evidence that perhaps Wilson is the author of the letters.[61]

Breau's satiric reading of the text appears to be supported by Wilson's satiric pseudonym. Beth Maclay Doriani argues that the pseudonym "Our Nig" is "a sarcastic comic retaliation at the culture which would deprive her of a true identity."[62] The quotations around the name allow Wilson to question the validity of the label. "To include 'our' challenges the idea of her belonging to someone;

to call herself 'nig' challenges the idea that her identity is defined only by her skin color and labels used by whites."[63] Henry Louis Gates argues that the pseudonym is used as a means to subjecthood: "Transformed into an *object* of abuse and scorn by her enemies, the 'object,' the heroine of *Our Nig* reverses this relationship by *renaming herself* not Our Nig, but 'Our Nig,' thereby transforming herself into a *subject*."[64] Wilson's assertion that the text was written by "Our Nig" parallels the assertion of many slave narratives that the narrative was indeed "written by himself (herself)." Thus Wilson does not rely on another to tell her tale, but retains authorial control.

Part of Wilson's authorial control is seen in her decision to blur the distinction between fiction and narrative. Although *Our Nig* is considered to be the first novel published in the United States by a black person, Wilson's text is not strictly fiction. Numerous scholars have addressed the autobiographical nature of the text, but the present concern is not the difference between fact and fiction, but the way in which Wilson's borrowings allowed her to create her own genre.[65] By linking her text to the slave narrative genre, Wilson is able to attain some of that genre's authority due to its basis in fact, but by writing a novel, she is not limited to a strict accounting of her life story. The sentimental novel tradition allows more artistic freedom for her depiction of Frado.

In his introduction, Gates notes the similarities between *Our Nig*'s plot and that of the "overplot" of nineteenth-century woman's fiction Nina Baym identifies in *Woman's Fiction: A Guide to Novels by and about Women in America, 1820–1870*. According to Baym, the plots of woman's fiction "all tell about a young woman who has lost the emotional and financial support of her legal guardians—indeed who is often subject to their abuse and neglect—but who nevertheless goes on to win her own way in the world."[66] Baym's woman's fiction is similar to sentimental fiction, particularly in its endorsement of a cult of domesticity:

> Domesticity is set forth as a value scheme for ordering all of life, in competition with the ethos of money and exploitation that is perceived to prevail in American society. The domestic ideal meant not that woman was to be sequestered from the

world in her place at home but that everybody was to be placed in the home and the world would hence become one. Then, to the extent that woman dominated the home, the ideology implied an unprecedented historical expansion of her influence.[67]

However, the concern will not be so much the way Wilson distinguishes herself from woman's fiction, but her treatment of domesticity and her revisions of sentimental fiction.

Just as Jacobs made crucial revisions, Wilson's changes are not idiosyncratic, but significant. Gates observes that not only does Wilson revise the traditional structure of woman's fiction, but also frequently inverts the most significant aspects of the structure.[68] By using a genre and then revising the key aspects, Wilson appears to be commenting on the form's inability to tell her particular story.

What makes Wilson's tale unsuitable for sentimental fiction is not simply that her protagonist is not white, but also that she becomes a single mother. While motherhood is celebrated in sentimental fiction, it is only a certain kind of motherhood. Mothers are responsible for maintaining and passing on good Christian values. Baym states that while the heroine of woman's fiction is liable to be abused by a number of people, "Least guilty are the mothers."[69] And in Stowe's woman-centered world, Rachel Halliday is presented as both the ideal mother and the ideal character. Yet in Wilson's text the mothers are far from ideal. Frado's mother abandons her and Mrs. Bellmont, a surrogate mother, abuses her. Thus Wilson is clearly offering a critique of mother rule celebrated in such texts as *Uncle Tom's Cabin*.

Wilson's critique is not a straightforward one, however. Although Mag and Mrs. Bellmont are far from ideal mothers, Frado is described as a struggling, but good mother. This difference in the portrayal of mothers appears to substantiate Elizabeth Ammons' argument that while Wilson is critical of mother rule, she has not completely abandoned the ideal. Although, Wilson describes the Bellmont household as a matriarchy substantiated by cruelty and abuse, behind this depiction is the longing for the mother-savior.[70] In her comparison of *Our Nig* and *Uncle Tom's Cabin*, Ammons argues that Wilson both inverts and echoes Stowe's maternal ideology. Wilson's depiction of

Mrs. Bellmont's tyrannical mother rule reveals that mother rule may be as bad or worse than white male rule. *Our Nig* implicitly critiques the belief that white mothers and Victorian maternal values will be the source of the nation's salvation. However, Ammons argues that *Our Nig* in a rather ironic fashion shares the sense of maternity espoused in *Uncle Tom's Cabin*. In Wilson's retelling of Marie St. Claire, the reader is horrified because Mrs. Bellmont transgresses our notions of mother.[71] Thus Ammons seems to believe that Wilson is not critical of mother rule as an ideal, but she reveals that even mother rule can go awry.

Even Stowe acknowledges this possibility with her portrayal of Marie; however, she balances Marie with numerous nurturing women such as Rachel Halliday. But in *Our Nig* there is essentially no reprieve from Mrs. Bellmont's sadism. Various characters wish to aid Frado, including Aunt Abby and Jane, but they are ineffectual in the face of Mrs. Bellmont's all-encompassing power; they are not mother-saviors. Their kindness is not enough to thwart Mrs. Bellmont; therefore, they are not effective protectors.[72] Aunt Abby and Jane's inability to aid Frado reveals that the idea of the mother-savior is merely a myth. Wilson's indictment of mother rule seems similar to Jacobs' critique of Mrs. Flint. Although these women are nothing like Mrs. Bellmont, their ineptitude and Mrs. Flint's misplaced anger suggest that social reform demands more than just a few well-meaning people; the system itself needs change. Whether the abusive party be male or female, society should not allow so much power to rest in one person's hand.

The problem with Stowe's concept of the mother-savior is that it is meant to work outside of the system. However, Jacobs and Wilson both question the feasibility of working outside of the social structure to create change within the structure. Both texts suggest that there does not exist a community of women to provide an alternative social structure. Ammons argues that in Wilson's text, "Domesticity is no sanctuary from capitalism . . . much less an alternative model for the reorganization of society." In fact, in *Our Nig*, "home" "manifests rather than contradicts capitalist values."[73] Thus for Wilson, maternal values are no match for capitalist values, but are themselves subsumed by capitalism. Frado's home with Mag as well as with the Bellmonts is guided by economics.

Mag's downfall begins with her seduction and subsequent pregnancy, but it is her poverty that seals her fate. She is first abandoned by her lover and then widowed when Jim dies. At the end of both relationships, Mag retires to a hovel to live in utter poverty. She then marries Seth, Jim's business partner. They did well when both were working, but eventually the business fails and they decide to leave the area to find work. In order to decrease their financial burden, Seth insists that they must give Mag's children (by Jim) away. Despite Mag's doubt that anyone would want anything of hers, Seth insists that pretty Frado would " 'be a prize somewhere.' "[74] Thus for the impoverished Mag and Seth, Frado becomes a commodity of which to be disposed.

Once it is apparent that her mother has abandoned Frado, the Bellmonts must decide what to do with her. " 'Send her to the County House,' said Mary. . . . 'Keep her,' said Jack. 'She's real handsome and bright, and not very black either' " (Wilson 25). The family discusses Frado's fate as though she were a stray dog that might be sent to the pound or kept by the family. As Mrs. Bellmont has difficulty keeping servants, she decides to keep Frado and train her as a servant. Frado's servitude, however, is not much better than slavery. Frado is overworked, underfed, and frequently beaten. Mrs. Bellmont, however, feels justified in her treatment of Frado because Frado's "time and person belonged solely to her" (41). Mrs. Bellmont clearly sees Frado's relationship with the family as an economic one. Her main concern is that she get her money's worth from Frado. In response to Mr. Bellmont's comment about the number of beatings Frado receives, Mrs. Bellmont declares: "'I'll beat the money out of her, if I can't get her worth any other way.' " (90). These beatings often take place in the kitchen, thus turning home into the site of an economic contract rather than a retreat from capitalism. In exchange for a home, Frado must perform certain duties.

This is the same position that Linda finds herself in at the end of *Incidents*. Both of these free women must serve another's family rather than perform these domestic duties for their own families. Agreeably Linda's position is not nearly as odious as Frado's, but despite the benevolent relationship between Linda and the Bruces, Linda cannot experience true freedom. Linda and Frado's inability to experience freedom within the domestic realm suggests that domesticity should not be celebrated for its own sake. There is nothing liberating about domesticity unless it is experienced within a certain context—with one's own family. This is what Linda still desires and what Frado hopes for if she can only earn enough money to care for her child.

As mothers, Linda and Frado both desire to care for their children. Both women fit Braxton's definition of the outraged mother: "The outraged mother embodies the values of sacrifice, nurturance, and personal courage. . . . Implied in all her actions and fueling her heroic ones is outrage at the abuse of her people and her person. She feels keenly every wrong done her children, even to the furthest generations."[75] Just as Linda's actions are guided by concern for her children, Frado's desperation to make money is fueled by her desire to take care of her son. One of the outraged mother's goals is "to impart a sense of identity and 'belongingness' to her child."[76] This goal appears to be the motivation behind each mother's desire for a home of her own. The fact that Frado has these maternal desires appears to substantiate Ammons' claim that Wilson is actually lamenting the absence of the mother-savior, rather than denying her possibility.

As mothers, Linda and Frado show concern for their children, but motherhood is also a means to their own fulfillment. Braxton argues that "Motherhood opens the pathway to greater self-awareness and, like sass, becomes a vehicle for the retrieval of lost self-respect."[77] Upon becoming mothers, both women base their actions on what is best for their children. Their sense of themselves as good mothers seems to increase their self-esteem. However, even before becoming mothers, both women use sass to gain some measure of self-respect. Neither Linda nor Frado are utter victims or completely without self-respect because they insist on standing up for themselves. Just as Linda tells Flint that he has no right to do what he would like with her, Frado refuses to continually cower before Mrs. Bellmont. One day as Mrs. Bellmont raises a stick to beat her, Frado orders her to desist, "'strike me, and I'll never work a mite more for you;' and throwing down what she had gathered [firewood], stood like one who feels the stirring of free and independent thoughts" (105). Mrs. Bellmont was so amazed by Frado's outburst that she picked up the wood and carried it into the house herself. Frado's display of sass parallels that of Linda and Cassy. Rather than use brute physical force as Douglass does with Covey, the women rely on their wit.

Although standing up to Mrs. Bellmont is probably her most satisfying display of sass, Frado makes use of her wit and cleverness on several occasions. For example, when Mrs. Bellmont wanted Frado to eat from her used plate, Frado has the dog lick it before she deigns to eat from it. Frado also displays her wit at school through several pranks. It seems significant that Frado does not turn to physical violence to protect herself. Unlike Linda and Cassy, she is not actually a slave and supposedly has some rights. She is also combating with other females—Mrs. Bellmont and Mary. Even when Mary tries to push her onto a plank across a stream, Frado does not appear to fight back. Frado is described as resisting, but this seems to mean merely refusing to go over the plank. Mary eventually falls into the stream in her attempt to push Frado, but it is Frado who is punished when Mary tells her mother that Frado pushed her. Thus it seems that Frado has much more success without the specter of physical violence. Wilson appears to support mental fortitude as the best means of bettering one's position. After all, it is the most morally bankrupt character, Mrs. Bellmont, who relies on physical abuse to have her way.

Critics have observed that Frado's brutal beatings serve to draw attention to her virtual enslavement, but Cynthia Davis extends the meaning of this violence to the body. Davis notes that "since the ideal white woman was virtually and (virtuously) bodiless, her black counterpart came to be defined as 'body' and little else."[78] The embodied status of the black woman is tied to stereotypical notions of her abnormal sexuality. According to popular stereotypes, black women were lascivious, but these writers seek to counter this misperception with the reality of their victimization. This line of thinking appears to underlie Jacobs' narrative. It is also evident in Pauline Hopkins' depiction of Sappho in *Contending Forces*.[79] Both Hopkins and Jacobs reveal the exploitation of black women in order to declare that the perceived promiscuity of black women does not come from within, but rather has been thrust upon them. Other writers, such as Frances E. W. Harper, respond to black women's supposed lasciviousness by depicting chaste black women.

Wilson, however, takes a slightly different approach by completely desexualizing Frado. This differs from Harper's tactic in
that Wilson removes any sexual tension from Frado's relationships.
Thus Frado's chastity is not questioned because sex is not an issue.
According to Davis, *Our Nig* challenges notions of black women's
inherent promiscuity by replacing the sexualized black woman with
the sexualized white woman—Frado's mother, Mag.[80] While Wilson
questions the purity of white women and their natural association
with "true womanhood," she does not merely reverse the stereotypes. Frado does not achieve the spirituality attributed to white
women. White women's designation as true women is connected to
their supposedly pious nature, and Frado has a rather ambivalent
attitude toward God and Christianity.

Frado's inability to achieve the spirituality attributed to white
women seems to be associated with her physicality. She seems
unable to reach the higher plane of spirituality because she is
enmeshed in her physical reality. Although Frado is not sexualized,
the physicality of her body is at the forefront of the text. Each
beating or whipping draws attention to Frado's body. Davis notes
the similarities between descriptions of Frado's beatings and classic representations of rape. Davis argues that "Wilson employs pain
in her narrative as a metonym for sexual exploitation."[81] According
to Davis, by emphasizing her physical pain, Wilson is able to address black women's experience as embodied beings without portraying black women as merely sexualized bodies.[82] This distinction
between body and sexualized body suggests Spillers' distinction
between "flesh" and "body." The sexualization of black bodies confines
them to the sphere of the flesh. Thus black women could be viewed
as merely a piece of meat to gratify (white) men. However, by
asserting their embodiment, but not their sexualization, Wilson
attempts to show black female bodies as human bodies that experience pain.

Wilson's approach at first seems quite different than that of
Jacobs, who focuses on the sexual degradation of female slaves, but
one actually sees more of Frado's beatings than Linda's sexual
harassment. In fact, Jacobs at once reveals and conceals Linda's
sexual abuse. The limitations of Jacobs' revelations are foreshad-
owed by the title of her narrative, which asserts that "incidents"

will be shared, not her entire life story. Jacobs' selectiveness is apparent in her interactions with Dr. Flint. She makes it clear to the reader that he made unsolicited sexual advances, but the reader is not given the content. For example, Linda tells the reader that Dr. Flint whispered awful things to her, but she does not reveal his actual words.

In analyzing descriptions of Linda's interactions with Flint, Foreman notes the discrepancy between Flint's reported actions and Linda's passionate responses. She suggests that "Jacobs transfers Linda's (unacknowledged) violated body to the body of the word. By serving for and providing the trope of physical abuse, words act both to describe her violation and to absorb it."[83] Foreman implies that Linda was indeed sexually violated by her master, but she uses her narrative to mask the attacks. Elizabeth Fox-Genovese comes to a similar conclusion when she states, "[I]t stretches the limits of all credulity that Linda Brent actually eluded her master's sexual advances."[84] Foreman and Fox-Genovese are not alone in their suspicions, however, one should ask: why would Jacobs deny an actual attack, yet acknowledge a consensual sexual relationship?

Rather than debate Jacobs' veracity on this point, I would like to look at the way in which language serves as a metonym for sexual abuse. Rather than depict actual abuse, Jacobs allows the reader to imagine the content of Flint's foul language. By forcing the reader to fill in the gaps, Jacobs can have it both ways—she can at once point to the slave's sexualized body and deny its existence. Even in discussing her relationship with Sands, Linda glosses over any mention of sexual intercourse, allowing the reader to fill in the blanks. By forcing the reader to supply the missing details, Jacobs also points to the reader's own collusion in the abuse of slaves. She seems to suggest that her northern readers, while not the actual proponents of slavery, are just as guilty by remaining silent.

Jacobs' tactics of both revealing and concealing her sexual history also seem to serve another purpose. Just as Wilson draws attention to Frado's physical abuse, Jacobs' pointing to her own violation allows her some measure of control. Davis asserts that Wilson takes control of her pain by documenting it. By using the pain instead of being used by it, Wilson effectively appropriates the power of her torturer.[85] In the first chapter, I discussed the way in which the female body is structured by its wounding. The torturer assigns meaning to the victim's body; however, Wilson reverses the power relations by focusing on Frado's abuse in such a way that she assigns meaning, rather than Mrs. Bellmont or Mary. Jacobs make a similar move as she calls attention to Dr. Flint's harassment and then responds with a sexual relationship of her own choosing.

This appropriation of victimization and pain works on two levels in both texts. As protagonists, Linda and Frado appropriate the power of their tormentors—Flint and Mrs. Bellmont—and as writers, Jacobs and Wilson maintain authorial control. Davis argues that in order for Frado to effectively use her pain she must first assert her voice.[86] This is exactly what she does when she stands up to Mrs. Bellmont. Just as Linda verbally challenged Flint, Frado challenges Mrs. Bellmont. According to Davis, by talking back to Mrs. Bellmont, Frado essentially recreates herself as a speaking body with agency rather than remaining a silenced body, which is acted upon at another's discretion.[87] This same argument may be extended to Linda as well. By expressing their pain, be it physical or sexual, both women are able to gain some power. I do not want to overstate this newfound power, but there is something to say for not being abject victims. Rather than remain silent about their victimization, they voice their pain and assert their right to their own bodies.

While the characters voice their pain, the authors also benefit from expressing their pain. Again, a connection can made between Jacobs' borrowings from sentimental fiction to write her narrative and Wilson's borrowings to write an allegory of a slave narrative. Both writers are "caught between a domestic ideology that relies on female sexual purity and an abolitionist discourse that insistently publicizes the sexual victimization of slave women." Because of their betwixt and between position, Jacobs and Wilson are able to demonstrate the way in which domestic ideology and abolitionist discourse both rely upon and contradict each other in reference to the documentation of the female slave's experience.[88] Fanny Nudelman argues that by using elements of sentimental fiction to tell her story, Jacobs "is able to expose the reliance of these structures on a mediated account of slave experience, and their inability to admit the slave woman's authorial agency."[89] A parallel may be drawn between Jacobs' position and Wilson's. As black women, both writers chose to depict the pain of black women rather than have that pain mediated through a white narrator. By asserting authorial agency, Wilson and Jacobs avoid having white women speak for them and thus unseat white women from their role of protectress. Both writers seem to be responding to the tendency of antislavery feminism to place black women in the role of victim, while casting white women as liberators. This, again, is what Jacobs finds so unsettling about Mrs. Bruce purchasing her freedom. However, this assertion of authorial control by Jacobs and Wilson resists this obligatory relationship with white women as well as mitigates the possibility of whites attaining sadistic pleasure by depicting black pain. The narrative agency that Jacobs and Wilson gain by telling their stories allows them to embody their heroines. Linda and Frado are not objectified by another; instead, they present themselves as subjects in pain. This is true of Frado despite the use of third person narration, since Wilson often collapses the distinction of first and third person by, for example, referring to Mag as "my mother," rather than as "her mother."

The narrative agency that Jacobs and Wilson gain by refashioning previous genres is indicative of the agency Linda and Frado seek in their reconfiguration of domesticity. Both writers make it a point to end their work very differently from the traditional sentimental novel, in which the just are rewarded and the villains are punished. In Linda and Frado's worlds, racism and economics often prevent the good and virtuous from receiving their reward. Neither Linda nor Frado are rewarded with a husband and happy home; however, that is not the reward they seek. Both would be satisfied with merely a home for their children, but even that is not to be.

Linda and Frado are not rewarded not because they are not deserving, but because they do not fit into the scheme of things. These women do not fit into the fabric of domesticity, but perhaps by telling their tales they can offer a critique of traditional expectations. While other sentimental texts, including *Uncle Tom's Cabin*, might celebrate feminine attributes while suggesting some change in family dynamics, they still retain a role for the father, the patriarch. This, however, is not the case in *Incidents* and *Our Nig,* which are both much more critical of the patriarch's role, whether black or white.

In *To Tell a Free Story*, William L. Andrews notes that abolitionists and slaveholders alike "claimed the institution of the family as the guiding ideal and the protection of the domestic well-being of black slaves" as one of their main concerns:

> For every James A. Thome who complained that "no ties of sacred home" were allowed to exist in the slave quarters, there was a C. G. Memminger to reply that under slavery "domestic relations become those which are most prized," since "each planter in fact is a Patriarch" who views the welfare of his "children and servants" as part of his sacred familial duty.[90]

Thus according to Memminger, Dr. Flint should not be seen as merely Linda's owner, but also as her father. However, Dr. Flint's incestuous suggestions clearly nullify him as a suitable father figure, and Sands is merely a shade better. Although Sands does not harass Linda, he clearly fails her and her children. Thus the two main "patriarchs" in Linda's life are proven to be ineffective protectors. With this type of history, it is no wonder that Linda does not pine away for some man to come and take care of her.

Wilson's text is also critical of so called "patriarchs." Almost every man in the text is criticized in some way. Mag's first lover is clearly shown to be a dastardly fellow and her second husband, Seth, is little better. Mag's lover leaves her to face poverty alone, while Seth encourages her to abandon one of her children in order to lessen their financial burden. Thus Seth shows that he is neither capable of supporting the family, nor is he willing to accept his (step)fatherly responsibilities. Seth's abdication of his fatherly duties is replicated when Frado enters the Bellmont household. Mr. Bellmont is in the position of a surrogate father to Frado, but he fails to protect her from his wife.

In many respects, he and Mrs. Bellmont enact a perverted version of the slave master and wife. While Jacobs' Dr. and Mrs. Flint represent the typical relationship, the Bellmonts are almost a reversal. Where Dr. Flint was Linda's tyrant, Mrs. Bellmont is Frado's. However, Mrs. Bellmont's extreme actions seem motivated by the same sexual jealousy that actuates Mrs. Flint. Mrs. Bellmont's jealousy is indicated by her concerns regarding Frado's complexion and beauty. For example, upon Frado's arrival, Jack describes her as "real handsome and bright, and not very black, either" (35). In response to this, Mrs. Bellmont does everything in her power to darken Frado's complexion and lessen her attractiveness. For instance, she has Frado out in the hot sun without a bonnet and cuts off her curls. These actions clearly indicate Mrs. Bellmont's envy in regard to Frado. Mrs. Bellmont compares Frado to Mary and seems to fear that Frado might be considered as good or better looking than her daughter: "She was not many shades darker than Mary now; what a calamity it would be ever to hear the contrast spoken of. Mrs. Bellmont was determined the sun should have full power to darken the shade which nature had first bestowed upon her as best befitting" (39). Although Mrs. Bellmont consciously directs her comparisons between Mary and Frado, I suspect that unconsciously she compares Frado to herself as well. Thus, although there is no indication of a sexual relationship between Mr. Bellmont and Frado, Mrs. Bellmont plays the role of the injured and enraged spouse.

But just as Mrs. Flint is unable to contain Dr. Flint, Mr. Bellmont is no match for his wife's wrath. Foreman argues that Mr. Bellmont's inability to protect Frado is due to his feminization. According to Foreman, Mr. Bellmont abandons his patriarchal role as head of the household and instead empowers Mrs. Bellmont to rule the roost.[91] Breau also reads Mr. Bellmont as feminized and contends that Mr. Bellmont's feminization is paralleled with Mrs. Bellmont's masculinization. Because she has gained access to masculine power, Mrs. Belmont's femininity and humanity have been perverted.[92] These depictions of Mr. and Mrs. Bellmont, however, should not be taken seriously. As Breau argues, they should be read within the context of a satire that includes "an inversion of traditional sexual politics, a satire against women modeled on male-authored misogynist satire, the satiric depiction of men as weak, effeminate, and hypocritical, and an exclusively female power struggle in which the evil women invariably defeat the good."[93] Hence, Wilson does not necessarily see women as innately tyrannical; rather, this impression is created by unequal gender standards. By playing with gender stereotypes, Wilson reveals that it is power, not gender, which is at issue. Mrs. Bellmont has been corrupted by excessive power—no one should feel as though one owns another human being.

As I mentioned previously, the excessive power that Mrs. Bellmont wields is also symbolic of the South's power. According to Carby, "The domestic realm, within which Wilson represented Mrs. Bellmont as the ultimate power, was the terrain of struggle over the treatment of Frado in which debates about the position and future of blacks in the United States are re-created."[94] Thus the effeminacy of Mr. Bellmont and his son James becomes symbolic of the North's inability to curtail slavery in the South.

Despite their sympathy for Frado, Mr. Bellmont and James were unwilling to actively resist Mrs. Bellmont. Mr. Bellmont's ineptitude is represented by his continual flights from home; rather than oppose his wife, he avoids witnessing her tyranny. James' flight from confrontation takes the form of illness. His mystery illness may be read as part of his feminization, since usually female characters are prone to pass away in this fashion. Ammons notes that there is a strong correlation between James' death and the death of Stowe's Eva. Although his death clearly echoes Eva's, Wilson does not depict the power of Christian conversion. While Eva's death inspires Tom and Tom's death inspires George Shelby to renounce slaveholding, James' death inspires Frado, who continues to have a miserable life.[95] Wilson is clearly critical of the Christian notion of the sacrificial victim. James' death has no enduring effect on his loved ones; yes, they love him and miss him, but they maintain the status quo. His death is not even enough to convert Frado to Christianity. According to Breau, James' poor health and his poor skills as a religious instructor symbolize the ineffectiveness of the abolitionist movement.[96] Thus one may read Wilson's allegory of a slave narrative not only as a critique of slavery, but also as a critique of northern racism and the ineffectiveness of the abolitionist movement.

In making her critique of northern abolitionists, Wilson utilizes the same metaphor that they use to justify their cause—the family. The pathological Bellmont family is a metaphor for an inept abolitionist movement. As I noted earlier, both sides of the slavery question utilized the sacredness of the family to support their positions. While Jacobs clearly illustrates that if slavery created an extended family, it was a dysfunctional family at best, Wilson makes a similar argument about the abolitionist family. The Bellmonts, Frado's surrogate family, are more concerned about Frado's usefulness to them than any sense of familial love and concern. Family members treat Frado as though she were a slave and the members that recognize Frado's abuse are powerless to prevent it. Thus Wilson criticizes this domestic relationship in order to suggest another possibility.

This new domestic order will begin with Frado, who does not have a mother-savior, but would like to be one for her son. However, before discussing Frado's motherhood, it is necessary to address the events that lead up to her motherhood. Although Frado does not experience her mother's "sexual fall," she does not fare much better in her selection of mates. Traditionally, the sentimental novel concludes with the marriage of the heroine, however, as Gates' observes, Frado's marriage to Samuel serves as "an ironic, false resolution," since homelessness and an infant then exacerbate her condition.[97] Foreman notes that Frado's abandonment by her husband echoes Mr. Bellmont's earlier abandonment; however, Samuel's abandonment is merely one of a long line of abandonments.[98] Frado was in a sense abandoned when her father died and also when Seth urged Mag to leave Frado behind. Mr. Bellmont, the patriarch who is unable to protect her from his wife, then emotionally abandons Frado. Thus each father figure or patriarch abandons her. This abandonment is merely continued when James dies without being able to protect her. Thus Frado's abandonment by her husband is merely a reenactment of previous disappointments.

Wilson's depiction of Frado's marriage appears to draw on elements of the seduction novel, but with a twist. Frado is deceived by Samuel and, like a seduced lover, is abandoned. However, unlike seduced and ruined heroines, Frado survives. Just at the point that should be her downfall, Frado turns her life around, "As soon as her babe could be nourished without his mother, she left him in charge of a Mrs. Capon, and procured an agency, hoping to recruit her health, and gain an easier livelihood for herself and child" (129). It is by working that Frado hopes to be a mother-savior for her son. She does not go out to find herself a husband and care-taker as her mother, Mag, had done with Jim and Seth, but instead Frado looks for employment. She exercises self-reliance by entering the public sphere and seeking work. Frado, like Linda, will not allow traditional expectations to break her spirit. Instead of allow-ing themselves to be victimized by a society that excludes them from true womanhood, Linda and Frado seek to define themselves as true women and mothers. It is this demand for self-definition that separates the feminist views of Jacobs and Wilson from that of Stowe. Rather than seek inclusion in a cult of womanhood defined by others, both writers revise ideals of womanhood and domesticity to allow women to be guided by their own ideas and values.

Jacobs and Wilson both use motherhood as a means to combat the dehumanization of slavery and racism. The slave economy viewed slaves as property or chattel, not human beings. Thus when a female slave bore children, she was seen in the same light as a broodmare contributing to her owner's stock. The denial of the female slaves' role as mother was just one part of a larger process to dehumanize slaves. However, slaves did not easily capitulate to this dehumaniza-tion. Female slaves were not only aware of the traditional African reverence of motherhood, but also of the importance placed on moth-erhood in American society. Therefore many female slaves turned to the role of the mother as a means to assert their personhood and womanhood. This movement is clearly depicted in the texts of Jacobs and Wilson. Both texts may be read as celebrations of the black mother. Karen Sánchez-Eppler argues that Jacobs' *Incidents* "pro-poses the role of the 'good mother' as a substitute for chastity. . . . This reinterpretation depends upon viewing the child not as a product of sexual activity, but as an object of maternal nature. . . . Motherhood replaces sexuality."[99] A similar reading is possible for Wilson's depic-tion of motherhood. Since Frado is desexualized, chastity is not at issue in *Our Nig*, but motherhood is advanced as a means to true womanhood. Despite Mrs. Bellmont's perversion of maternal values, it is maternal values and concern for her child's welfare that guide Frado's personal development. Thus maternity becomes an access to power for both Wilson and Jacobs, who combated negative stereo-types that demeaned black womanhood.

4

Tragic Mulattas
Inventing Black Womanhood

J ust as Harriet Jacobs and Harriet E. Wilson use motherhood as a means to combat the dehumanization of slavery and racism, Frances E. W. Harper and Pauline Hopkins employ a maternal consciousness to engender their protagonists. Under the rubric of the sentimental novel, Harper and Hopkins address the stereotype of the promiscuous black woman. However, like Wilson, these writers reconfigure the sentimental novel formula to better address their racial concerns. Their particular adaptations may also be read as a means of talking back to Harriet Beecher Stowe's *Uncle Tom's Cabin*. While many later writers revise and extend the work of their predecessors, Harper and Hopkins, clearly interact with Stowe in a call and response fashion. Like Jacobs and Wilson, they share Stowe's maternal consciousness, but they envision a different unfolding of this consciousness that is explicitly

93

racialized. Harper's *Iola Leroy* and Hopkins' *Contending Forces*, like Harriet Jacobs' *Incidents* respond to the exclusion of black women from the cult of true womanhood, but unlike Jacobs, Harper and Hopkins seek to include black women within this idea of womanhood, while Jacobs attempts to dismantle the ideology. Despite this difference, *Iola Leroy* and *Contending Forces* remain critical of the exclusionary nature of the cult of true womanhood. Harper and Hopkins address this omission by depicting their protagonists as mothers or mother figures, who by virtue of their maternity or maternal consciousness must be considered true women.

Writers such as Harper and Hopkins, who wrote after Reconstruction, were still affected by the legacy of slavery. Despite previous efforts to rescue the black woman's good name from the stereotypes developed during slavery, myths of the black woman's illicit sexuality persisted. Although the end of the Civil War brought the end of slavery, it did not eradicate a racist mindset. Technically the slaves were freed, but emancipation did not guarantee gender perrogatives; many whites continued to deny African American males and females the status associated with the titles "men" and "women." This resistance led some writers to address the issue in their writing. While some scholars have interpreted African-American writers' preoccupation with issues of sexual purity as a means of emulating white standards, Catherine Clinton argues black women's pursuit of respectability and virtue was foremost an issue of survival.[1] Both Harper's *Iola Leroy, or Shadows Uplifted* (1892) and Hopkins' *Contending Forces* (1900) respond to negative portrayals of black womanhood through their reworking of the tragic mulatta figure.

Although the use of the mulatta character by black writers is often disparged as merely an attempt to placate a white readership, these writers deploy the mulatta to question racial and gender contructs. In both novels, mulatta characters are subjected to sexual assaults on the basis of their race. One moment Iola is a respected white woman of the planter aristocracy, but upon learning of her black blood, she is relegated to the status of sexual object for which no indignity is too great. Grace suffers through a similar experience in *Contending Forces*; she is transformed to sexual object only when her race is questioned. In both these texts, the mulatta illustrates the interconnection of race and gender constructs. This mulatta character is used as a figure of mediation to reveal that even black women are true women. Unlike the stereotypical tragic mulatta, these women do not bemoan their mixed blood or desire acceptance by white society. For Grace, this is not an issue because her actual race remains ambiguous, but both Iola and Sappho, also of *Contending Forces*, do not take the opportunity to pass despite their ability to do so. The issue of passing will be taken up later, but I wish to call attention to the complexity of both writers' use of the mulatta.

Rather than use the white blood of their protagonists as an inroad to respectability and true womanhood, Harper and Hopkins employ maternal ideology. Iola and Sappho are both presented as caring, nurturing women. Although Iola does not become a mother during the course of the novel and Sappho is separted from her child for most of the book, both women are shown caring and providing for the larger black community as mother figures. Thus while motherhood is not as central to these texts as that of Jacobs' and Wilson's, the black woman is presented as a nurturing, maternal force in the black community.

Elizabeth Ammons observes that Harper shares Stowe's maternal ideology. She, like Stowe, appeals "to a sisterhood of mothers and argue[s] in favor of maternal values as the ethical alternative and logical correction to racial injustice in America."[2] Harper's knowledge of Stowe's writing is evident even prior to the publication of *Iola Leroy*. In response to *Uncle Tom's Cabin*, Harper wrote at least three poems: "Eliza Harris," "To Harriet Beecher Stowe," and "Eva's Farewell."[3] Although Harpers' poetry is not limited to the topics of race and slavery, according to Francis Smith Foster, "Harper's poems have been recognized as providing the most authentic rendition of the slaves' points of view available to nineteenth-century readers."[4] Antislavery poems make up approximately one third of the various versions of Harper's *Poems on Miscellaneous Subjects*. The prominent theme of these poems is the ability of ordinary people emboldened by their integrity and conviction to perform heroic feats. Heroic women, such as Eliza Harris, predominate in these poems.[5] Sisterly affection and maternal instincts serve as sources of strength for these heroic women. Harper returns to these themes in *Iola Leroy*. Although Harper's heroine is not a mother, the text is very much concerned with maternal values as the means to uplift the black community. Thus Harper's project is in line with a larger feminist tradition that equates feminine values with maternal values. Unlike Hortense Spillers, Harper does not critique this conjunction, but expands it to include black women.

Harper's celebration of maternal values is just one of the many similarities between *Iola Leroy* and Stowe's *Uncle Tom's Cabin*. Both writers use the sentimental tradition to explore the similar issues of racism and slavery. Harper's work may be seen as both an extension and a revision of Stowe's work. Stowe calls attention to the immorality of slavery, while Harper focuses on the aftermath of slavery. Stowe wishes the slaves to be free, but in "their proper place" away from white society, while Harper wishes for the former slaves to take their rightful place as members of an integrated society. Harper continues Stowe's work in another way as well. Some critics have lauded the feminist implications in *Uncle Tom's Cabin*, but Harper's text goes much further in its presentation of strong female characters and its articulation of feminist principles. Iola Leroy is portrayed not only as an enthusiastic supporter of the black race, but also as a budding feminist. Harper and Stowe appear to have similar aims in their attack against slavery and racism, but they have very different agendas in that Stowe wishes to morally strengthen the status quo, while Harper seeks to dismantle it completely.

As an example of race literature, *Iola Leroy* rewrites the portrayal of blacks in literature to facilitate the social movement of the black community. According to Richard Yarborough, much of African-American fiction written prior to World War I sought to elicit the reader's sympathy even if it meant overemphasizing or misrepresenting African-American life.[6] Like Stowe, Harper used sympathy as one of her main tactics of her protest novel. Although both writers wrote protest novels, Stowe, a pre-Emancipation writer, protested slavery, while Harper, a post-Emancipation writer, protested racial inequality. Both authors use sentimentality to create a sense of commonality between the reader and the characters. One of the aims of sentiment is to reduce the distance between two groups. It is the writers' hope that if the readers are able to sympathize with the sufferings of the characters, they will eventually see the injustice of the characters' situation.

Throughout her novel, Stowe attempts to draw sympathy from white women readers by appealing to their motherly instincts. Stowe's desire to elicit sympathy from fellow mothers is an aspect of the central position of women in her novel. According to Ammons, Stowe argues that motherhood must not remain in service to the patriarchy. However, as I argue in my second chapter, despite Stowe's attempt to present a woman centered utopia, she still accepts the tenets of the cult of true womanhood. Her white women characters are molded by this tradition, which insisted that women be pious, pure, submissive, and domestic. In other words, Stowe wishes to present powerful women who are still true women as defined by men.

The cult of true womanhood is also present in Harper's text, but with a revisionist twist. Hazel Carby describes the predicament facing black women writers: "They had to define a discourse of black womanhood which would not only address their exclusion from the ideology of true womanhood but, as a consequence of this exclusion, would also rescue their bodies from a persistent association with illicit sexuality."[7] This is why Harper emphasizes Iola's chastity. Even as a slave she resists the sexual overtures of her masters. This is Harper's attempt to rewrite previous portrayals of black women. She attempts to persuade the white reader that her black characters represent the true characteristics of blacks. She also wants the reader to sympathize with her characters and realize that they should not be subjected to injustice.

Both *Iola Leroy* and *Uncle Tom's Cabin* protest injustice, but while Stowe opposes slavery she does not address the racism that justified slavery. It is this racism that Harper wishes to eradicate. Both novels begin in the midst of slavery, but Harper's covers the period of the Civil War and Reconstruction. For Harper, the end of slavery is a reality, but for Stowe, it is merely a hoped-for reform. This difference in time has a significant effect on the messages of both novelists. *Uncle Tom's Cabin* is an abolitionist novel. Barbara Christian observes that "the novel constructed as a romance had been one of the most effective propaganda techniques that the abolitionists had used in their fight to change public opinion about slavery."[8] Stowe's text confronts the patriarchy's view of slavery as right and just and reveals its inhumanity and immorality.

Harper also attacks the patriarchy, but she takes her arguments much further. Her critique of the patriarchy is not merely an issue of gender, but also a racial issue. She speaks as a black woman who is subjugated because she is female and black. The patriarchy she seeks to destroy is a racialized patriarchy.[9] Harper does not seek to reform the ideas of men as Stowe does, and thus support the patriarchy; rather, she wishes to completely dismantle the hierarchical nature of a patriarchy that values one gender and one race over others.

Besides confronting the hierarchical nature of the patriarchy, Harper's text provides a different perspective on the Civil War by presenting the view of a black woman, rather than that of a white male. According to Elizabeth Young's "Warring Fictions," "Harper embeds the war in a narrative trajectory of maternal quest and reunion, simultaneously feminizing war narrative and using this literary form to represent the importance of maternal and familial structures in the black community."[10] Harper's text at once feminizes and colors the war by both foregrounding the heroism of black men and women and by depicting the war in the context of black family life.[11] This double movement of the text appears to support Ammons' contention that Harper views maternal values as the corrective to injustice; however, according to Young, Harper illustrates this through maternal absence, not presence.

Harper's focus on maternal absence, like Wilson's depiction of an antimother, draws the reader's attention to the importance of maternity. The black soldiers are portrayed in relation to their mothers: Robert runs away to join the army in part because his mistress sold his mother away from him and Harry joins a black regiment in order to increase the likelihood of finding his mother. Nonsoldiers, such as Ben Tunnel, are also described in relation to their mothers. For instance, Ben will not run away because his mother cannot go with him. Each of these men is responding to either the desire for reunion with or the fear of separation from their mother. Young contends, "*Iola Leroy* frames the war in terms of maternal *absence*." Her mother's disappearance marks the beginning of Iola's contact with the war and her search for her mother parallels the duration of the war.[12] It is only at the war's end that she reunites with her mother.

Although Iola does not find her mother until the war's end, during her stint as a nurse, she plays the role of mother for the troops. In her role as nurse, Iola provides a link between the two realms of mothering and warfare; thus, as nurse, Iola feminizes the war.[13] Harper's utilization of the nurse figure as well as other aspects of her maternal ideology clearly links her text to that of white women writers who depicted the war. Middle-class white women frequently served as nurses during the war; however, unlike Iola, they already occupied the home front, and thus had a position from which to expand. Iola, on the other hand, does not have a recognizable position at home, thus her entrance on the war front is much more vexed.[14] Harper not only feminizes the war by providing a woman's perspective; she also expands the definition of womanhood by portraying a black nurse-mother. Harper's focus on the black mother also serves to illustrate the primacy of familial relations within the black family. Young notes that Iola's maternal search is shared by Harry and Robert; thus the black mother serves as a focal point for the black community. Reconstruction can only begin after the reunion of families.[15]

Harper's text revises the claims for a national identity by stressing the importance of the family. In other words, Harper uses the family unit as the means to American identity. The desire for family unity is antithetical to the American slavery system, which sought to destroy familial bonds. By asserting the importance of family bonds, however, slaves assert their personhood and their right to freedom. Throughout the text, the characters are forced to decide which claims are more important: the family, liberation, or American citizenship. The slaves are in an anomalous position; they are in America, but not of it. They wish to be a part of the "American family" (not just a family in America, but part of America as family), but they are torn between the claims of their genetic family, the slave community, and the master's family.

Harper's text implies that the allegiance of the blacks should be with the black community. This does not mean separatism; indeed, Harper endorses interaction between the white and black communities, but ultimately the responsibility of racial uplift lies with the black community. Harper's endorsement of racial allegiance is apparent in her treatment of passing. Like Stowe, Harper uses passing to explore the color line; however, unlike Stowe's mulattos, who pass for white, Creole, or Spanish in their attempt to escape from slavery, Harper's mulattos never actively attempt to pass for white. Harper's mulattos pass by omission; they never explicitly claim to be white. By having her characters mistaken for white, Harper may question the color line without weakening her character's allegiance to the black community.

For example, Dr. Latimer refuses to pass for white in return for the support and recognition of his paternal grandmother. He will not betray his mother or her people. Despite his allegiance to the black community, Dr. Latimer does in a sense pass for white when he socializes with Dr. Latrobe. He does not say that he is white, but Dr. Latrobe assumes that he is and Dr. Latimer allows this assumption to continue so that he might later shake up Dr. Latrobe's conception of blacks. Dr. Latrobe "had thought he was clear-sighted enough to detect the presence of negro blood when all physical traces had disappeared."[16] Dr. Latimer, however, proves that this was not the case.

In fact, all of Harper's characters who could receive personal gain by passing refuse to do so. Some might argue that Harper's mulatto characters could have subverted the color line by passing for white, but this would not weaken the color line because passing does not interrogate the underlying principles upon which the color line is based. However, by refusing to pass explicitly, but inadvertently passing, these characters break down the color line because their blackness is not apparent. Neither their physical nor their intellectual characteristics give them away. They disprove the theories of Dr. Latrobe and those like him because their black blood does not in any way make them inferior. Thus it is only when an act of passing is revealed or thought to have taken place that the arbitrariness of the color line is revealed. The fact that a number of Harper's characters are mistaken for white reveals to the reader that race is merely a performance. In other words, the characters are racialized based on their actions, not inherent features.

Although Harper's depiction of race reveals race to be a biological fiction, Harper does accept race as a political concept. Despite her desire for a color-blind society, Harper realizes that society is indeed very color-conscious. This realization of the importance that color plays in American society probably affected her depiction of full-blooded blacks and mixed blacks. Harper presents the reader with both educated and uneducated full-blooded blacks. The presence of Lucille Delany and Reverend Carmicle serves to dispel the myth of black ignorance. These blacks are shown to be as worthy as, if not more worthy than, the mixed blacks. It is significant that Lucille is more educated than the mulatta heroine. In her presentation of full-blooded and mixed blacks, Harper questions the belief that white blood is necessary to create an intelligent person. This is not the case for Stowe, who only has mulatto characters who appear intelligent, enterprising, or genteel. Harper appears to be reworking Stowe's work in such a way as to salvage the moral force of her abolitionist ideals and to provide a corrective for Stowe's misappropriation of romantic racialization.

Besides addressing the color line, Harper also explores the need for the black community to elevate itself. According to Harper, this must be done in part through education. The major characters in the novel are all educated to some degree and they use their education to elevate their race. They are following Dr. Gresham's advice: "Out of the race must come its own defenders" (321). Toward the end of the novel, the black intellectuals are shown to be self-sufficient, as the white characters have virtually disappeared. Harper acknowledges the need for a new role for black intellectuals. According to Carby, "Iola's dismissal of the assistance of white patriarchal power was symptomatic of Harper's wider plea that the black community look toward itself for its future, not toward assistance and support from or alliance with the forces represented by the various white characters in the novel."[17] This seems to be the idea behind the "conversazione."

In the chapter "Friends in Council," a group of black men and women meet to share different views of various aspects of the race question. Bishop Tunster presents a paper based on emigration to Africa, but the others do not believe self-exile is the answer. This is another point of difference between Stowe and Harper. Stowe sends George and his family out of the country, while the majority of Harper's characters reject emigration as an option. The group discusses several points, but the most agreed upon is the need for scholastic and moral education. It is significant that this education is intended for both men and women and that women are also expected to be teachers, not just students.

The importance of the woman's role in racial uplift is apparent in the paper presented by Iola, "Education of Mothers." Iola's paper argues for the need for enlightened mothers. Her argument is readily accepted by the other members of the group. Iola urges that in light of the homelessness and absence of legal marriage due to the history of slavery, the black community must instill the belief that " 'the true strength of a race means purity in women and uprightness in men' " (437). This moral education of the community would fall upon the women. Reverend Eustace asserts that they " 'need a union of women with the warmest hearts and clearest brains to help in the moral education of the race.' " Iola endorses this by asserting, " '[I]f we would have prisons empty we must make the homes more attractive' " (438). Thus Harper's *Iola Leroy* clearly shares Stowe's maternal values.

Carby observes that in both *Iola Leroy* and Harper's lectures, "what shaped her work was an assertion of what she saw to be female virtues, values, and actions to counteract rampant commercial and mechanistic interests."[18] The views expressed in Iola's Education of Mothers" appear to echo those of Harper's 1983 address before the Brooklyn Literary Society, "Enlightened Motherhood." In this speech, Harper asserts: "We need mothers who are capable of being character builders, patient, loving, strong, and true, whose homes will be an uplifting power in the race. This is one of the greatest needs of the hour. No race can afford to neglect the enlightenment of its mothers."[19] It is clear that Harper believed in women's ability to mold the future. A year after the publication of *Iola Leroy*, Harper declares in "Woman's Political Future" that "today we stand on the threshold of woman's era, and woman's work is grandly constructive. In her hand are possibilities whose use or abuse must tell upon the political life of the nation, and send their influence for good or evil across the track of unborn ages."[20] Harper's ideal of women actively leading the elevation of the black community is evident in Iola's maternal values and feminist ideals.

The importance Iola places on motherhood and maternal values may remind one of Stowe's woman-centered world. As I mentioned in the previous chapter, Stowe supported a separate spheres ideology. Rachel, Mrs. Bird, and Mrs. Shelby do not have power outside of the domestic sphere. As mothers and wives, it is their responsibility to see to the family's moral upbringing. With the exception of Marie St. Clare, it is the women in the novel who represent a private, domestic brand of liberal morality.[21] The women are expected to share their morality with their husband and children and thus guide them along the proper path. Critics such as Myra Jehlen argue that by adhering to a separate-spheres ideology, Stowe "did not seek to advance the cause of women's self-rule, in fact, she affirmed their feudal placement."[22] Stowe's text is ultimately quite conservative in that it reaffirms male hierarchy despite suggestions of female superiority.

Harper neither reaffirms male hierarchy, nor suggests female superiority; rather she argues for equality between the sexes. Although Harper is not a supporter of a separate-spheres ideology, she does seem to adhere to a belief in sexual difference. Her attitude toward maternity implies that there is a distinction between feminine and masculine perspectives, but they are equally valued. One might question Harper's ability to be at once egalitarian and a staunch supporter of maternal values; however, the affirmation of maternal values is not without the concomitant assertion of the importance of paternal involvement. When Reverend Eustace offers his agreement that enlightened mothers are necessary, Lucille adds that enlightened fathers are also necessary. She states, " 'If there is anything I chafe to see it is a strong, hearty man shirking his burdens, putting them on the shoulders of his wife, and taking life easy for himself' " (437). Just as the father has a role within the domestic sphere, the mother has a role in the public sphere.

Equality between the sexes allows females to leave the domestic realm if they so choose. Iola is a staunch supporter of a woman's right to work. Although her Uncle Robert assures her that she need not work, she believes it is necessary for her independence. She tells him, " 'I think that every woman should have some skill or art which would insure her at least a comfortable support. I believe there would be less unhappy marriages if labor were more honored

among women'" (399). Iola does not look at woman's work simply
as preparation for marriage, but as crucial to her own sense of
well-being. She scolds Dr. Latimer for his assumption that Lucille's
qualities would make her a good wife: " 'Now isn't that perfectly
manlike. . . . Did any of you gentlemen ever see a young woman of
much ability that you did not look upon as a flotsam all adrift until
some man had appropriated her?' " (428). This question clearly
reveals that Iola does not believe that a woman needs a man to
constitute her worth. Iola has been working and engaging in community concerns because she does not believe that marriage should
be her sole concern.

Even as a single woman, Iola has something to contribute to her
community. Iola takes part in discussions about the black community, but she wants to do something more—she wants to do some
lasting service for her people. Dr. Latimer suggests, " 'Why not . . .
write a good, strong book which would be helpful to them? I think
there is an amount of dormant talent among us, and a large field
from which to gather materials for such a book' " (444). Iola's first
thought is that no one would expect anything good from "the black
Nazareth." However, Dr. Latimer immediately responds by telling
her, " '[O]ut of the race must come its own thinkers and writers' "
(444). He does not believe that whites can do justice to the black
experience because they cannot put themselves in the black man's
place. Iola then agrees to write a book, but she wishes to make
Dr. Latimer her hero. Dr. Latimer proposes instead that she tell
her own story. The suggestion that Iola write a book has feminist
implications. Dr. Latimer does not naturally assume that a male
must write the book, nor does he assume that the book must be
about a male. Women are expected to take a full part in the work
for the progress of their people. All of the female characters take
some form of action to help the community, whether it is in the
form of Aunt Linda's advice or Lucille's teaching. Writing a book
is merely the natural extension of the community service Iola
provides.

Dr. Latimer's urging of Iola to write a book echoes the historical
circumstances surrounding Stowe's writing of *Uncle Tom's Cabin*.
According to the story, her sister-in-law, Mrs. Edward Beecher, wrote
Stowe a letter stating: "If I could use a pen as you can, I would

write something that will make this whole nation feel what an accursed thing slavery is."[23] This echoing, however, is not merely coincidental; rather Harper is responding to the notion that Stowe could write about the black experience. Harper, like Dr. Latimer, seems to question the limits of sympathy and empathy. It is not that Harper does not see the value of sentimentality, but, like Jacobs, she does not want sympathy to negate difference. While one might sympathize with another's experiences, this is not the same as having them; therefore one's perspective is never the same. For example, although Stowe sympathizes with her black characters, she still describes her black characters as inferior to whites. Her racism is not from a lack of sympathy, but perhaps from a lack of understanding. One may argue that despite the presentation of Tom as the hero of her text, she does not valorize black characters and experiences. I contend that Stowe's text was addressed to whites and her primary concern was not the experience of the slaves, but the response of whites to slavery. Harper, on the other hand, is not only writing about the black experience, but also writing for the black community and from within the community, which allows her to portray black characters in another light.

Harper's different background from Stowe allows her to make feminist concerns a more integral part of her text. Since racism, not merely slavery, is Harper's prime concern, she argues that men and women of the black community must work together. Upper-class and lower-class blacks must also come together to elevate the black community as a whole. Since all members of the black community are subject to racism, there is no room for sexism or classism to divide what must be a united struggle. Stowe, on the other hand, has no need to call for social elevation, only moral elevation. Thus she turns to women, the moral superiors, to aid men in their moral life. To call women to take a more active role within the public arena would upset a patriarchal system that Stowe does not seek to disrupt. Stowe probably did not see a need to build a social system for her white readers because one was already in place that only needed mending in the area of morals. Harper, however, addresses a newly freed people who are excluded from the American social system and do not have a system recognized by the dominant society, and thus might be more open to her egalitarian beliefs.

Throughout the novel, Iola is presented as a self-sufficient woman. Although she does not need a man to make her whole, Iola does agree to marry Dr. Latimer, a black male, after refusing to marry Dr. Gresham, a white male. Her acceptance of Dr. Latimer's proposal and rejection of Dr. Gresham's is not only a statement of Iola's racial allegiance, but also a rejection of traditional marital relations.[24] Dr. Gresham presents his proposal in terms of chivalric rescue: "All the manhood and chivalry of his nature rose in her behalf, and . . . he resolved to win her for his bride." He says to Iola, " 'Miss Leroy, you need not be all alone. Let me claim the privilege of making your life bright and happy' " (274-75). Iola's rejection of Dr. Gresham's offer to protect her and her secret seems to comment on her mother's earlier decision to accept just such a proposal from Eugene Leroy. The disastrous results of the Leroy marriage appear to inform Iola's decision to reject secrecy and submissiveness. Instead, Iola openly acknowledges her connection to the black race and intends to work with her husband for the good of the community. Iola and Dr. Latimer's marriage will be one of mutual commitment to a shared dream. Harper describes their relationship as an equal partnership:

> Kindred hopes and tastes had knit their hearts; grand and noble purposes were lighting up their lives; and they esteemed it a blessed privilege to stand on the threshold of a new era and labor for those who had passed from the old oligarchy of slavery into the new common wealth of freedom. (453)

Rather than give up her life's work to marry, Iola marries a man who is willing to share her work. Iola and Dr. Latimer's egalitarian relationship may be explained in part by Claudia Tate's discussion of black female desire in sentimental narratives. According to Tate, an integral part of black women's postbellum sentimental fiction is the revision of the conventional gender conduct of husbands and wives. By blurring the distinctions between masculine and feminine decorum, the patriarch is divested "of the presumed rights to unquestioned authority over household management and absolute deference from women and children."[25] Iola may still be traditional in that she is a wife and she works in a traditionally female field, but she has not allowed marriage to form her self-image.

And as with most sentimental novels, with the marriage comes the end of the text. Unlike *Incidents* and *Our Nig*, *Iola Leroy* does end on a positive note like most sentimental texts. The text proper concludes with the note: "The shadows have been lifted from all their lives; and peace, like bright dew, has descended upon their paths. Blessed themselves, their lives are a blessing to others" (461). Then in the note following the text, Harper expresses her hope that her text will "awaken in the hearts of our countrymen a stronger sense of justice and a more Christlike humanity" (462). Harper clearly believed that books like hers would help to lift the shadows, hence her title: *Iola Leroy, or Shadows Uplifted*. Not only does this book reaffirm the need for black writers to write about their experience, but it also acknowledges that women may write about their experiences and that their experiences are worth reading about. This novel is in essence the book that Dr. Latimer suggests that Iola write.

Not only does Harper's text confirm the value of black women's experiences, it also presents a veiled argument against the exclusive nature of the cult of true womanhood. The cardinal virtues of piety, purity, submissiveness, and domesticity traditionally excluded female slaves, since they were usually unable to meet the purity requirement, due to the sexual exploitation associated with slavery. Iola, however, is able to maintain her purity even during her period of enslavement. Harper does not delineate Iola's sexual harassment with the same detail that Jacobs provides, but it is clear from the following passage that she rejects attempts to sully her chastity: "Tom was very anxious to get word to the beautiful but intractable girl who was held in durance vile by her reckless and selfish master, who had tried in vain to drag her down to his own low level of sin and shame" (256). Ammons, however, reads Iola as a victim of rape. She suggests that Harper's reticence allows her to only hint at Iola's sexual victimization.[26] Although Iola's ability to protect her virtue may seem as unbelievable as Linda's resistance to Dr. Flint, I prefer to suspend disbelief; after all, this is a matter of fiction and thus need not be completely probable. Despite the unlikelihood of a female slave being able to protect her virtue, the important point is that in Harper's text, Iola is supposedly successful.

Regardless of the extent of Iola's victimization, Harper clearly is not placing the blame on the slaves, but on masters who abuse their power. This point is particularly evident in the discussion between Alfred Lorraine and Eugene Leroy prior to Eugene and Marie's marriage. Alfred is horrified that Eugene would even consider marrying his slave, but Eugene is appalled that he would be ostracized for doing what is right. He asks, " '[S]hould not society have a greater ban for those who, by consorting with an alien race, rob their offspring of a right to their names and to an inheritance in their property, and who fix their social status among an enslaved and outcast race?' " (280). Alfred attempts to justify his position by refering to the reputed promiscuity of female slaves, but Eugene argues that it is white men who are the villains in this scenario.

Iola, however, is able to resist the sexual attacks to which female slaves so often suffer, and thus she maintains her purity. Not only is Iola pure, she is also pious and domestic. Although Iola does not limit herself to the domestic realm, she is well versed in domestic responsibilities. Thus, with the exception of submissiveness, Iola lives up to the ideals of true womanhood. However, within Harper's text, Iola's lack of submissiveness does not "unwoman" her; rather, Harper redefines submissiveness so that it is more egalitarian. Iola is shown to be respectful of her Uncle Robert and her husband, but she is ruled by neither. Harper implies that Iola and Dr. Latimer will have an egalitarian relationship in which both partners are submissive to each other; in other words, theirs will be a compromising partnership. Not only does Harper reconfigure the definition of true womanhood, she also implies that true manhood shares these same virtues. During the "conversazione," the group not only calls for pure women, but also upright men. The call for enlightened fathers also implies that the domestic realm is not solely the woman's. Piety is also a virtue expected of men, as the text is replete with Christian virtues and concern for the moral progress of the black community. Thus for Harper, enlightened motherhood and fatherhood entails being true women and men, and the requirements of both are the same: purity, piety, domesticity, and respect. It is these virtues that will aid in the elevation of the black community.

Harper's concerns with racial uplift and maternal values are shared by another sentimental novel, Hopkins' *Contending Forces*.

In her essay, "Pauline Hopkins: Our Literary Foremother," Claudia Tate hypothesizes about the appeal of the sentimental formula: "The popular success of white women in depicting their heroines' necessity of making their own way in the world despite injustice provided a ready and fertile context within which black women writers might also place their fair-haired black heroines and dramatize racial protest."[27] Although on the surface sentimental novels often appear to be insignificant, moralizing, domestic narratives with nothing more to them than exaggerated emotion, women's sentimental novels "generally appropriate the conventions of sentimentality to mask the heroine's growing self-consciousness, rationality, and ultimately her desire to redefine feminine propriety."[28] The fact that Hopkins uses sentimental fiction in order to deliver a political message is evident in her preface: "I have presented both sides of the dark picture—lynching and concubinage—truthfully and without vituperation, pleading for that justice of heart and mind for my people which the Anglo-Saxon in America never withholds from suffering humanity."[29] Thus like, Jacobs, Hopkins seeks compassion as a precursor to political action.

The political action that writers like Hopkins, Harper, Wilson, and Jacobs call for entails the end of racial discrimination, but all of their heroines are also tools to redefine true womanhood. Like Jacobs, Hopkins appears to challenge the cult of true womanhood on the basis of its exclusion of black women. Hopkins points to the frequent rape of black women as an impediment to the preservation of their virtue. Sappho, a victim of rape, serves as Hopkins' tool in the questioning of the definition of true womanhood. According to the contemporary definition of true womanhood, Sappho would be discredited as a true woman because of her sexual history, despite the fact that she was an unwilling participant. Sappho must struggle with a sense of shame as a result of her victimization. During a meeting of the sewing circle in which Mrs. Willis has been urging the importance of morality in the uplifting of the black community, Sappho says to Mrs. Willis, " 'So many of us desire purity and think to have found it, but in a moment of passion, or under the pressure of circumstances which we cannot control, we commit some horrid sin, and the taint of it sticks and will not leave us and we grow to loathe ourselves' " (Hopkins 154). However, Mrs.

Willis states that " 'We are not held responsible for compulsory sin, only for the sin that is pleasant to our thoughts and palatable to our appetites' " (154–55). Thus according to Mrs. Willis, Sappho should not consider her rape as a sin for which she is responsible. This is a reinterpretation of the cult of true womanhood that would hold a woman responsible in the event of her rape by no longer considering her virtuous. By alluding to her sexual experience, Sappho reveals that she does not meet the definition of a true woman, but through Mrs. Willis, Hopkins questions this definition.

Just as Jacobs' questioning of ideal womanhood reveals that "to be bound to the conventions of true womanhood was to be bound to a racist, ideological system,"[30] so does Hopkins' critique. While Jacobs reveals the inability of slave women to meet the strictures of true womanhood, Hopkins argues that continued racism leaves the free black woman just as susceptible to sexual exploitation as the female slave was, and thereby just as excluded from the cult of true womanhood. Hopkins makes this connection by presenting the reader with two violated heroines—Grace and Sappho. Grace's story is set during the antebellum period and thus exemplifies the experience of the female slave, while Sappho's postbellum experience represents the plight of free black women. Although both women are victims of rape, their fates are quite different. Tate argues in *Domestic Allegories of Political Desire* that "[t]he antebellum discourse binds Grace to the conventional fate of the sexually violated heroine—death. By contrast, the postbellum discourse allows Mabelle to choose her own life as Sappho Clark."[31] The conventional fate that Tate refers to is the fate of heroines of seduction novels. Seduction novels are closely related to sentimental novels in that the reader's sentiments are played upon, however, seduction novels may be seen as a subgenre in which a helpless, virtuous woman is pursued by a man until she eventually gives in to his demands and then dies. Although Hopkins clearly borrows from the seduction novel genre, she uses Sappho to rewrite the fate of the violated woman. Just as Jacobs presents Linda as a virtuous woman despite her sexual encounters, Hopkins presents Sappho as virtuous despite her rape. Tate asserts that "the novel presents a heroine whose virtue is not simply the product of sexual innocence; she qualifies herself as a virtuous person through the strength of her character."[32] Thus for Hopkins, Sappho need not be virginal to be virtuous.

This is an important revisionist twist by Hopkins in a tradition in which, as Carby notes, "the black woman repeatedly failed the test of true womanhood because she survived her institutionalized rape, whereas the true heroine would rather die than be sexually abused."[33] Before addressing Hopkins' revision, I will first address her depiction of Grace, which more closely follows the traditional pattern of violated heroines. I have been discussing Grace as a sexually violated woman; however, this violation is merely implied. From the moment Anson Pollock first sees her, he desires her. The reader is told of his "determination to possess the lovely Grace Montfort at all hazards" (45). He makes his feelings known to Grace, but she rejects him. Pollock eventually exacts his revenge by having Grace whipped. In the previous chapter, I discussed the metonymic relationship between beatings and rape, and Grace's beating clearly fits within this rubric. I am indebted to Carby for her very convincing reading of Grace's whipping as a displaced account of rape:

> Her clothes were ripped from her body, and she was "whipped" alternately "by the two strong, savage men." Hopkins's metaphoric replacement of the "snaky, leather thong" for the phallus was a crude but effective device, and "the blood [which] stood in a pool about her feet" was the final evidence that the "outrage" that had been committed was rape.[34]

Grace faints frequently during her attack and then drowns herself at the first opportunity. Since she could not prevent the attack, Grace does the next best thing by killing herself. This would be the expected response of any true woman.

Grace's response to her rape and, in fact, the rape itself is connected with the issue of race. It is the rumor of Grace's black blood that leaves her vulnerable to such an attack. Before Pollock kills Montfort and steals his family and possessions, he sets the stage by spreading two rumors: Montfort plans to free his slaves and Grace has black blood. The community would not have tolerated such violence to an upstanding family of white slave owners. The ambiguity about Grace's ancestry is essential for the story. Since Hopkins does not reveal Grace's ancestry, it is unknown whether her inability to survive her victimization is a result of her racial heritage. By leaving Grace's ancestry ambiguous, Hopkins opens up the possibility that a black woman could not survive such a vicious attack. This would go against popular racist beliefs that justified the atrocities of slavery by the fact that the slaves could endure them.

Despite the fact that Hopkins questions the ability of a black woman to survive such violence, her depiction of Sappho critiques the expectation that no true woman would survive such degradation. Although Grace fits the traditional definition of a true woman, Sappho clearly fails to meet these standards. Not only does she survive her rape, but she also bears a child whom she abandons. However, as Tate argues, Hopkins does not abandon her heroine to some insidious fate; instead, the text "transforms Sappho from a passive and impure heroine—the sexually experienced object of perverse male desire—into an active female-hero, the subject of her own desire."[35] This transformation is brought about by first revealing Sappho's sense of shame and guilt about her sexual history. In speaking with Mrs. Willis, she expresses concern that black women have been deemed immoral due to their history as rape victims. Sappho asks whether God will hold black women responsible for their illegitimate children, and Mrs. Willis responds, that virtue is only assessed when one has a choice. Sappho's conversation with Mrs. Willis reveals that she is still dealing with the consequences of her rape. She is not sure if she is still virtuous even though she was forcibly raped and not a willing participant.

Sappho almost confides her history to Mrs. Willis, but then stops short. However, it is not until she stops hiding from her past that Sappho can consider herself a true woman despite her rape. According to Carby, Sappho's "journey to retrieve her own identity and understand and accept the consequences of her womanhood meant that she also had to acknowledge her position as mother and to accept the child she had denied, a child that represented her rape."[36] Thus like our other heroines, Linda and Frado, Sappho's sense of womanhood is connected to her motherhood. Under different circumstances each of these heroines is separated from her child(ren), and it is the reunion or hoped for reunion that makes them whole.

It is only by returning to the child she abandoned and confronting her past that Sappho overcomes her victimization. The realization that "innocent or guilty, our deeds done in the flesh pursue us with relentless vigor unto the end of life" (341) leads Sappho to reclaim her child and her role as mother. Her aunt supports her decision and reminds her that " 'in doing [her] duty, happiness will come to [her], the greater and more abiding for the trouble which has preceded it' " (344). Her aunt is proven correct, since at the end of the novel Sappho is rewarded with marriage. She and Will are reunited, and he accepts her and her child. Thus, unlike those of Linda and Frado, Sappho's story ends with marriage—by the end of the text, Hopkins' violated woman is redeemed and rewarded in the manner of a true woman.

Although their conclusions are quite different, Hopkins' and Jacobs' texts operate in the same manner. Their heroines' stories are used to analyze the conventions of true womanhood. The analysis centers on the tension between the protagonists' life experiences and these ideals. This is different from the tactics of Harper and Wilson. Rather than reveal tension between the ideals and her heroine's life, Harper depicts her heroine as an icon of true womanhood, while Wilson takes the opposite route by undermining the connection between whiteness and true womanhood with her depiction of Mrs. Bellmont.

Hopkins, like Jacobs, urges her readers to use sympathy unconventionally by understanding the very different experience of the black woman. She and Jacobs suggest that people should be judged within their contexts and not by rigid expectations and definitions. They do not stop at questioning the definition of true womanhood, however; they also imply that a woman's self-esteem is not the same as her virginity. Thus although Sappho may not have been a "true woman" based on the standards of her day, Hopkins questions the justification of those standards and suggests that women be judged by more than their sexual purity. This is quite similar to Jacobs' argument that a female slave should be judged by different standards. However, unlike Jacobs, Hopkins does not allow for willing sexual encounters outside of marriage. What preserves

Sappho's virtue is that she was forcibly raped as a child. Thus one's virtue is still contingent on sexual purity, but it is not the sole arbiter. Morality may be defined differently by Hopkins, Harper, Wilson, and Jacobs, but its importance serves as a common theme in their texts.

For these writers, morality is not always a strictly black and white issue but one filled with shades of gray. The ability to see shades of gray appears to be an attribute of what Tate defines as the "mother's law." Mrs. Willis represents the "mother's law," while the "father's law" is represented by Luke. Tate notes that the characters turn to the mother's law for instruction as they realize the inappropriateness of the father's law.[37] Luke expresses "the father's law of patriarchal judgment" when he describes Mabelle's (Sappho's) rape and refers to her as a "ruined woman." John then "corroborates patriarchal judgment when he uses his knowledge of Sappho's history to try to force her into becoming his *fille de joie*."[38] Thus the father's law is shown to uphold the cult of true womanhood that Hopkins seeks to reconfigure. According to the patriarchal definition of womanhood, Sappho is irreparably ruined. Sappho tries to avoid the condemnation of the father's law by creating a new identity, but John's actions lead her to believe that the father's law is inescapable. She eventually runs away, considering herself an unworthy bride for Will.[39] Thus, according to Tate, the father's law entails the maintenance of purity at all costs. An impure woman is no longer a true woman, regardless of the circumstances.

The mother's law, however, is more forgiving. It is the mother's law as enacted by the Sisters of the Holy Family that initially protects Sappho. After her vicitimization, Sappho sought refuge with the sisters and they helped to conceal her identity: "I did not die. The good Sisters gave out that story in order to destroy my identity" (328–29). Although most religious orders cherish veracity, in this case, the sisters chose to conceal the truth. By hiding the truth, the sisters appear to be practicing Tate's ideal of the mother's law.

The principal proponent of the mother's law, however, is Mrs. Willis. This is evident in the advice she gives to Sappho regarding women's virtue. In her talk, "The Place Which the Virtuous Woman Occupies in Upbuilding a Race," Mrs. Willis asserts the importance of virtue, but she does not formulate a concrete list of do's and don'ts to determine another's virtue. The omission of a concrete list of virtuous and nonvirtuous acts separates the mother's law from the father's law, which is less forgiving. Tate argues that Mrs. Willis' "advice does not sanction the father's law; instead, she insists that man's view is finite, while God's judgment is infinite."[40] This is not to say that the mother's law is less virtuous than the father's law, but it takes into account the circumstances surrounding one's deeds. According to Tate, "The mother's law centers a black matricentric morality, it metes out reward and punishment in direct proportion to the moral character of one's deeds, privileges a female-centered ethical context, and serves as a broader basis for defining a virtuous woman other than on grounds of sexual chastity."[41] A parallel may be drawn between Tate's discussion of the father's law and mother's law and Spillers' argument that patriarchal law has a different meaning within the slave economy. Under slavery, she argues that the father's law establishes property, not gender; however, Luke and John attempt to reclaim patriarchal authority by designating what constitutes a proper woman. Although Hopkins' text is set after slavery, the legacy of slavery remains. One element of this legacy appears to be the maternal mark to which Spillers refers. She suggests that female slaves not only passed on the condition of slavery, but also established a female line of descent. Will, Sappho's future husband, is a product of this female descent. Mr. Smith, Will's father, died years ago and thus has no patriarchal authority. Essentially raised by his mother, Will reminds one of Spillers' discussion of the African-American male being touched or molded by his mother in ways that are inescapable.[42] This handling by his mother is what allows Will to marry Sappho despite her past; he is able to follow the more forgiving mother's law. It is through the mother's law that Hopkins is able to redefine true womanhood in a way that would include the black woman's very different experience of womanhood.

Hopkins' portrayal of the mother's law seems to echo Stowe's concept of mother rule. She like Stowe, envisions a community of women who nurture society. However, the racial dynamics at play affect Hopkins' maternal ideology. While she seems to accept the tenets of true womanhood for the most part, she has a different

interpretation of purity. Since African-American women were often
the victims of rape, physical purity was often unattainable, but
Hopkins' seems to offer mental purity as another option. In other
words, women could still be seen as pure if they did not willingly
consent to sexual relations. This view of purity is more responsive
to the reality of black women's lives. Although this might seem like
a rather insignificant shift in emphasis, it does have important
repercussions. A strict definition of purity is much more serviceable
in the patriarchal goal of policing women's bodies, but by bringing in
the issue of consent, Hopkins provides women with more control
over the way in which they are defined. Thus the mother's law does
not merely represent women policing patriarchal regulations, but
instead, represents the beginning of a rethinking of social relations.

Hopkins' interest in true womanhood is most apparent in her
portrayal of Mrs. Willis. She is depicted as the ideal race woman,
but she is not alone, as "every city or town from Maine to New York
has its Mrs. Willis" (144). Thus Hopkins does not believe that strong,
capable black women like Mrs. Willis are rare. Nor does she believe
that women like Mrs. Willis develop by accident. Hopkins explains
that Mrs. Willis consciously chose to be a race woman: "The best
opening, she decided after looking carefully about her, was in the
great cause of the evolution of true womanhood in the work of the
'Woman Question' as embodied in marriage and suffrage" (146).
Mrs. Willis clearly believes that women are particularly suited for
elevating the race. Hopkins' depiction of Mrs. Willis implies that
true womanhood also includes a political consciousness. This observation has also been made by Yarborough, who notes that unlike
"many of her fellow novelists, Hopkins also continually stresses . . .
that Afro-American women are just as politically conscious and
active as men like [Will] Smith and [Arthur] Lewis."[43]

The political consciousness of the women is displayed in the
meeting of the sewing circle. The women gather regularly to discuss important issues, such as " 'the place which the virtuous woman
occupies in upbuilding a race' " (148). During the meeting, Mrs.
Willis indoctrinates the young women with the duties of "race
women": " 'Shortly, you must fill the positions now occupied by your
mothers, and it will rest with you and your children to refute the
charges brought against us as to our moral irresponsibility, and the

low moral standard maintained by us in comparison with other races' " (148). Mrs. Willis' belief in black women's ability to uplift the race echoes Iola's sentiments expressed at the "converzione," which also included men.

Both meetings discuss issues pertinent to the black women's club movement. The inclusion of these scenes in both texts point to the historical importance of the movement. The black women's club movement developed in response to the portrayal of black women as immoral. The negative stereotypes of black women grew out of the female slave's inability to protect herself from rape. Mrs. Willis appears to be responding to this stereotype when she tells the girls that " 'the native African woman is impregnable in her virtue' " and that virtue was later " 'pushed one side by the force of circumstances' " (149). She then explains her belief that black women should not be blamed for the illegitimacy of her children when they resulted from compulsion rather than choice. Mrs. Willis' comments come in response to Sappho's question, " 'Do you think, then, that Negro women will be held responsible for all the lack of virtue that is being laid to their charge today?' " (149). Sappho's question is not unwarranted, for as Yarborough observes, turn-of-the-century black women were "held accountable not only for their own moral condition but also for the sexual degradation associated with their collective slave past."[44] The sewing circle was a means to mobilize in order to combat this stigma.

Hopkins' women, however, are not limited to discussing issues of morality. Sappho and Dora also discuss the virtues of industrial education and the need for the vote. Dora shares Arthur's view of the race problem with Sappho: " 'His argument is, as I understand it, that industrial education and the exclusion of politics will cure all our race troubles' " (124). While Dora admits that she generally accepts what men tell her, Sappho quickly dismisses Arthur's view. She attempts to persuade Dora of the importance of the ballot for black men. Sappho argues, " 'If we lose the franchise, at the same time we shall lose the respect of all other citizens' " (125). Dora's response to Sappho's criticism of Arthur's ideas is to state that " 'Arthur thinks that women should be seen and not heard, where politics is under discussion' " (126). This comment, however, does not dissuade Sappho. She clearly has firm ideas about the political needs of her people.

Sappho is obviously much more outspoken than Dora; however, this seems true only within the private sphere. Although she is critical of Dora's willingness to allow men to think for her, Sappho does not share her views in public forums such as the American Colored League meeting. Tate notes that "Sappho endorses perhaps unwittingly the ideology of female reticence; for although she makes no public discourse on racism and sexism, she shares a critique on both practices with her friend Dora."[45]

Sappho's reticence seems to echo Hopkins' own reluctance to go too far in her critique of sexism. Such reluctance is apparent in her construction of Mrs. Willis "as a successful but problematic professional woman."[46] It is not her views that are problematic; Hopkins appears to endorse Mrs. Willis' expressions of the mother's law. However, Hopkins depicts her as rather repulsive: "Keen in her analysis of human nature, most people realized, after a short acquaintance, in which they ran the gamut of emotions from strong attraction to repulsion, that she had sifted them thoroughly, while they had gained nothing in return" (144). Sappho experiences this sense of repulsion just as she is about to unburden her secret. Tate suggests that Hopkins sought to contain her contemporaries' discomfort with "female will to power" by having Sappho voice and control their objections:

> Hence by characterizing an effective but not idealized professional black woman, who constructs a social cover of feminine civility to mask her political ego, the text provides its first readers with a ready target for anticipated allegations of feminine impropriety, while simultaneously challenging them to decide whether gender prescriptions should silence the expression of wisdom and inhibit ability.[47]

Although Hopkins does not idealize Mrs. Willis, the fact that she does embrace her views suggests that wisdom should supersede gender conventions. It is, after all, Mrs. Willis' articulation of the mother's law that ultimately allows Sappho to escape the father's law and the traditional fate of the violated heroine. As Sappho escapes the bonds of the sentimental heroine, so Hopkins escapes the confines of the sentimental novel by writing a narrative about a black female who may not meet the requirements of true womanhood, but is still deemed a "true woman."

It is the mother's law that accords true womanhood status upon Sappho. She must also take responsibility for her child because a true woman would not abandon her children. Maternal, nurturing qualities are celebrated by both Hopkins and Harper. These are the qualities that prove that their heroines are true women. Thus although their stories are different from each other and from the texts of Wilson and Jacobs, all four writers turn to a maternal consciousness as a means of engenderment. This theme will recur in twentieth-century texts as well, but these later writers are more critical of the conflation of maternity with feminity.

5

The Haunting Effects of Slavery

While nineteenth-century black women writers responded to negative slavery myths by showing that black women are maternal and thus true women, twentieth-century black women writers used maternity to assert womanhood while also questioning the relationship between maternity and womanhood. Texts such as Toni Morrison's *Beloved*, Sherley Williams' *Dessa Rose*, and Gayl Jones' *Corregidora* illustrate the continued effect of slavery myths, but they offer slightly different solutions than their nineteenth-century predecessors. While Harriet Jacobs and Harriet E. Wilson focus on gender and maternity and Frances E. W. Harper and Pauline Hopkins foreground gender and sexuality, these later writers analyze the simultaneous interconnection of gender, maternity, and sexuality. Their three protagonists can only construct their gender identity after coming to terms with their sexuality and their maternity. Morrison's Sethe escapes the narrow confines of maternity and becomes a complete person only after negotiating

121

her sexuality and her maternity; she can exclude neither. Dessa must realize that despite her inability to nurse her son, she is still a mother and a woman. Jones' Ursa faces a slightly different problem in that she cannot bear children, but she must learn that this does not diminish her as a woman. All of these characters eventually determine that maternity is merely one aspect of femininity and they are persons in their own right apart from their roles as mothers. Together these texts demonstrate the lasting effects of slavery upon black women's gender development.

While these contemporary texts have a different style from their predecessors, they do share similar concerns. Jacobs, Wilson, Harper, and Hopkins all wrote in the sentimental tradition. Although Morrison has not written a sentimental novel, Nancy Armstrong argues that *Beloved* "situates itself squarely within the tradition of sentimental fiction."[1] In other words, even though *Beloved* is not classified as a sentimental novel, Morrison still addresses similar issues. She "exposes the sentimental options— 'Give me purity or give me death!'—as a fantasy that could materialize only for members of an elite minority."[2] Thus Morrison shares in the critique leveled by Jacobs, who argued that black women were unfairly stigmatized for surviving their degradation. Unlike Jacobs, Morrison's attack comes not in the form of a slave narrative, but a novel about slavery, a fictive slave narrative. Morrison's position as a fiction writer returning to the site of slavery, brings one to the discussion of the real versus representation. In "The Site of Memory," Morrison describes her predicament as a fiction writer discussing the process of writing memoirs. She compares her task to that of the authors of slave narratives. She notes that as a black woman writing over a hundred years after slavery, her role is quite different. "My job becomes how to rip that veil drawn over 'proceedings to terrible too relate.' "[3] Morrison explains that she is "looking to find and expose a truth about the interior life of people who didn't write it."[4] In other words, Morrison is attempting to imagine and then re-present the real. However, as Peggy Phelan notes: "As a representation of the real the image is always, partially, phantasmatic."[5] Thus it is particularly appropriate that Morrison's attempt to imagine the real takes the form of a ghost story. Rather than lament the inability to present an accurate re-presentation, one should take advantage of the possibilities available in partial representation. Phelan argues that: "Representation follows two laws: it always conveys more than it intends; and it is never totalizing. The 'excess' meaning conveyed by representation creates a supplement that makes multiple and resistant readings possible."[6]

This paradox of excess and failure is echoed in the conclusion of *Beloved*. In a text about the necessity of remembering, Morrison concludes with the notion that: "It was not a story to pass on."[7] The novel concludes with the communal exorcising of the ghost, Beloved. Marianne Hirsch argues that Beloved represents memory. She is the memory of slavery come to challenge a community that has been trying to forget its past.[8] If, indeed, Morrison's text does advocate the necessity of remembering, why is this not a story to pass on? In her reading of the text, Jean Wyatt notes the ambiguousness of this phrase. While Beloved's story "cannot by passed on from teller to teller, . . . it also cannot 'pass on,' or die."[9] Perhaps it is not enough to merely remember; one must remember differently. Hirsch contends that Morrison's rememory is a maternal memory, which can offer resistance and opposition. She defines rememory as "memory combined with the threat of repetition; it is neither noun nor verb, but both combined." Rememory allows Morrison to offer a different way of remembering what has been repressed.[10] Thus Morrison's text is not seeking to document a repressed history of slavery, but to create ruptures and gaps in society's cultural amnesia. *Beloved* is not so much a reminder of what one has forgotten, but that one has forgotten. The acknowledgment of amnesia allows for the reinterpretation of the present.

This then returns one to the project of *Women in Chains*; by remembering slavery and using it as a lens to interpret black women's texts, new layers of meaning become available. This discussion begins with the analysis of an actual slave narrative and then moves to fictive nineteenth-century texts that are less and less explicitly about slavery and now the project addresses a fictive slave narrative written in the twentieth century that is explicitly about slavery, but also not "true." Thus the legacy of slavery survives across time and genres. The legacy that these texts share is that they all in some way respond to the same assumption that developed during slavery: "that slave women are not mothers; they are 'natally dead,' with no obligation to their offspring or their own parents."[11] *Beloved*, like *Incidents, Our Nig, Contending Forces,* and *Iola Leroy*, takes issue with this characterization of female slaves and her descendants. Thus maternity becomes the site to engender African-American females.

While Jacobs and Wilson are critical of societal definitions of ideal motherhood and Hopkins and Harper assert the fitness of black mothers, Morrison goes even further in her critique of motherhood. It is not merely that Sethe is a disenfranchised mother, but that motherhood as defined in patriarchal culture is itself limiting for women.[12] Morrison's text appears to support Shirley Stave's contention that although motherhood has been privileged, that privilege has been based on fear and the wish to control the mother.[13] The mother must be controlled because she is used to symbolize important aspects within society. In *Bordering on the Body*, Laura Doyle argues that: "Because of the mother's alignment with the body and her function as reproducer of the group as a social body, the mother comes to signify, often ambivalently, a bodily and collective past."[14] The mother figure is not merely a repository of a nation's history; she is central to the project of nation building. It is by controlling the mother and her reproduction that the borders of nations are policed. As the creator of boundaries, the mother is neither within nor without the border but on the border. According to Doyle:

> In the race-bounded economy the mother is a maker and marker of boundaries, a generator of liminality, both vertically and horizontally. She is forced across a border, or she is prohibited from crossing a border; in either case her function is to reproduce, through offspring, the life of that border.[15]

An example of mother as border is the slavery doctrine that declared that the child followed the condition of the mother. This ruling created a means of increasing the slave population as well as justifying the importance of white women's purity. A promiscuous white woman not only brought shame to her family, but also jeopardized the purity of the nation's borders. Doyle asserts:

Under kinship patriarchy women are both central and mar-
ginal in that they serve the central role of creating the group's
margins. . . . She becomes an instrument in the formulation of
crucial categories of difference: fit or unfit, black or white,
Nordic or Mediterranean, wayward or eugenic.[16]

Thus motherhood, which is described as the epitome of femininity,
is not about women's desires, but the patriarchy's. Motherhood is
not defined by women, but created by men's fictions. According to
Stave, patriarchal definitions and fantasies of motherhood have
been imposed on women in such a way that women cannot possibly
meet the standards.[17] As with many ideals, the ideal mother is an
untenable position, particularly for the already marginalized female slave. *Beloved* not only critiques the glorification of motherhood, but also society's exclusion of other aspects of womanhood.

While Morrison turns to motherhood as a site to engender Sethe,
she also insists that womanhood does not equal motherhood. Before addressing the way in which womanhood is separated from
motherhood, however, the engendering role of maternity will be
addressed. Slaves are not supposed to be troubled by family bonds;
female slaves are not expected to experience mother love. Baby
Suggs contemplates the familial disruption common to slaves: "men
and women were moved around like checkers. . . . What she called
the nastiness of life was the shock she received upon learning that
nobody stopped playing checkers just because the pieces included
her children" (Morrison 29). Sethe is fortunate that the same man
fathered her children and none had been sold away from her, but
Baby's eight children had six fathers and she was only able to keep
one child.

Although Sethe's children are not sold, she has been separated
from her own mother; she has experienced the effects of slavery
and its disruption of families. For slaves, family and motherhood
must have different meanings because they are first and foremost
slaves; their masters may or may not observe kinship relations. In
The Mother/Daughter Plot, Hirsch explains that "the economy of
slavery circumscribes not only the process of individuation and
subject-formation, but also heightens and intensifies the experience of motherhood—of connection and separation."[18] This point is

supported by Paul D's observation that: "This here new Sethe didn't know where the world stopped and she began" (202). Doyle asserts that Sethe's sense of boundlessness jeopardizes the boundary making process:

> Beloved's supposed ability to look through floors is a mirror image of Sethe's blindness to boundaries between herself and the world. The mother and daughter transgress boundaries, penetrate boundaries, sabotaging their prescribed cultural function to create and reproduce boundaries.[19]

Sethe cannot maintain the proper boundaries because her love is "too thick." It is this thick love that leads Sethe to kill her daughter and attempt to kill her other children before schoolteacher can capture them and return them to slavery.

Hirsch explains Sethe's drastic response in terms of her heightened experience of loss; mothers experience loss more acutely when they cannot own their children, let alone themselves.[20] Sethe rejects Paul D's criticism of her love as too thick. She knows what it felt like to be measured and studied by schoolteacher, and she does not want that for her children. Sethe attempts to justify her actions to Beloved by explaining that she acted out of love. For Sethe, murder becomes symbolic of mother love, but her actions appear incomprehensible to others. For example, one of the Garner boys asks, "What she go and do that for? On account of a beating? Hell, he'd been beat a million times and he was white. . . . But no beating ever made him . . . I mean no way he could have . . . What she go and do that for?" (184–85). He doesn't understand that Sethe is not responding to the beatings associated with slavery; rather, she is responding to the ownership entailed in slavery. Instead of allowing her children to be owned by schoolteacher, she wanted to own them. Morrison describes Sethe's gathering of her children as collecting "every bit of life she had made, all the parts of her that were precious and fine and beautiful." (200). For Sethe, a slave who could not own her children or herself, love means ownership.

When Sethe escapes from slavery, it becomes an opportunity to own herself and her children. As a slave she had been seen as a breeder, not a mother, but once she escapes, she can claim the mother role for herself. However, Sethe's conception of motherhood is framed by her experiences as a slave. Her vision of motherhood is not the same as that of her mistress, Mrs. Gardner, because "motherhood occurs in specific historical contexts framed by interlocking structures of race, class, and gender."[21] Thus Sethe does not respond to her exclusion from the maternal realm by merely mimicking those that are included, rather she reinterprets mothering from the perspective of an escaped slave. Motherhood becomes a means of asserting both her humanity and her femininity—it becomes a site of engenderment.

By claiming maternity as a site of engenderment, I do not wish to imply that nonmothers are not gendered or that Sethe was degendered prior to her escape, but there is a moment of change for Sethe. Prior to her escape her owners did not recognize her as a gendered person, let alone a mother, because she was property. Although Sethe has a fondness for Mrs. Garner, schoolteacher recognizes Sethe's ultimate position when he refers to her as "the breeding one" and her fetus as a foal (279). She and her family are property just like the plantation animals. Sethe tries to explain to Paul D the difference that freedom meant, "I was big, Paul D, and deep and wide and when I stretched out my arms all my children could get in between. I was *that* wide. Look like I loved em more after I got here. Or maybe I couldn't love em proper in Kentucky because they wasn't mine to love" (198–99). Escaping slavery in some way authorized Sethe to love and to mother in a different manner.

Although the text clearly celebrates Sethe's escape from slavery, it is more critical of her mothering. While motherhood becomes Sethe's means of claiming personhood and gender, it is also described as suffocating. Motherhood should not equal womanhood, but merely be one aspect of womanhood. Carole Boyce Davies describes motherhood as confining: "Sethe's body is multiply captive. And, significantly, while she can flee slavery, she cannot flee motherhood or the body that has been captured by the needs of her children."[22] Sethe is not just physically trapped within motherhood, but also psychologically. The mother/daughter relationship becomes paralyzing for Sethe when her love for Beloved becomes consuming. In the text, love is often used "as the justification for acting upon the beloved, for scripting the beloved purely within the narrative of the lover, for denying the integral self of the beloved."[23] The mother/daughter relationship becomes perverted by selfishness. For Sethe's part, her selfishness appears to arise from her newfound freedom. When she tells Paul D about her pride and joy in escaping with her children, Sethe admits, "It was a kind of selfishness I never knew nothing about before. It felt good" (198).

While I contend that Sethe's consuming love is based on a newfound selfishness once she is in a position to claim ownership of herself and her children, Stave views Sethe and Beloved's relationship as one of love and hate. In support of this contention, Stave points to the epigraph, "I will call them my people, which were not my people; and her beloved, which was not beloved," to argue that Sethe's aberrant love obscures her hatred of Beloved. According to Stave, the epigraph implies Sethe's hostility toward Beloved for being "all-consuming and destructive, a vampire who drains Sethe's life-blood as well as her breasts."[24] Beloved's all-consuming love is suggested in the repetition of the phrase: "I am Beloved and she [Sethe] is mine." Beloved views Sethe as an extension of herself, "I am not separate from her there is no place where I stop her face is my own and I want to be there in the place where her face is and to be looking at it too" (259). Beloved's desire for union with her mother is a form of cannibalism as she feeds off Sethe's love.

According to Stave, Beloved, as the eternal child, demands eternal motherhood from Sethe. This eternal motherhood excludes any other aspects of personhood. Sethe is denied any role besides mother, as Beloved feeds off her love like a vampire.[25] As Sethe begins to fade away, "Beloved ate up her life, took it, swelled up with it, grew taller on it" (307). Beloved attempts to punish Sethe with slow murder. Instead of forgiveness or understanding, Beloved seeks revenge. Beloved has already suffered through separation from her mother and thus, desires reunion. However, since she cannot return to the womb, Beloved seeks reunion through death. It is not enough to be together in life because they are two separate beings; death comes closest to approximating the unification experienced in utero.[26] Thus the mother/daughter relationship, which should be built upon love, becomes parasitic, as Beloved slowly sucks away Sethe's life-blood.

Although this parasitic relationship may seem quite extreme, Freud describes the child's cannibalistic urges as a common response to weaning. In his essay "Femininity," Freud observes that "the reproach against the mother which goes back furthest is that she gave the child too little milk—which is construed against her as lack of love."[27] In Luce Irigaray's rereading of Freud, she argues that:

> We should rather understand it as nostalgia for the earliest nourishment, for which the child is "altogether insatiable" as it never "gets over the pain of losing its mother's breast." . . . One could equally, however, see the child's manifest resistance to weaning as a symptom of the trauma occasioned by the *final break in material contact with the inside of the mother's body:* rupture of the fetal membranes, cutting of the umbilical cord, denial of the breast. . . . Could its "insatiable hunger" perhaps be the need to reabsorb its material cause? This would imply the inadmissible urge to devour the mother, to destroy this original nature-body from which one must eternally separate and be separated but to which one must eternally return and refer back.[28]

Thus Beloved is not merely seeking revenge against Sethe for killing her, but also for denying her milk.

Sethe is aware of the importance of her milk to her children and thus conceives of motherhood as having "milk enough for all" (242). In telling Paul D about her flight to freedom, Sethe focuses upon her desire to bring her milk to her daughter. Sethe sent her children ahead to freedom, but she wants her baby to know that "the milk would be there and [she] would be there with it" (20). The milk actually supersedes Sethe's importance.

The precedence of the milk is exemplified in Sethe's recitation of her beating. She tells Paul D that the boys stole her milk and after she told on them they beat her with a cowhide. Paul D is incredulous that they would beat her while she was pregnant, but for Sethe the important part was that they took her milk. Sethe's obsessive desire to bring milk to her baby is a response to her own hunger as a child. She was not nursed by her mother, but by Nan

and only after the white babies: "The little whitebabies got it first
and I got what was left. Or none. There was no nursing milk to call
my own" (246). For Sethe, her mother's absence is translated as
milk deprivation; therefore, she will mother her children with an
abundance of milk.

Sethe loves her children enough to not only bring them milk, but
to kill them before allowing them to be remanded to slavery. These
two aspects of Sethe's mother love come together as Denver nurses
from Sethe's bloody breast. According to Doyle:

> in nursing from her mother's bloody breast after the murder
> of her sister, Denver drinks in the ghost of her mother's dis-
> placed daughterly self, for it is that displaced self, as we have
> seen, that drives Sethe to murder. Or, to put it differently, the
> ghost is both milk sister and blood mother to Denver, the
> latter in so far as the ghost is a reembodiment of her mother
> as a child.[29]

This scene not only serves as a baptism of sorts for Denver, but also
marks Sethe's inclusion in the practice of infanticide. Both Ella and
Sethe's mother killed babies born to them by white men. Ella recalls, "She had delivered, but would not nurse, a hairy white thing,
fathered by 'the lowest yet.' It lived five days never making a sound"
(318). Nan has told Sethe that her mother threw away the children
she bore for the white crew. Both women refused to claim babies
they did not want, but Sethe's infanticide was not a sign of disgust
and outrage, but an act of love. Sethe acts upon the desire that
Linda in *Incidents* can only think about, but both women wish to
protect children they love.

Why Sethe acts and Linda merely contemplates is unclear, but
I would argue that the difference lies in their upbringing. Linda
knew her family, while Sethe only knew her mother by a mark
below her breast: "Right on her rib was a circle and a cross burnt
right in the skin. She said, 'This is your ma'am. This,' and she
pointed" (76). At this point, Sethe does not understand the meaning
of the mark and is slapped when she asks to be marked. In her
reading of this scene, Hirsch notes that in this one moment of
significant interaction between mother and daughter, Sethe is

marked by her mother's history of infanticide that Sethe then repeats.[30] This maternal mark that Hirsch refers to appears to be the same maternal mark to which Hortense Spillers refers to in "Mama's Baby, Papa's Maybe."[31] This marking is not physical, but psychological; however, Sethe cannot begin to understand the significance of her mother's mark and her relation to it until she, herself, is marked.

Sethe's back retains the marks of the cowhide whipping. Her scarred back, like her mother's mark, mark her as a slave. This is why her mother slapped her for asking for a mark; the mark was not something to be cherished, but a symbol of her enslavement: "It was the mark of ownership by the master who had as much as written 'property' under her breast. Yet . . . her mother had transformed a mark of mutilation, a sign of diminished humanity, into a sign of recognition and identity."[32] Like her mother's mark, Sethe's scarred back does not have one meaning, but changes with the eye of the beholder. When Amy sees Sethe's back, rather than seeing repulsive scars, she sees a tree, "A chokecherry tree. See, here's the trunk—it's red and split wide open, full of sap, and this here's the parting for the branches" (97). Thus Amy "reads and renames her marking so that it suggests life and not death."[33] When Paul D sees Sethe's back for the first time, he describes her sculptured back as "the decorative work of an ironsmith too passionate for display" (21). He then responds by kissing every ridge and leaf of her tree, but he cannot sustain the tree imagery. After their lovemaking, Paul D saw Sethe's tree as "a revolting clump of scars. Not a tree, as she said. Maybe shaped like one, but nothing like any tree he knew because trees were inviting; things you could trust and be near" (27). In noting the fluctuating meaning of Sethe's scars, Davies observes that:

> Sethe, then, is a marked woman, marked physically by abuse, pregnancy, motherhood and other societal inscriptions by white female, by Black male and by the white male inflicter of the abuse, which marks her initially. The marking which is reidentified as the branches of a tree itself sometimes resonates as life, with myriad reference points. For when looked at differently it also becomes the signifier for captivity.[34]

Thus the scars on Sethe's back constitute a text to be read. Mae Henderson suggests that the whip marks represent a past that Sethe represses, but cannot remember nor forget. The marks are at once "*his*tory and *her*story."[35] Sethe, however, only has mediated access to both stories. Because her back "(symbolizing the *presence* of her *past*)" is marked, Sethe can only read herself through others' eyes.[36] Even when Paul D insists upon hearing Sethe's version, she can only repeat Amy's description of her scarred back. Henderson asserts that as an illiterate female slave, Sethe is the object of white male written discourse and the subject of white female and black male spoken discourse.[37] To support her contention, Henderson observes that Baby Suggs, a black female, does not speak of Sethe's scarred back. When Baby sees Sethe's back, she is too overcome for words: "Baby Suggs hid her mouth with her hand. . . . [W]ordlessly the older woman greased the flowering back" (114). Thus the black woman may read, but not comment. According to Henderson, this presumes that black women have no voice or history. They represent the ultimate Other who defines the presence of white or male subjects. Thus Sethe's scarred back represents a *tabula rasa* upon which others inscribe their identity.[38] The inscriptions on Sethe's back are extension of the cataloguing process that schoolteacher teaches to his nephews. He has the boys observe slaves and then list human and animal characteristics alongside each other. Both the whipping and the cataloguing are methods to define and contain the slave.

Schoolteacher's methods of inscription are similar to that of Nehemiah in Sherley Anne Williams' *Dessa Rose*. Nehemiah is in the process of writing a book about a foiled slave insurrection and he interviews Dessa in hopes of receiving useful information. When Dessa asks him what he will use her comments for, Nehemiah responds, " 'I write what I do in the hope of helping others to be happy in the life that has been sent them to live.' "[39] Although Nehemiah describes his project in benevolent terms, it is clear that he has a particular opinion that he wishes to present as fact. In response to Dessa's recitation of the facts, "Nehemiah hesitated; the 'facts' sounded like some kind of fantastical fiction. He didn't for a minute believe that was all there was to the young buck's attack on his master—a busted banjo!" (Williams 35).

Throughout the text, the reader is told of Nehemiah's disbelief; clearly he has not come in search of "facts," but for material to fit into his version of history. If Nehemiah is skeptical of Dessa's account, Dessa is equally skeptical of his project and white people in general. Just as Baby Suggs saw blacks as pieces in a checker game, Dessa saw blacks as mere marks: "That's what we was in white folks' eyes, nothing but marks to be used, wiped out" (185). Suspicious of the motives of whites, Dessa resists being manipulated. She believes that whites see blacks as pawns, and she refuses to capitulate to the attempts of others to define her and her history.

Ashraf Rushdy notes: "Chattel does not know its history, and part of the strategy of making chattel of humans is to make them ignorant of their histories, both collective and personal."[40] Nehemiah attempts to do this by naming Dessa, documenting her history, and returning her to slavery. He insists on calling her Odessa, despite her insistence that her name is Dessa. He then questions her account of the insurrection because it does not fit his story. He also makes it his personal vendetta to remand her to slavery after her second escape. Mae Henderson observes that like the biblical Adam, Nehemiah uses the privilege of naming to assert ownership. Thus Nehemiah seeks to suppress Dessa's voice as well as remand her to slavery.[41] Nehemiah's naming is not limited to the exchange of Odessa for Dessa, but also extends to nicknames. Marta E. Sánchez notes that although Nehemiah refers to Dessa's race with the term darky, he usually employs gendered slurs such as slut, sly bitch, and devil woman.[42] Thus it is not merely Dessa's race that is being held in contempt, but her gender as well.

The gender specificity of Nehemiah's insults parallels the gender specificity of Dessa's marking by her master: "They lashed her about the hips and legs, branded her along the insides of her thighs" (143). Henderson observes that whipping and branding Dessa near her genitalia suggests an attempt to connect the sign of slavery with the area that designates her as female.[43] Perhaps it is more than coincidence that Dessa's brand is near her pubic area, while Sethe's mother was marked beneath her breast. Both of these markings appear to link slavery and sex. In reference to *Dessa Rose*, Henderson argues that "the effect is to attempt to deprive the slave woman of her femininity and render the surface of her skin a parchment upon which meaning is etched by the whip (pen) of white patriarchal authority and sealed by the firebrand."[44] Dessa is so ashamed of these markings that she wants to keep them hidden. In a scene similar to the one between Sethe and Paul D, Dessa shares her scars with Harker. After their lovemaking, Dessa covers her scars, but Harker assures her that he knows about the scars and " 'It ain't impaired you none at all. . . . It only increase your value' " (208). Harker treasures Dessa's womanhood despite her master's attempt to deny her femininity.

The master's actions appear to be part of his desire to dehumanize his slaves and render them chattel. Thus the branding and whipping of slaves becomes a means of objectification. Therefore through whipping and branding, Dessa, like Sethe, becomes a text to be read. Thus "in escaping from Nehemiah, Dessa seizes physical freedom, but she does not escape the text of slavery."[45] Anyone who sees her scars may read Dessa and recognize her as a slave or former slave. Dessa is careful to keep her scars hidden "because she knows that to 'read' her is to 'own' her."[46] The only way for Dessa to own her own story is to determine who will read it.

For example, Harker persuades Dessa to share her scars with him, but she continues to keep them hidden from Rufel. Dessa is probably more willing to expose herself to Harker, another former slave, because he would read her with sympathetic eyes. His sympathetic reading is later repeated by Aunt Chole, who is brought in by the sheriff to determine whether or not Dessa is the escaped slave Nehemiah has been searching for. After her inspection, Aunt Chole reports, " 'I ain't seed nothing on this gal's butt. She ain't got a scar on her back' " (254). This is an interesting ruse on Aunt Chole's part because she misrepresents the situation without actually lying—Dessa does not have scars on her back and Aunt Chole does not see any scars on Dessa's bottom because she never looks at it. This seems to contradict Henderson's contention that the black female can never comment on her reading because clearly Aunt Chole is offering a counterreading of Dessa's body. Although Dessa has received sympathetic readings from a black male and a black female, she does not trust Rufel, a white female, enough to reveal her scars. Despite Rufel's desires to see and read her scars,

Dessa conceals them. McDowell argues that revealing her scars to
Rufel would be akin to a slave auction. The scars represent the
master's text and his myths and fantasies. But by concealing the
scars from Rufel, Dessa claims the rights of her body, her text.[47]
Dessa's desire to own her body/text operates on two levels. She
wants control over her physical body and the way in which it is
read, but she also wants control over her personal text or (her)story
that Nehemiah seeks to interpolate into his text.

One way in which Dessa asserts ownership of her story is by
demanding her proper name. She remarks, " 'my name Dessa, Dessa
Rose. Ain't no O to it' " (256). Both Nehemiah and Rufel have been
calling her Odessa, rather than Dessa. By rejecting the O, Dessa
signals her rejection of others inscripting her body.[48] Dessa not only
claims her own name and story, she also disrupts Nehemiah's attempts to contain her within his text. According to Henderson,
Dessa disrupts Nehemiah's discourse with singing, evasion, silence,
nonaquiescence, and that also allows her to make her escape and
ultimately control her own story.[49] Thus Dessa does not merely
disrupt Nehemiah's text, but also creates her own text. Dessa has
the last word of her text as she tells her story to her grandchild.
She ensures the accuracy of her story by having it read back to her.
This double-checking is a means of avoiding the type of misreading
that she encountered in Nehemiah's attempt to twist her story to
suit his ends.

While one of the themes of *Dessa Rose* is about textuality and
storytelling, the book is also very much about maternity. Dessa
initially tells her story to her son and then to his children. The
familial network is a significant driving force in Dessa's life. Like
Linda and Sethe, Dessa initially escapes slavery to prevent her
child from being born into slavery. When Rufel asks why she ran
away, Dessa responds, " 'Cause, cause I didn't want my baby to be
slaved.' " (149). Upon learning of her pregnancy, Kaine asks Dessa
to see Aunt Lefonia and obtain an abortion, but Dessa suggests
that they run away instead. She knows that if she does not flee,
there would be no way of protecting her child from her master.

Dessa is rescued from prison prior to the birth of Desmond, so
her master is no longer an immediate threat. Although Dessa saves
her child from slavery, she is unable to nurse him. Unlike Sethe,

she does not have enough milk. However, Rufel does have sufficient milk for her child and Dessa's. Thus Williams replaces the image of the black mammy with that of the white mammy. Sánchez argues that with this reversal, Williams encourages the reader to briefly picture an environment in which the female body and maternal instincts are a common reference point for womanly behavior.[50] However, this communal moment is quickly replaced by the shocked response of the black slaves, Ada and Harker. The discomfort of Harker and Ada vindicates Rufel. Rufel's sense of triumph transforms this moment of sympathy into one that establishes the social context of whites and blacks. "By means of the female body and feeling, Rufel transgresses a white value system; but, ironically her action also allows for the regeneration of the social hierarchy and the moral order that it apparently would violate."[51] In other words, what at first appears to be a moment of sympathy between a white woman and a black child actually becomes a moment for Rufel to reassert her superiority over blacks because she is willing to transgress white values to provide sympathy.

Williams does not present Rufel as merely nursing Desmond out of kindness; rather, her decision to nurse him is fraught with her own racism. She begins to nurse him without thought but when she becomes conscious of Desmond's blackness against her white skin, she becomes embarrassed. She first assures herself that she will not be found out and then when Ada and Harker discover her, she uses their shock to justify her superior morality. Although she relishes their confoundment, she feels " 'some mortification at becoming wet nurse for a darky' " (105–6). Rufel is presented as having a complex set of emotions ranging from a feeling of wonder at the baby, a sense of the necessity of nursing, and repulsion from blackness. Thus Rufel is not acting merely out of sympathy. Williams is complicating the notion of sentimentality. In chapter 3's discussion of *Incidents in the Life of a Slave Girl*, I noted the way in which Jacobs sought to create a sympathetic bond between the reader and the slaves, but she also refuses to completely elide their differences. Williams, however, appears to be more critical of sympathy or empathy as a means to attain community.

While Rufel is not simply sympathetic, Dessa is also not merely thankful. Dessa at first resists acknowledging her lack of milk and

Rufel's nursing of Desmond. However, she must face reality when Ada informs her that Rufel is "the only nursing woman on the place" (122). With this information she had to confront her suspicions: "Dessa had suspected from the way the baby turned from her, fretting and in tears, that she had no milk to speak of. Her baby, nursing—Her breathing quickened and her heart seemed to pound in her ears. There was more, but Dessa turned away" (122). Part of Dessa is horrified by the thought of Rufel nursing Desmond. This horror is in part frustration at her own inability to nurse: "It hurt me to my deepest heart not to nurse my baby. Made me shamed, like I was less than a woman" (183).

Dessa's conception of her femininity is tied to her sense of maternity. For Dessa, to be a woman is also to be a mother and to be unable to nurse questioned her identity as mother. Interesting complexes of feelings come together for Dessa around mothering. It is only when she realizes that she is pregnant that she decides to escape slavery. As a slave she could not be the kind of mother that she would like to be because she would have no authority over her offspring. As a slave she was not seen as a mother or a woman, but by escaping Dessa could claim motherhood, womanhood, and freedom.

Not only is Dessa jealous of Rufel's ability to nurse, she is also shocked at the thought of a white woman nursing her baby: "It went against everything she had been taught to think about white women but to inspect that fact too closely was almost to deny her own existence" (123). Rather than explore that fact, Dessa challenges Rufel by questioning her relationship with Mammy. In chapter 2, I provide a discussion of the image of Mammy as well as an analysis of Rufel and Dessa's argument regarding M/mammy, but I would like to note the way in which their argument problematizes sympathy. When Dessa says, " 'Wasn't no "mammy" to it,' " (124) she disrupts romantic notions of both a white mammy and a black mammy. Sánchez argues that Dessa's assertion that Rufel doesn't have a mammy asks readers to question romantic notions about the charity whites offer to blacks. Readers are forced to reexamine the history of black women nursing the children of others, only to have their own names forgotten.[52] By denying Rufel's relationship with Mammy, Dessa refuses to allow Rufel to assume a similar romanticized notion of herself in relation to Desmond. Just as Rufel had feelings of repulsion toward Desmond, perhaps Mammy/Dorcas also had feelings of resentment toward Rufel. Williams will not allow sympathy to elide the crucial power differential. Rufel cannot be like Mammy because she has the power to refuse that Mammy did not have. Nor could Mammy love Rufel like her own child because she did not have the power to choose her community of loved ones. This is not to say that Mammy could not have loved Rufel, but the power dynamics at play taint her ability to love freely.

Despite Williams' critique of simple sympathy, there are moments of sisterly connection between Rufel and Dessa; however, they never move beyond the superficial acknowledgment of similarity. The first moment of connection comes when Dessa helps Rufel get Oscar out of her bed. After this incident, Dessa realizes, "the white woman was subject to the same ravishment as me" (220). This thought keeps Dessa awake as she rethinks her relationship with Rufel: "I wasn't so cold with her no more. I wasn't zactly warm with her, understand; I didn't know how to be warm with no white woman" (220). Thus Dessa recognizes that as women she and Rufel have something in common—"white mens wanted the same thing, would take the same thing from a white woman as they would from a black woman. Cause they could" (220). But in spite of this recognition, there is still a significant distance between them. Dessa notes that after their experience they could not help developing some closeness, but she also expresses her reluctance to discuss certain things with Rufel. She does not share very much that is personal. Dessa realizes "this was a white woman and I don't think I forgot it that whole, entire journey." Yes they are both women, but Rufel is a free white woman, while Dessa is an escaped slave.

Although Dessa is reluctant to share herself with Rufel, Rufel considers them to be friends. When Dessa refers to Rufel as "Mis'ess" and apologizes for speaking when it wasn't her place, Rufel responds with anger, " 'Well, I ain't talking no "place," ' she was yelling now, 'no "mistress." ' . . . I'm talking friends,' she scream" (239-40). Rufel wants to move beyond the power dynamics and be friends—equals. However, it is Rufel's superior social position that allows her to save Dessa from Nehemiah: "Friend or not, best she could do for me then was to prove I wasn't nothing but her slave" (252). By assuming the role of Dessa's mistress and superior, Rufel is able to protect her from Nehemiah, but in his anger Nehemiah lumps Rufel with Dessa: " 'You-all in this together'—grabbing at [them]—'womanhood'. . . . 'All alike. Sluts' " (255). In his eyes, they are both the same—mere women. Clearly they do have some things in common; they have shared experiences and come to know each other. Reflecting on her close call, Dessa thinks, "I wanted to hug Ruth. I didn't hold nothing against her, not 'mistress,' not Nathan, not skin." But despite this closeness, they "couldn't hug each other, not on the streets, not in Arcopolis, not even after dark" (256). Williams will not allow for the uncomplicated happy ending; despite their feelings for each other, they cannot get beyond the power differential.

Although Dessa's relationship with Rufel is an important aspect of the novel, Dessa's own development is even more important. This novel is not only about escaping slavery, but attaining womanhood. Dessa, like Sethe, must learn to work through her painful history. Both women must heal their physical and psychological scars. While their scars are directly related to slavery, Gayl Jones' Ursa Corregidora is also haunted by the legacy of slavery even though she was never a slave. Ursa is haunted by the memory of Corregidora, the Brazilian slavemaster who fathered her grandmother and mother. Ursa is consumed with hatred for Corregidora and plagued by the instruction to "make generations" to bear witness to the horrors of slavery. When she must have a hysterectomy as a result of an argument with her husband, Ursa is forced to come to terms with a womanhood that does not entail motherhood.

Before beginning my analysis of the text, it may be fruitful to address the significance of Ursa's surname. Adam McKible notes that *corregidore* is Portuguese for colonial magistrate, while *corregidora* is Spanish for wife of a chief magistrate. Thus her surname implies the extent of Corregidora's power, including his psychosexual domination, as the Corregidora women are effectively his wives. However, *corregidora* also suggests the meaning of its French root word—*corregir*—to correct.[53] Therefore Ursa, whose name in Latin means "bear,"[54] must somehow negotiate the painful memories of slavery. After slavery was abolished all the papers were burned, thereby erasing history, but the Corregidora women responded with their own oral history: " 'My great-grandmama told my grandmama the part she lived through that my grandmama didn't live through and my mama told me what they all lived through and we were suppose to pass it on like that from generation to generation so we'd never forget.' "[55] However, in order for this oral narrative to continue the family tree must continue to bear fruit; thus Great Gram insists that the Corregidora women bear children who are then able to testify to the experience of their foremothers. Great Gram explains that because the officials burned all the evidence of slavery, the Corregidora women must leave evidence of their enslavement. According to Amy Gottfried, by instructing her descendants to "bear witness," Great Gram Corregidora supplants "sexual commodification" with "a deliberate, political self-definition. But as Ursa . . . discovers, this political move has a double-edged drawback: The Corregidoras' agenda severely limits their sexual identities, a limitation which in turn provokes domestic violence."[56] In other words, just as Corregidora prostituted their bodies, Great Gram is in a sense prostituting their wombs.

Corregidora ran a whorehouse and Great Gram had been *"his favorite. 'A good little piece. My best. Dorita. Little gold piece' "* (10). Great Gram and Gram are his golden pussies; "a woman's vagina equals her economic value and that economic value equals her essence."[57] Commodification was built into the slavery system in which slaves were valued for their labor. In the case of many female slaves this often meant being valued for sexual labor as whores or reproductive labor as breeders. For the Corregidora women this meant having golden pussies. Even though Ursa was not one of Corregidora's women, she has inherited the sexual commodification of her body. Her relationship with Mutt is based on ownership: " 'My pussy, ain't it, Ursa?' 'Yes, Mutt, it's your pussy' " (156). According to Gottfried, Ursa reenacts Great Gram's role as Corregidora's gold piece by becoming Mutt's pussy. Overcome by the political agenda of the Corregidora women, Ursa defines herself in terms of her vagina and womb and thus allows Mutt to own her vagina and soul.[58] Corregidora treated his whores as gaping vaginas, but the Corregidora women respond by glorifying their wombs as the source of evidence with which to condemn Corregidora.

Although the Corregidora women redefine themselves as wombs rather than vaginas, they have not abandoned Corregidora's objectification. Great Gram and Gram still do not allow themselves to own their own bodies nor do they recognize children as separate beings.[59] Ursa and her mother are not expected to have their own lives; rather, they are to be mouthpieces for the recitation of the experiences on Corregidora's plantation and breeders to continue the family legacy. Thus when Tadpole asks Ursa what she wants, she responds, " 'What all us Corregidora women want. Have been taught to want. To make generations' " (22). This goal is so well entrenched by Great Gram and Gram that Ursa's mother considered it a natural desire. She explains to Ursa that she had not been looking for a man, but she knew " 'it was something my body wanted, just something my body wanted. . . .' 'It was like my whole body wanted you, Ursa' " (116–17). Her mother's explanation reveals that for Corregidora women, womanhood is reduced to anatomy; a real woman is a womb.

Thus when Ursa looses her womb, she must completely rethink her sense of womanhood. Ursa reports the results of her fall very matter-of-factly, "The doctors in the hospital said my womb would have to come out. Mutt and me didn't stay together after that" (4). The fact that she loses Mutt is presented as a natural consequence of losing her womb. She does not investigate the ins and outs of their relationship, rather, the reader is left to assume that without her womb there is no longer a need for Mutt. She does not spend much time mourning the loss of their relationship, but she does mourn for her womb. She now has to reimagine herself because her womb was much more than an organ—it was the site of dreams. Ursa describes the loss she feels: "I lay on my back, feeling as if something more than the womb had been taken out" (6). It is not just that her womb is barren; her entire future now appears barren.

Her inability to bear children leads Ursa to question her worth to a man, " 'Now, what good am I for a man?' "(25). She does not even see her vagina as a source of value without her womb. Ursa collapses her vagina and womb as she reflects on her barrenness: "No warm ones, only bruised ones, not even bruised ones. No seeds. . . . It ain't a pussy down there, it's a whole world. . . . The center of a woman's being. Is it? No seeds" (45–46). Her vagina and womb come together to create the essence of her womanhood. Without her womb she can no longer enjoy vaginal stimulation. After she remarries, she cannot enjoy sex with Tadpole. He doesn't understand why a hysterectomy would effect her sexual fulfillment. Tadpole says to Ursa, " 'Damn, you still got a hole, ain't you? As long as a woman got a hole, she can fuck' " (82). But despite the presence of her vagina and clitoris, Ursa does not experience pleasure: "He was inside, and I felt nothing. I wanted to feel, but I couldn't" (82). The hysterectomy has left a psychological scar that impairs her sexual pleasure.

When Ursa finds Tadpole with Vivian, he justifies his actions with her sexual frigidity. He is angry that she does not experience orgasm with him and suggests that it is Ursa's fault that he turned to Vivian for sexual pleasure. The only time that Ursa had experienced pleasure with Tadpole is when he stimulated her clitoris: "I was struggling against him, trying to feel what I wasn't feeling. Then he reached down and fingered my clitoris, which made me feel more" (75). This moment of satisfaction, however, is short lived, as it becomes painful. Although the pain may have been real, it is also probably symptomatic of her discomfort with a desire that is not centered in either the vagina or the womb.

According to Madhu Dubey, "Ursa has to find a new story for herself that can account for her lack of a womb, and a new conception of feminine desire that is not centered around reproduction."[60] Ursa attempts to quell her fear that her hysterectomy has degendered her by reaffirming her heterosexuality and marrying Tadpole. However, while having intercourse with Tadpole, Ursa realizes that she no longer feels any sexual pleasure except when he fingers her clitoris. Dubey argues that this new awareness of clitoral pleasure opens up a place outside the reproductive system, however, at this point, Ursa cannot admit this new sexual awareness.[61] Ursa expresses this fear while reflecting on Tadpole's infidelity and her previous conversation with Cat, "*Afraid only of what I'll become, because those times he didn't touch the clit, I couldn't feel anything, and then he...*" (89). She both fears the desire she did not experience as well as the one she did. If she can experience pleasure from her clitoris, this opens up the possibility of lesbianism because a man would not be necessary. It is at this point that she "admits what she would not say earlier, her fear that the failure of heterosexual relationships threatens to dissolve her very sense of herself."[62] Even after Ursa admits her fear, lesbianism remains an undeveloped possibility.

At this point Ursa is no longer capable of operating within a reproductive sexuality and is uncomfortable with a lesbian or clitoral sexuality. One way that Ursa responds to this dilemma is through her music. Joyce Pettis contends, "Ursa's visible sexuality versus her difficulty in giving and receiving sexual pleasure, clearly related to the history of the women in her family, is a vigorous source of tension in her development and in the narrative, a tension communicated through the blues."[63] Ursa claims, "I sang because it was something I had to do" (3). The blues were Ursa's way of explaining what she couldn't explain; it was a way to cope with her family's history. She was looking for a song to say it all, "I wanted a song that would touch me, touch my life *and* theirs. A Portuguese song, but not a Portuguese song. A new world song" (59). Ursa's blues were her version of the family oral narrative: "Unlike the Corregidora women's story, Ursa's blues, accommodating as it does the contrary emotions of pleasure and pain, tenderness and violence, desire and hatred, constitutes an alternative narrative form that can represent the contradictory nature of black feminine sexuality."[64] It is this contradictory sexuality that Ursa must come to terms with.

Gottfried argues that Ursa's sexuality is not only restricted by her family's past but further frustrated by their insistence that she leave evidence.[65] After a history of forced concubinage, Great Gram and Gram are not going to have a healthy view of sexuality to pass on to their children. In fact, they have no need for sex outside of procreation; they desire progeny, not sexual fulfillment. It is only after Ursa loses her womb that she realizes the emptiness of a solely reproductive sexuality. Ursa's mother describes their reproductive sexuality as though it was completely natural—"my whole body wanted you" (117) —but Ursa sees what she will not explain: "Desire, and loneliness . . . screaming, fury in her eyes" (101). Ursa is able to see what her ancestors' reproductive myth represses:

Her mother's deepest and most inchoate desires cannot be expressed within this reproductive economy. . . . Ursa's mother's first giving of herself in childbirth, far from exhausting all that she has to give, instead creates a residue that cannot be given within the terms of a reproductive system.[66]

According to the ideology of motherhood and the Corregidora version of that ideology, motherhood should be a woman's source of self-fulfillment, but it is not enough for Ursa's mother and it is too much for some women. Dubey asserts that the novel demythicizes reproductive ideology through Ursa's memories of May Alice and the Melrose woman. May Alice is ruined when she is impregnated and abandoned by her boyfriend. The Melrose woman commits suicide when she suspects she is pregnant. These memories "when juxtaposed with her ancestors' pride in their reproductive capacity, betray the contradictory nature of her society's ideology of motherhood: at once a source of pride and shame."[67] However, once Ursa can no longer include herself within this frame, she realizes its inability to account for all of her desires.

The Corregidora women respond to their abuse by repressing their sexuality and focusing on their womb, rather than their vagina. Ursa in turn redefines herself by changing her focus from her womb to her clitoris, however as Gottfried observes, Ursa is still defining her sexuality by limiting her desire to one location.[68] Throughout the text, Ursa has been trying to realize her sexual self. Clearly the legacy of sexual abuse Ursa inherits affects her view of sexuality, but beyond that she must deal with her realization that "a man always says I want to fuck, a woman always has to say I want to get fucked" (89). However, by performing fellatio Ursa appears to reverse this scenario as she takes the active role. One might argue that Ursa is still being fucked because she is still providing an orifice for Mutt's penis, but the fact that she initiates the act is significant. This moment recalls the time in which Mutt pulled Ursa on top of him and asked if she has had it this way. When she says no, he responds, " 'Well, you ain't getting it' " (156). This could have been a moment for Ursa to take the active role and in a sense fuck Mutt, but he will not allow it. However, when they reunite Ursa takes the initiative and responds to their desire: "I knew what he wanted. I wanted it too" (184). Unlike their previous sexual encounters, which revolved around Mutt's desires, Ursa is responding to her own sexual needs.

As Ursa begins to perform fellatio, she tries to imagine what Great Gram had done to Corregidora to inspire such love and hate:

> In a split second I knew what it was, and I think he might have known too. A moment of pleasure and excruciating pain at the same time, a moment of broken skin but not sexlessness, a moment just before sexlessness, a moment that stops just before sexlessness, a moment that stops before it breaks the skin: "I could kill you." (184)

This is a moment of power and vulnerability: "Seeing this simultaneously powerful and powerless position, she at last admits that she fears her own vulnerability in emotional and sexual intimacy; the admission is essential for any reestablishment of her relationship with Mutt."[69] Keith Byerman provides a slightly different reading of the power dynamics at work in this scene:

> This moment of choice between life and death, between manhood and unmanning is the moment of female power. But this power, which manifests itself when the woman seems most clearly in a posture of submission, expresses itself most effectively by not being exercised. Its latency becomes its greatest proof, and also its greatest excitement. To not kill keeps the power in reserve as a constant reminder to the oppressor of his vulnerability.[70]

This point appears to be sustained by Mutt and Ursa's declaration that they do not want a woman or man that will hurt them. Three times Mutt states that he does not want a woman that will hurt him and each time Ursa responds, " 'Then you don't want me.' " But in the last lines of the text they come to an understanding: "He shook me till I fell against him crying. 'I don't want a kind of man that'll hurt me neither,' I said. He held me tight" (185). At this point, they both realize the other's power to cause pain. Ursa realized Mutt's power as she fell down the stairs, but now he knows that she can also hurt him. Although they express their ability to inflict pain in physical terms, this may also be seen as symbolic of the emotional pain they are capable of inflicting. By asserting her power, Ursa is leveling the playing field and presenting herself as an equal. She appears to be telling Mutt that she will no longer just wait to be fucked. Ursa's desire to initiate sexual intimacy parallels her desire to be an equal partner with Mutt.

Dubey argues that "the novel's conclusion, returning Ursa to her husband, attempts a nonreproductive but heterosexual adjustment of Ursa's desire. . . . [A]s Ursa performs fellatio on Mutt, she exercises a feminine power outside the reproductive system."[71] According to Dubey:

> fellatio, as a sexual act that is superfluous to a reproductive exchange of energy, situates Ursa at the very margins of heterosexuality (at a moment that stops just short of "sexlessness"). This boundary is perhaps the only space where an exercise of feminine power is possible. For the woman fully enclosed within the heterosexual, reproductive system (May Alice, the Melrose woman) power is entirely inaccessible. And the woman who finds her pleasure outside this system (Cat) is divested of all power. Ursa's position, both inside and outside, invests her with a sexual power, which, in a heterosexual context, is necessarily a power of potential violence ("a moment that stops just before it breaks the skin").[72]

Thus by the text's conclusion, Ursa has negotiated competing sexual ideologies and found one that responds to her desires and allows her some personal agency.

Ursa, like Dessa and Sethe, has been scarred by slavery, but each of their stories ends with healing. McDowell notes that while black men wrote the majority of slave narratives, black women wrote most of the contemporary novels about slavery. More significantly, these novels dramatize "not what was *done* to slave women, but what they *did* with what was done to them."[73] I would argue that in essence what they, like the nineteenth-century black women writers, did was to engender themselves. Slavery operated on the basis that female slaves were akin to animals and thus should not be accorded the gendered attributes of white women; however, female slaves rejected this definition of themselves. Female slaves constructed a vision of gender that incorporated African traditions, American traditions, and the history of slavery to formulate a different gender. Contemporary feminists acknowledge that gender is relational and thus there cannot be one feminine gender. Even all black women do not share the same gender conception, but I would argue that due to the history of slavery black women constructed a sense of gender significantly different than white women and it is this articulation of gender that I address in these texts by black women. Although all African-American women writers are not concerned with the issue of maternity, it does provide an interesting site from which to analyze gender since motherhood was something previously denied them. In my reading of these texts, I have argued that maternity becomes both a site of engenderment and a site of critique. These writers at once assert that their characters are capable of mothering while also arguing that women are more than mothers.

Conclusion

In these texts, motherhood becomes a lens from which to gaze at issues of gender and sexuality. For Jacobs, her task was to address the exclusive nature of the cult of true womanhood, which was based on a purity that female slaves were frequently unable to sustain due to forced concubinage. Wilson also interrogates this ideal womanhood, but with a slightly different slant. While Jacobs is particularly interested in the issue of purity, Wilson sidesteps that issue by desexualizing Frado and focusing instead upon the issues of motherhood and domesticity. Both Wilson and Jacobs depict single mothers who reconfigure the traditional family. Although Wilson avoids the issue of purity, Harper and Hopkins create characters who are concerned with purity. Harper's Iola is presented as an icon of true womanhood who happens to be black. Harper assures her readers that this is an ideal that black women can achieve. Hopkins' Sappho, however, is not pure in the traditional sense and like Jacobs' Linda must reconfigure the ideal of true womanhood. Although Harper and Hopkins address the issue of purity differently, they have similar views of domestic relations. Their characters are not (or do not remain) single mothers, but their marriages are presented as egalitarian matches that are not as invested in a separate-spheres ideology. Although these writers focus on different issues, all of these issues are related to the characters' conception of womanhood. Linda and Sappho's concerns about their purity are related to their sense of femininity, while Frado and Iola's concerns about domestic relations are connected to their views of the female role.

The twentieth-century texts are not as explicitly concerned with the cult of true womanhood, but they are invested in some related concerns. Sethe, Dessa, and Ursa are each concerned with their womanhood, which for all of them is in some way connected to motherhood. Sethe and Dessa's visions of freedom are bound up with their views of motherhood. They seek freedom for their children and to be better mothers, but in the process they also realize that as women they are more than mothers. Ursa, on the other hand, must come to accept her barrenness and realize that even though she cannot bear children, she is still a woman and a sexual being. Thus for all of these texts I would argue that the legacy of slavery lives on in them as the female characters must cope with depictions of femininity that are in some way at odds with the history of slavery.

All of these writers "pass on" the maternal as they remember black female slavery. In these acts of rememory, the writers create projects that in Hortense Spillers' words, gain "the *insurgent* ground as female social subject."[1] Their texts not only record but exemplify the "culturally forbidden maternal mark."[2] Slavery sought to eradicate the black maternal role, but instead it engendered a maternal line of descent. Rather than apologize for what has become termed a pathological situation, these writers celebrate the power of the maternal once it is defined by the woman and not by society. Maternity becomes a means to acknowledge femininity and humanity. These female characters come to realize that not only are they women and mothers, but also persons in their own right. The legacy of slavery has not crippled black women, but it has affected their self-concept.

Notes

Introduction

1. Hazel V. Carby, *Reconstructing Womanhood: The Emergence of the Afro-American Woman Novelist* (New York: Oxford UP, 1987) 6.

2. bell hooks, *Ain't I A Woman: Black Women and Feminism* (Boston: South End P, 1981) 124.

3. I should note that in my use of femininity, I am not ascribing any particular characteristics. My focus is on the way in which the denial of femininity or gender was used by proponents of slavery to deny the humanity of female slaves and justify practices of slave breeding and the sale of family members without regard for familial bonds.

4. Morrison, *Playing in the Dark: Whiteness and the Literary Imagination* (Cambridge: Harvard UP, 1992) 21.

1. The Breeding Ground

1. Drucilla Cornell, *Beyond Accommodation: Ethical Feminism, Deconstruction, and the Law* (New York: Routledge, 1991) 20.

2. Jane Gallop "Reading the Mother Tongue: Psychoanalytic Feminist Criticism," *Critical Inquiry* 13.2 (1987): 318.

3. Nancy Chodorow, *The Reproduction of Mothering: Psychoanalysis and the Sociology of Gender* (Berkeley: U of California P, 1978) 92–110.

4. Chodorow 173–90.

5. Chodorow 68.

6. Chodorow 32.

7. Elizabeth V. Spelman, *Inessential Woman: Problems of Exclusion in Feminist Thought* (Boston: Beacon Press, 1988) 88.

8. Maxine Hong Kingston, *The Woman Warrior* (New York: Knopf, 1976).

9. Spelman 113.

10. Judith Butler, *Gender Trouble: Feminism and the Subversion of Identity* (New York: Routledge, 1990) 1.

11. Butler 3.

12. Butler 6. In order to differentiate between sex and gender, throughout this text female and male will be used in reference to sex and woman and man in reference to gender.

13. Julia Kristeva, "Stabat Mater," *The Kristeva Reader,* ed. Toril Moi (New York: Columbia UP, 1986) 161.

14. Kristeva 160–61.

15. Cornell 43.

16. Cornell 48.

17. Harriet Jacobs, *Incidents in the Life of a Slave Girl.* 1861. *The Classic Slave Narratives,* ed. Henry Louis Gates Jr. (New York: Penguin, 1987) 387. Future references to this work appear parenthetically in the chapter.

18. Cornell 48–49.

19. Angela Davis, *Women, Race & Class* (New York: Random House, 1981) 5.

20. Hortense Spillers, "Mama's Baby, Papa's Maybe: An American Grammar Book," *Diacritics* 17.2 (1987): 72.

21. Davis, *Women* 6.

22. Dorothy Sterling, *We Are Your Sisters: Black Women in the Nineteenth Century* (New York: W. W. Norton, 1984) 13.

23. Sterling 13.

24. Moses Grandy, *Narrative of the Life of Moses Grandy: Late a Slave in the United States of America* (Boston: 1844), *Flight from the Devil: Six*

Slave Narratives, ed. William Loren Katz (Trenton: Africa World Press, 1996) 230–31. Although Grandy dictated his narrative to George Thompson and narratives that utilize an amanuensis are seen as less reliable, the fact that he recounts a process that is recounted by other former slaves points to the truthfulness of his own experience.

25. Sterling 39.

26. Jacqueline Jones, *Labor of Love, Labor of Sorrow: Black Women, Work, and the Family from Slavery to Present* (New York: Basic Books, 1985) 20.

27. Elizabeth Fox-Genovese, *Within the Plantation Household: Black and White Women of the Old South* (Chapel Hill: U of N. Carolina P, 1988) 307.

28. Spelman 42.

29. Davis, *Women* 6.

30. bell hooks, *Ain't I A Woman: Black Women and Feminism* (Boston: South End P, 1981) 71.

31. Spillers, "Mama's" 67.

32. Kaja Silverman, "*Histoire d'O*: The Construction of a Female Subject," *Pleasure and Danger: Exploring Female Sexuality,* ed. Carol S. Vance (Boston: Routledge & Kegan Paul, 1984) 325.

33. Silverman 325.

34. Silverman 332.

35. Mae G. Henderson, "Speaking in Tongues: Dialogics, Dialectics, and the Black Woman Writer's Literary Tradition," *Changing Our Own Words: Essays on Criticism, Theory, and Writing by Black Women* (New Brunswick, N.J.: Rutgers UP, 1989) 26.

36. Spillers, "Mama's" 73.

37. Abel 188.

38. Spillers, "Mama's" 80.

39. Davis, *Women* 7.

40. Kenneth M. Stampp, *The Peculiar Institution: Slavery in the Ante-Bellum South* (New York: Vintage Books, 1989) 340.

41. Spillers, "Mama's" 74–75.

42. Davis, *Women* 7.

43. Cornell 194.

44. Patricia Hill Collins, "Shifting the Center: Race, Class, and Feminist Theorizing about Motherhood," *Representations of Motherhood,* ed. Donna Bassin, Margaret Honey, and Meryle Mahrer Kaplan (New Haven: Yale UP, 1994) 56.

45. Marianne Hirsch "Maternity and Rememory: Toni Morrison's *Beloved,*" *Representations of Motherhood,* 99.

46. Cynthia Griffin Wolff, "'Margaret Garner': a Cincinnati Story," *Massachusetts Review* 32.3 (1991) 417–40.

47. There continues to be debate regarding the nature and extent of slave breeding. However, for my purpose I'm less concerned with the existence or absence of slave breeding and more interested in the fact that gendered notions of motherhood were not extended to female slaves. I do, however, believe slave breeding did take place and probably to a greater degree than we will ever be able to document. For more information regarding slave breeding, see Catherine Clinton, " 'Southern Dishonor': Flesh, Blood, Race, and Bondage," *In Joy and In Sorrow: Women, Family, and Marriage in the Victorian South, 1830–1900* (New York: Oxford UP, 1991) 52–68; Wilma King, " 'Suffer with Them Till Death': Slave Women and Their Children in Nineteenth-Century America"; and Claire Robertson, "Africa into the Americas? Slavery and Women, the Family, and the Gender Division of Labor," in *More Than Chattel: Black Women and Slavery in the Americas* (Bloomington: Indiana UP, 1996) 3–40, 147–68.

48. Qtd. in Stampp 245.

49. Stampp 248.

50. Spillers, "Mama's" 79.

51. Abel 189.

52. Spillers, "Mama's" 80.

53. Abel 188.

54. Spillers, "Interstices: A Small Drama of Words," *Pleasure and Danger: Exploring Female Sexuality*, ed. Carol S. Vance (Boston: Routledge & Kegan Paul, 1984) 88.

55. Sterling Stuckey, *Slave Culture: Nationalist Theory & The Foundations of Black America* (New York: Oxford UP, 1987), 10–11. See also Philip

Curtin, *The Atlantic Slave Trade* (Madison: U of Wisconsin P, 1969) and James H. Rawley, *The Transatlantic Slave Trade* (New York: W. W. Norton, 1981).

56. Kamene Okonjo, "The Dual-Sex Political System in Operation: Igbo Women and Community Politics in Mid-Western Nigeria," *Women in Africa: Studies in Social and Economic Change,* ed. Nancy J. Hafkin and Edna G. Bay (Stanford: Stanford UP, 1976) 45.

57. Okonjo 48.

58. Niara Sudarkasa, " 'The Status of Women' in Indigenous African Societies," *Women in Africa and the African Diaspora,* ed., Rosalyn Terborg-Penn, Sharon Harley, and Andrea Benton Rushing (Washington, D.C.: Howard UP, 1987) 33.

59. Sudarkasa 35.

60. Annie M. D. Lebeuf, "The Role of Women in the Political Organization of African Societies," *Women of Tropical Africa,* ed., Denise Paulme, trans. H. M. Wright (Berkeley: U of California P, 1963) 114.

61. Sudarkasa 32.

62. Sudarkasa 36.

63. Sudarkasa 31.

64. Christie Farnham, "Sapphire? The Issue of Dominance in the Slave Family, 1830–1865," *"To Toil the Livelong Day": America's Women at Work, 1780–1980,* ed, Carol Groneman and Mary Beth Norton (Ithaca, N.Y.: Cornell UP, 1987) 73.

65. Farnham 72.

66. Farnham 80.

67. White, "Female" 256.

68. Claire Robertson, "Africa into the Americas? Slavery and Women, the Family, and the Gender Division of Labor," *More Than Chattel: Black Women and Slavery in the Americas,* ed. David Barry Gaspar and Darlene Clark Hine (Bloomington: Indiana UP, 1996) 9–12.

69. Herbert S. Klein, "African Women in the Atlantic Slave Trade," *Women and Slavery in Africa,* ed, Claire C. Robertson and Martin A. Klein (Madison: U of Wisconsin P, 1983) 35.

70. Fox-Genovese appears to be limiting her comments to Euro-American modernity and particularly the middle classes as white women have

performed labor without loosing their feminine gender designation. For example, white female serfs labored in the fields of England and American frontiers' women worked on farms and ranches.

71. Jacqueline Jones, "Race, Sex, and Self-Evident Truths: The Status of Slave Women During the Era of the American Revolution," *Half Sisters of History: Southern Women and the American Past*, ed. Catherine Clinton (Durham: Duke UP, 1994) 24–25.

72. Fox-Genovese 193.

73. Davis, *Women* 12.

74. hooks 71.

75. Judith Van Allen, "'Aba Riots' or Igbo 'Woman's War'? Ideology, Stratification, and the Invisibility of Women," *Women in Africa: Studies in Social and Economic Change* (Stanford: Stanford UP, 1976) 80–81.

76. Barbara Welter, *Dimity Convictions: The American Woman in the Nineteenth Century* (Athens: Ohio UP, 1976) 21–23.

77. Calvin C. Hernton, *Sex and Racism in America* (New York: Grove P, 1965) 125.

78. Denise Paulme, ed., *Women of Tropical Africa,* trans. H. M. Wright (Berkeley: U of California P, 1963) 3.

79. Eugene D. Genovese, *Roll, Jordan, Roll: The World the Slaves Made* (New York: Pantheon Books, 1974) 458.

80. Michele Wallace, *Black Macho and the Myth of the Superwoman* (New York: Dial P, 1979) 139.

81. The fact that some African societies also included clitordectomy as part of their puberty rites does question the degree of sexual freedom allowed to women since this procedure makes sexual intercourse quite painful. Despite this contradiction, we still have a society with different mores and customs, rather than an immoral society.

82. John Blassingame, *The Slave Community: Plantation Life in the Antebellum South* (New York: Oxford UP, 1979) 161–62.

83. Herbert G. Gutman, *The Black Family in Slavery and Freedom, 1750–1925* (New York: Pantheon Books, 1976) 75.

84. Blassingame 161.

85. Barbara Christian, *Black Feminist Criticism: Perspectives on Black Women Writers* (New York: Pergamon P, 1985) 213.

86. Christian, *Black Feminist* 213–14.

87. Monique Gessain, "Coniagui Women (Guinea)," *Women of Tropical Africa* 34.

88. Fox-Genovese 301.

89. Stampp 340.

90. Fox-Genovese 290.

91. Wallace 22.

92. Stampp 343.

93. Fox-Genovese 193.

94. Fox-Genovese 193.

95. E. Franklin Frazier, *The Negro Family in the United States* (Chicago: U of Chicago P, 1966) 102.

96. Daniel Patrick Moynihan, *The Negro Family: The Case for National Action* (Washington, D.C.: Government Printing Office, 1965).

97. Robert William Fogel and Stanley Engerman, *Time on the Cross: The Economics of American Negro Slavery* (Boston: Little, Brown, 1974) 141.

98. Genovese 491–92.

99. Deborah G. White, "Female Slaves: Sex Roles and Status in the Antebellum Plantation South," *Journal of Family History* 8.3 (1983): 253.

100. White's emphasis on childcare may appear to contradict Fox-Genovese's assertion that female slaves did not devote themselves to caring for their own children and houses, but Fox-Genovese's point is that this was not their primary duties. It was also quite common for female slaves to provide childcare for other slaves' children, so this "feminine" role was not necessarily connected to familial responsibilities. White 254.

101. Davis, *Women* 18.

102. Davis, "Reflections on the Black Woman's Role in the Community of Slaves," *The Black Scholar* 3.4 (1971): 7.

103. Davis, "Reflections" 7.

104. White, "Female" 251–52.

105. White, "Female" 255.

106. Jacobs 342.

107. Sterling 13.

108. Joyce A. Ladner, "Racism and Tradition: Black Womanhood in Historical Perspective," ed. Filomina Chioma Steady (Cambridge: Schenkman, 1981) 275.

109. hooks 70.

110. Fox-Genovese 292.

111. Although I am primarily concerned with the degendering of female slaves, a similar process is seen in the treatment of male slaves. Fox-Genovese discusses the images of Sambo and Buck (291) who are basically male versions of Mammy and Jezebel. As with Mammy and Jezebel, Sambo and Buck are polar opposites. Sambo represented the docile servant, while Buck represented the virile sexually active black male.

112. Fox-Genovese 291.

113. Spillers, "Interstices" 76.

2. The Cult of True Womanhood

1. Barbara Welter, *Dimity Convictions: The American Woman in the Nineteenth Century* (Athens: Ohio UP, 1976) 21.

2. Welter 21 (emphasis mine).

3. Catherine Clinton, *The Plantation Mistress: Woman's World in the Old South* (New York: Pantheon Books, 1982) 87.

4. Clinton 100.

5. Nancy F. Cott, *The Bonds of Womanhood: "Woman's Sphere" in New England, 1780–1835* (New Haven: Yale UP, 1977) 199.

6. Cott 189.

7. Cott 84.

8. Nancy Tanner, "Matrifocality in Indonesia and Africa and Among Black Americans," *Woman, Culture, and Society*, ed. Michelle Zimbalist Rosaldo and Louise Lamphere (Stanford: Stanford UP, 1974) 132.

9. Tanner 131.

10. Deborah Gray White, *Ar'n't I A Woman?: Female Slaves in the Plantation South* (New York: W. W. Norton, 1985) 56.

11. Cott 91.

12. Mary P. Ryan, *Womanhood in America: From Colonial Times to the Present* (New York: Franklin Watts, 1983) 144.

13. Ryan 144.

14. Clinton 155.

15. White 56.

16. Clinton 201.

17. Sherley Anne Williams, *Dessa Rose* (New York: Berkley Books, 1986) 124–30. Future references to this work appear parenthetically in the chapter.

18. I think it is significant that Williams distinguishes the two views of Mammy through capitalization. Rufel's Mammy has the formal capital letter, while Dessa's mammy has the less formal, more familial lowercase spelling.

19. Clinton 202.

20. Moses Grandy, *Narrative of the Life of Moses Grandy: Late a Slave in the United States of America.* 1844. *Flight from the Devil: Six Slave Narratives*, ed. William Loren Katz (Trenton: Africa World Press, 1996) 230.

21. Carole Boyce Davies, *Black Women, Writing and Identity: Migrations of the Subject* (London: Routledge, 1994) 143.

22. Davies 144.

23. Joanne M. Braxton, *Black Women Writing Autobiography: A Tradition within a Tradition* (Philadelphia: Temple UP, 1989) 21.

24. Braxton, *Black Women* 33.

25. Davies 136.

26. Gillian Brown, *Domestic Individualism: Imagining Self in Nineteenth-Century America* (Berkeley: U of California P, 1990) 33.

27. Harriet Beecher Stowe, *Uncle Tom's Cabin or, Life among the Lowly* (1852; New York: Penguin, 1986) 521. Future references to this work appear parenthetically in the chapter.

28. Harryette Mullen, "Runaway Tongue: Resistant Orality in *Uncle Tom's Cabin, Our Nig, Incidents in the Life of a Slave Girl,* and *Beloved,*"

The Culture of Sentiment: Race, Gender, and Sentimentality in Nineteenth-Century America, ed. Shirley Samuels (New York: Oxford UP, 1992) 262.

29. Sojourner Truth, *Narrative of Sojourner Truth; A Bondswoman of Olden Time* (1878; New York: Arno Press and New York Times, 1968) 134.

30. Davies 136.

31. Richard Yarborough, "Strategies of Black Characterization in *Uncle Tom's Cabin* and the Early Afro-American Novel," *New Essays on Uncle Tom's Cabin,* ed. Eric J. Sundquist (Cambridge: Cambridge UP, 1986) 46.

32. Mullen 244.

33. Yarborough, "Strategies" 72.

34. Elizabeth Ammons, "Stowe's Dream of the Mother-Savior: *Uncle Tom's Cabin* and American Women Writers before the 1920s," *New Essays on Uncle Tom's Cabin,* ed. Eric J. Sundquist (Cambridge: Cambridge UP, 1986) 176.

35. Mullen 244.

36. Herbert Ross Brown, *The Sentimental Novel in America 1789–1860* (Durham: Duke UP, 1940) 176.

37. Philip Fisher, *Hard Facts: Setting and Form in the American Novel* (New York: Oxford UP, 1985) 93.

38. Jane Tompkins, *Sensational Designs: The Cultural Work of American Fiction 1790–1860* (New York: Oxford UP, 1985) 125.

39. Tompkins 126.

40. Barbara Christian, *Black Women Novelists: The Development of a Tradition, 1892–1976* (Westport, Conn.: Greenwood Press, 1980) 20.

41. Harriet Jacobs, *Incidents in the Life of a Slave Girl.* 1861. *The Classic Slave Narratives,* ed. Henry Louis Gates Jr. (New York: Penguin, 1987) 335. Future references to this work appear parenthetically in the chapter.

42. Fisher, *Hard Facts* 105. Fisher's assumption that suffering elicits compassion is problematized by the fact that it may also encourage sadism, hence the appreciation of horror films. I'd like to thank Carole-Anne Tyler for pointing this out to me.

43. Fisher, "Partings and Ruins: Radical Sentimentality in *Uncle Tom's Cabin,*" *Amerikastudien American Studies* 28.3 (1983): 280.

44. William L. Andrews, *To Tell a Free Story: The First Century of Afro-American Autobiography, 1760–1865* (Urbana: U of Illinois P, 1986) 15.

45. Marion Wilson Starling, *The Slave Narrative: Its Place in American History* (Washington, D.C.: Howard UP, 1988) 311.

46. Charles T. Davis and Henry Louis Gates Jr., eds., *The Slave's Narrative* (Oxford: Oxford UP, 1985).

47. Frederick Douglass, *Narrative of the Life of Frederick Douglass.* 1845. *The Classic Slave Narratives*, ed. Henry Louis Gates Jr. (New York: Penguin Books, 1987) 255, 256, and 257. Future references to this work appear parenthetically in the chapter.

48. See William Wells Brown, *Narrative of William W. Brown, A Fugitive Slave* (Boston: Anti-Slavery Office, 1847).

49. See Mary Prince, *History of Mary Prince, A West Indian Slave.* 1831. *The Classic Slave Narratives,* ed. Henry Louis Gates Jr. (New York: Penguin, 1987).

50. See Elizabeth Keckley, *Behind the Scenes. Or, Thirty Years a Slave and Four Years in the White House* (1868; New York: Oxford UP, 1988).

51. Starling 242.

52. Tompkins 125.

53. Yarborough, "Strategies" 66.

54. G. Brown 38.

55. G. Brown 18.

56. Angela Davis, *Women, Race & Class* (New York: Random House, 1981) 29.

57. Davis, *Women* 27.

58. Davis, *Women* 29.

59. Davis, *Women* 31.

60. Marie St. Claire is an exception since her husband is clearly her moral superior. Yellin briefly discusses this exception in her essay "Doing It Herself: *Uncle Tom's Cabin* and Woman's Role in the Slavery Crisis."

61. Myra Jehlen, "The Family Militant: Domesticity Versus Slavery in *Uncle Tom's Cabin*," *Criticism* 31.4 (1989): 392.

62. Jehlen 399.

63. Nancy F. Cott, "Passionlessness: An Interpretation of Victorian Sexual Ideology, 1790–1850," *A Heritage of Her Own: Toward a New Social History of American Women*, eds. Nancy F. Cott and Elizabeth H. Pleck (New York: Simon & Schuster, 1979) 162–81. Although Cott bases her study on women in New England, it is useful in generalizing about the country's views about sex and gender.

64. Ann duCille, *The Coupling Convention: Sex, Text, and Tradition in Black Women's Fiction* (New York: Oxford UP, 1993) 32.

65. duCille 33.

3. Reclaiming True Womanhood

1. William Andrews, introduction, *Six Women's Slave Narratives* (New York: Oxford UP, 1988) xxxi–xxxii.

2. Mary Prince, *The History of Mary Prince, A West Indian Slave*. 1831. *Six Women's Slave Narratives*, ed. William Andrews (New York: Oxford UP, 1988).

3. Andrews, intro. xxxiv.

4. For the narratives of Old Elizabeth and Mattie Jackson, see *Six Women's Slave Narratives*, ed. William Andrews (New York: Oxford UP, 1988).

5. Jean Fagan Yellin, introduction, *Incidents in the Life of a Slave Girl*, by Harriet A. Jacobs (1861; Cambridge: Harvard UP, 1987) xviii.

6. Yellin, intro. xix.

7. Hazel V. Carby, *Reconstructing Womanhood: The Emergence of the Afro-American Woman Novelist* (New York: Oxford UP, 1987) 45.

8. John Blassingame, *The Slave Community: Plantation Life in the Antebellum South* (New York: Oxford UP, 1979) 373.

9. Blassingame 368.

10. Carby 46.

11. See Jean Fagan Yellin, "Texts and Contexts of Harriet Jacobs' *Incidents in the Life of a Slave Girl Written by Herself*," *The Slave's Narrative*, ed. Charles T. Davis and Henry Louis Gates Jr. (New York: Oxford UP, 1985).

12. Mary Vermillion, "Reembodying the Self: Representations of Rape in *Incidents in the Life of a Slave Girl* and *I Know Why the Caged Bird Sings*," *Biography: An Interdisciplinary Quarterly* 15.3 (1992): 249.

13. Jane Tompkins, *Sensational Designs: The Cultural Work of American Fiction 1790–1860* (New York: Oxford UP, 1985) 126.

14. Harriet Jacobs, *Incidents in the Life of a Slave Girl.* 1861. *The Classic Slave Narratives,* ed. Henry Louis Gates Jr. (New York: Penguin, 1987) 335. Future references to this work appear parenthetically in the chapter.

15. Tompkins 140.

16. Yellin, intro. xxx.

17. Barbara Welter, *Dimity Convictions: The American Woman in the Nineteenth Century* (Athens: Ohio UP, 1976) 23.

18. Welter 41.

19. Mary Helen Washington, *Invented Lives: Narratives of Black Women 1860–1960* (Garden City, NY: Doubleday, 1987) 4.

20. Carby 47.

21. Michele Wallace, *Black Macho and the Myth of the Superwoman* (New York: Dial P, 1979) 144.

22. Elizabeth Keckley, *Behind the Scenes. Or, Thirty Years a Slave and Four Years in the White House* (1868; New York: Oxford UP, 1988) 39.

23. Dana D. Nelson, *The Word in Black and White: Reading "Race" in American Literature, 1638–1867* (New York: Oxford UP, 1992) 143.

24. Welter 21.

25. Yellin, intro. xxx.

26. Kari J. Winter, *Subjects of Slavery, Agents of Change: Women and Power in Gothic Novels and Slave Narratives 1790–1865* (Athens: U of Georgia P, 1992) 95.

27. Yellin, intro. xxxiii.

28. Carby 50.

29. Karen Sánchez-Eppler, *Touching Liberty: Abolition, Feminism, and the Politics of the Body* (Berkeley: U of California P, 1993) 90.

30. Harriet Beecher Stowe, *Uncle Tom's Cabin or, Life among the Lowly* (1852; N.Y.: Penguin, 1986) 506–7. Future references to this work appear parenthetically in the chapter.

31. Nelson 136.

32. Braxton, *Black Women* 30–31. Although Braxton is speaking in reference to women, the trickster figure need not be female, or even human. For example Brer Rabbit is a popular trickster figure in African American folklore.

33. Nelson 135.

34. Wallace 26.

35. Nelson 137.

36. Vermillion 247.

37. Carla Kaplan, "Narrative Contracts and Emancipatory Readers: *Incidents in the Life of a Slave Girl*," *Yale Journal of Criticism* 6.1 (1993): 101–2.

38. Kaplan 103.

39. Kaplan 103.

40. See Foreman 322 and Valerie Smith, "Form and Ideology in Three Slave Narratives," *Self-Discovery and Authority in Afro-American Narrative* (Cambridge: Harvard UP, 1987).

41. Frederick Douglass, *Narrative of the Life of Frederick Douglass.* 1845. *The Classic Slave Narratives*, ed. Henry Louis Gates Jr. (New York: Penguin Books, 1987) 249.

42. Fisher, *Hard Facts* 118.

43. For a discussion of the gender iniquity in antimiscegenation and rape laws, see Karen A. Getman, "Sexual Control in the Slaveholding South: The Implementation and Maintenance of a Racial Caste System," *Harvard Women's Law Journal* 7 (1984): 115–52.

44. Wallace 138.

45. This is not to say that since Africans have been diluted with Anglo blood they are now above the condition of slavery. Rather, this should bring into question the idea of race as a marker of slavery. By acknowledging the intermixing of white and black, one realizes the impossibility of continuing to distinguish the races because the gray area between white and black continually expands.

46. Hortense Spillers, "Mama's Baby, Papa's Maybe: An American Grammar Book," *Diacritics* 17.2 (1987): 79.

47. This is not to say that such a child would face a better fate since according to the narrator, such offspring were often killed or sent away,

but it would be different. See Karen A. Getman, "Sexual Control in the Slaveholding South: the Implementation and Maintenance of a Racial Caste System," *Harvard Women's Law Journal* 7 (1984): 115–52 for further discussion of mulatto children born to white mothers. While the master's offspring born to female slaves would be seen as a valuable contribution to the plantation's holdings, children born to white women but fathered by slaves were merely viewed as shameful evidence of a ruined woman. This double standard is clearly a reflection of a male-dominated society.

48. Nina Baym, *Woman's Fiction: A Guide to Novels by and about Women in America 1820–70* (Urbana: U of Illinois P, 1993) xxix–x.

49. Nelson 137.

50. Nelson 144.

51. Nelson 142.

52. Jean Fagan Yellin, *Women & Sisters: The Antislavery Feminists in American Culture* (New Haven: Yale UP, 1989) 79.

53. Yellin, *Women & Sisters* 79.

54. The fact that one should apologize for single motherhood is particularly salient in arguments like that found in the Moynihan report in which Daniel Moynihan finds such arrangements to be pathological and debilitating to the black community.

55. P. Gabrielle Foreman, "The Spoken and the Silenced in *Incidents in the Life of a Slave Girl* and *Our Nig*," *Callaloo* 13.2 (1991): 323.

56. Although both Jacobs and Wilson blur genres, Jacobs' text is considered a slave narrative and thus part of the autobiographical realm, while Wilson's text is viewed as a novel despite its autobiographical aspects. The difference is the degree of "truth" expected from the genres. As a slave narrative, *Incidents* is expected to be a more truthful in its representation of Jacobs' life as a slave, while Wilson is allowed more license to play with the details of her life.

57. Carby 43.

58. Carby 44–45.

59. Elizabeth Breau, "Identifying Satire: *Our Nig*," *Callaloo* 16.2 (1993): 457.

60. Breau 457.

61. Breau 458.

62. Beth Maclay Doriani, "Black Womanhood in Nineteenth-Century America: Subversion and Self-Construction in Two Women's Autobiographies," *American Quarterly* 43.2 (1991): 212.

63. Doriani 212.

64. Henry Louis Gates Jr., introduction, *Our Nig; or, Sketches from the Life of a Free Black*, by Harriet E. Wilson (1859; New York: Random House 1983) li.

65. See Gates' introduction. See also: David Ames Curtis and Henry Louis Gates Jr., "Establishing the Identity of the Author of *Our Nig*," *Wild Women in the Whirlwind: Afra-American Culture and the Contemporary Literary Renaissance*, ed. Joanne M. Braxton and Andrée Nicola McLaughlin (New Brunswick, N.J.: Rutgers UP, 1990); Barbara A. White, " 'Our Nig' " and the She-Devil: New Information about Harriet Wilson and the 'Bellmont' Family," *American Literature* 65.1 (1993): 19–52; and Eric Gardner " 'This Attempt of Their Sister' ": Harriet Wilson's *Our Nig* from Printer to Readers," *New England Quarterly* 66.2 (1993): 226–46.

66. Baym ix.

67. Baym 27.

68. Gates xlvi.

69. Baym 37.

70. Elizabeth Ammons, "Stowe's Dream of the Mother Savior: *Uncle Tom's Cabin* and American Women Writers before the 1920s," *New Essays on Uncle Tom's Cabin*, ed. Eric J. Sundquist (Cambridge: Cambridge UP, 1986) 185.

71. Ammons 177.

72. See Angelyn Mitchell, "Her Side of His Story: A Feminist Analysis of Two Nineteenth-Century Antebellum Novels—William Wells Brown's *Clotel* and Harriet E. Wilson's *Our Nig*," *American Literary Realism* 24.3 (1992): 7–21 for a different reading in which Mitchell argues that Alfrado is provided with several surrogate mothers such as Aunt Abby, Jane, and Mr. Bellmont.

73. Ammons 182.

74. Harriet E. Wilson, *Our Nig; or, Sketches from the Life of a Free Black* (1859; New York: Random House, 1983) 17. Future references to this work appear parenthetically in the chapter.

75. Braxton, "Ancestral Presence: The Outraged Mother Figure in Contemporary Afra-American Writing," *Wild Women in the Whirlwind: Afra-American Culture and the Contemporary Literary Renaissance*, ed. Joanne M. Braxton and Andrée Nicola McLaughlin (New Brunswick, N.J.: Rutgers UP, 1990) 300–1.

76. Braxton, *Black Women* 21.

77. Braxton, *Black Women* 33.

78. Cynthia J. Davis, "Speaking the Body's Pain: Harriet Wilson's *Our Nig*," *African American Review* 27.3 (1993): 391.

79. See chapter 2 for a fuller discussion of *Contending Forces*.

80. C. Davis 394.

81. C. Davis 397.

82. C. Davis 398.

83. Foreman 318.

84. Elizabeth Fox-Genovese, *Within the Plantation Household: Black and White Women of the Old South* (Chapel Hill: U of N. Carolina P, 1988) 392.

85. C. Davis 399.

86. C. Davis 399.

87. C. Davis 401.

88. Fanny Nudelman, "Harriet Jacobs and the Sentimental Politics of Female Suffering," *ELH* 59 (1992): 942.

89. Nudelman 950

90. William L. Andrews, *To Tell a Free Story: The First Century of Afro-American Autobiography, 1760–1865* (Urbana: U of Illinois P, 1986) 242.

91. Foreman 320.

92. Breau 461.

93. Breau 461.

94. Carby 44.

95. Ammons 185.

96. Breau 462.

97. Gates xlviii.

98. Foreman 321.

99. Sánchez-Eppler 100–101.

4. Tragic Mulattas

1. Catherine Clinton, "Reconstructing Freedwomen," *Divided Houses: Gender and the Civil War*, ed. Catherine Clinton and Nina Silber (New York: Oxford UP, 1992).

2. Elizabeth Ammons, "Stowe's Dream of the Mother Savior: *Uncle Tom's Cabin* and American Women Writers before the 1920s," *New Essays on Uncle Tom's Cabin*, ed. Eric J. Sundquist (Cambridge: Cambridge UP, 1986) 176–77.

3. Francis Smith Foster, ed., *A Brighter Coming Day: A Frances Ellen Watkins Harper Reader* (New York: Feminist Press, 1990) 11.

4. Foster 54.

5. Foster 55.

6. Richard Yarborough, "Strategies of Black Characterization in *Uncle Tom's Cabin* and the Early Afro-American Novel," *New Essays on Uncle Tom's Cabin*, ed. Eric J. Sundquist (Cambridge: Cambridge UP, 1986) 78.

7. Hazel V. Carby, *Reconstructing Womanhood: The Emergence of the Afro-American Woman Novelist* (New York: Oxford UP, 1987) 32.

8. Barbara Christian, *Black Feminist Criticism: Perspectives on Black Women Writers* (New York: Pergamon P, 1985) 168.

9. One could also add class to this litany, however, my focus is on race and gender, and I will only address class as it impinges on these two issues.

10. Elizabeth Young, "Warring Fictions: *Iola Leroy* and the Color of Gender," *American Literature* 64.2 (1992): 274.

11. Young 277.

12. Young 279.

13. Young 280.

14. Young 281.

15. Young 281.

16. Frances E. W. Harper, *Iola Leroy, or Shadows Uplifted*. 1892. *Three Classic African American Novels*, ed. Henry Louis Gates Jr. (New York: Vintage, 1990) 425. Future references to this work appear parenthetically in the chapter.

17. Carby 93.

18. Carby 93–94.

19. Foster 292.

20. Harper, "Colored Woman's Political Future," *World's Congress of Representative Women*, ed. May Wright Sewall (Chicago: Rand McNally, 1894) 433–34.

21. Myra Jehlen, "The Family Militant: Domesticity Versus Slavery in *Uncle Tom's Cabin*," *Criticism* 31.4 (1989): 392.

22. Jehlen 399.

23. Harriet Beecher Stowe, *Uncle Tom's Cabin or, Life among the Lowly* (1852; New York: Penguin, 1986) 8.

24. Young 284.

25. Claudia Tate, "Allegories of Black Female Desire; or, Rereading Nineteenth Century Sentimental Narratives of Black Female Authority," *Changing Our Own Words: Essays on Criticism, Theory, and Writing by Black Women*, ed. Cheryl A. Wall (New Brunswick: Rutgers UP, 1989) 119.

26. Elizabeth Ammons, *Conflicting Stories: American Women Writers at the Turn into the Twentieth Century* (New York: Oxford UP, 1991) 30.

27. Tate, "Pauline Hopkins: Our Literary Foremother," *Conjuring: Black Women, Fiction, and Literary Tradition*, ed. Marjories Pryse and Hortense Spillers (Bloomington: Indiana UP, 1985) 56.

28. Tate, "Allegories" 103.

29. Pauline Hopkins, *Contending Forces: A Romance Illustrative of Negro Life North and South* (1900; New York: Oxford, 1988) 15. Future references to this work appear parenthetically in the chapter.

30. Carby 50.

31. Tate, *Domestic Allegories of Political Desire: The Black Heroine's Text at the Turn of the Century* (New York: Oxford UP, 1992) 161.

32. Tate, *Domestic* 161.

33. Carby 34.

34. Carby 132.

35. Tate, *Domestic* 148.

36. Carby 142–43.

37. Tate, *Domestic* 174.

38. Tate, *Domestic* 175.

39. Tate, *Domestic* 175.

40. Tate, *Domestic* 175.

41. Tate, *Domestic* 174.

42. Spillers, "Mama's" 80.

43. Richard Yarborough, introduction, *Contending Forces*, by Pauline E. Hopkins (1900; New York, Oxford UP, 1988) xxxix.

44. Yarborough, intro. xxxiii.

45. Tate, *Domestic* 165.

46. Tate, *Domestic* 164.

47. Tate, *Domestic* 164.

5. The Haunting Effects of Slavery

1. Nancy Armstrong, "Why Daughters Die: The Racial Logic of American Sentimentalism," *The Yale Journal of Criticism* 7.2 (1994) 14.

2. Armstrong 17.

3. Toni Morrison, "The Site of Memory," *Inventing the Truth: The Art and Craft of Memoir*, ed. William Zinsser, Rev. ed. (Boston: Houghton Mifflin, 1995) 91.

4. Morrison, "Site" 93.

5. Peggy Phelan, *Unmarked: The Politics of Performance* (London: Routledge, 1993) 1.

6. Phelan 2.

7. Morrison, *Beloved* (New York: Signet, 1991) 336. Future references to this work appear parenthetically in the chapter.

8. Marianne Hirsch, "Maternity and Rememory: Toni Morrison's *Beloved*," *Representations of Motherhood*, eds. Donna Bassin, Margaret Honey, and Meryle Mahrer Kaplan (New Haven: Yale UP, 1994) 105.

9. Jean Wyatt, "Giving Body to the Word: The Maternal Symbolic in Toni Morrison's *Beloved*," *PMLA* 108.3 (1993) 484.

10. Hirsch, "Maternity" 96.

11. Morrison, *Playing* 21.

12. See Ann Dally's *Inventing Motherhood: The Consequences of an Ideal* (London: Barnett Books, 1982) in which she argues that idealization is used to keep women in their place.

13. Shirley A. Stave, "Toni Morrison's Beloved and the Vindication of Lilith," *South Atlantic Review* 58.1 (1993) 58.

14. Laura Doyle, *Bordering on the Body: The Racial Matrix of Modern Fiction and Culture* (New York: Oxford UP, 1994) 6.

15. Doyle 27.

16. Doyle 27.

17. Stave 58.

18. Hirsch, *The Mother/Daughter Plot: Narrative, Psychoanalysis, Feminism* (Bloomington: Indiana UP, 1989) 6.

19. Doyle 220–21.

20. Hirsch, "Maternity" 6.

21. Collins, "Shifting" 56.

22. Carole Boyce Davies, *Black Women, Writing, and Identity: Migrations of the Subject* (London: Routledge, 1994) 139.

23. Stave 59.

24. Stave 59. I would also like to offer another possible reading of the epigraph: perhaps the people refers to all enslaved Africans whether they are actually blood relations or not and the beloved is loved by the slave community if not by the slave master's family.

25. Stave 61.

26. Stave 61.

27. Sigmund Freud, "Femininity," *The Standard Edition of the Complete Psychological Works of Sigmund Freud*, Ed. James Strachey, Volume XXII, (London: Hogarth Press, 1964) 122.

28. Luce Irigaray, *Speculum of the Other Woman*, Trans. Gillian C. Gill (Ithaca: Cornell UP, 1985) 40.

29. Doyle 226.

30. Hirsch, "Maternity" 102.

31. Hortense Spillers, "Mama's Baby, Papa's Maybe: An American Grammar Book," *Diacritics* 17.2 (1987) 79.

32. Mae G. Henderson, "Toni Morrison's Beloved: Re-Membering the Body as Historical Text," *Comparative American Identities: Race, Sex, and Nationality in The Modern Text*, ed., Hortense J. Spillers (New York: Routledge, 1991) 77.

33. Davies 140.

34. Davies 138.

35. Henderson, "Toni" 68.

36. Henderson, "Toni" 69.

37. Henderson, "Toni" 69.

38. Henderson, "Toni" 69.

39. Sherley Anne Williams, *Dessa Rose* (New York: Berkley Books, 1986) 41. Future references to this work appear parenthetically in the chapter.

40. Ashraf H. A. Rushdy, "Reading Mammy: The Subject of Relation in Sherley Anne Williams' *Dessa Rose*," *African American Review* 27.3 (1993) 371.

41. Mae G. Henderson, "Speaking in Tongues: Dialogics, Dialectics, and the Black Woman Writer's Literary Tradition," *Changing Our Own Words: Essays on Criticism, Theory, and Writing By Black Women* (New Brunswick: Rutgers UP), 25.

42. Marta E. Sánchez, "The Estrangement Effect in Sherley Anne Williams' *Dessa Rose*," *Genders* 15 (1992) 27.

43. Henderson, "Speaking" 26.

44. Henderson, "Speaking" 26.

45. Deborah McDowell, "Negotiating Between Tenses: Witnessing Slavery After Freedom—Dessa Rose," *Slavery and the Literary Imagination,* eds. Deborah E. McDowell and Arnold Rampersad (Baltimore: Johns Hopkins UP, 1989) 150.

46. Sánchez 33.

47. McDowell 154.

48. Henderson, "Speaking" 32.

49. Henderson, "Speaking" 31.

50. Sánchez 29.

51. Sánchez 29.

52. Sánchez 31.

53. Adam McKible, " 'These are the Facts of the Darky's History': Thinking History and Reading Names in Four African American Texts," *African American Review* 28.2 (1994) 232.

54. Amy S. Gottfried, "Angry Arts: Silence, Speech, and Song in Gayl Jones's *Corregidora*," *African American Review* 28.4 (1994) 560.

55. Gayl Jones, *Corregidora* (Boston: Beacon Press, 1975) 9. Future references to this work appear parenthetically in the chapter.

56. Gottfried 559.

57. Gottfried 560.

58. Gottfried 560.

59. Gottfried 560.

60. Madhu Dubey, *Black Women Novelists and the Nationalist Aesthetic* (Bloomington: Indiana UP, 1994) 76.

61. Dubey 76.

62. Dubey 77.

63. Joyce Pettis, " 'She Sung Back in Return': Literary (Re)vision and Transformation in Gayl Jones's *Corregidora*," *College English* 52.7 (1990) 795.

64. Dubey 86.

65. Gottfried 559.

66. Dubey 79.

67. Dubey 79.

68. Gottfried 562–63.

69. Missy Dehn Kubitschek, *Claiming the Heritage: African-American Women Novelists and History*, (Jackson: UP of Mississippi, 1991) 150.

70. Keith E. Byerman, *Fingering the Jagged Grain: Tradition and Form in Recent Black Fiction* (Athens: U of Georgia P, 1985) 181.

71. Dubey 80.

72. Dubey 80.

73. McDowell 146.

Conclusion

1. Spillers, "Mama's Baby, Papa's Maybe: An American Grammar Book," *Diacritics* 17.2 (1987) 80.

2. Elizabeth Abel, "Race, Class, and Psychoanalysis? Opening Questions," *Conflicts in Feminism,* ed. Marianne Hirsch and Evelyn Fox Keller (New York: Routledge, 1990) 189.

Bibliography

Abel, Elizabeth. "Race, Class, and Psychoanalysis? Opening Questions."
Conflicts in Feminism. Ed. Marianne Hirsch and Evelyn Fox Keller.
New York: Routledge, 1990. 184–204.

Ammons, Elizabeth. *Conflicting Stories: American Women Writers at the
Turn into the Twentieth Century*. New York: Oxford UP, 1991.

———. "Stowe's Dream of the Mother-Savior: *Uncle Tom's Cabin* and
American Women Writers before the 1920s." *New Essays on Uncle Tom's
Cabin*. Ed. Eric J. Sundquist. Cambridge: Cambridge UP, 1986. 155–95.

Andrews, William L. "Reunion in the Postbellum Slave Narrative: Frederick
Douglass and Elizabeth Keckley." *Black American Literature Forum*
23.1 (1989): 5–16.

———. *To Tell a Free Story: The First Century of Afro-American Autobiography, 1760–1865*. Urbana: U of Illinois P, 1986.

Armstrong, Nancy. "Why Daughters Die: The Racial Logic of American
Sentimentalism." *The Yale Journal of Criticism* 7.2 (1994): 1–24.

Baym, Nina. *Woman's Fiction: A Guide to Novels by and about Women in
America 1820–70*. Urbana: U of Illinois P, 1993.

Benjamin, Jessica. *The Bonds of Love: Psychoanalysis, Feminism, and the
Problem of Domination*. New York: Pantheon Books, 1988.

Berry, Mary Frances. "Judging Morality: Sexual Behavior and Legal Consequences in the Late Nineteenth-Century South." *The Journal of
American History* 78.3 (1991): 835–56.

Berzon, Judith R. *Neither White Nor Black: The Mulatto Character in American Fiction*. New York: New York UP, 1978.

Blassingame, John. *The Slave Community: Plantation Life in the Antebellum South*. New York: Oxford UP, 1979.

———. *Slave Testimony: Two Centuries of Letters, Speeches, Interviews and Autobiographies*. Baton Rouge: Louisiana State UP, 1977.

Braxton, Joanne M. "Ancestral Presence: The Outraged Mother Figure in Contemporary Afra-American Writing." *Wild Women in the Whirlwind: Afra-American Culture and the Contemporary Literary Renaissance*. Ed. Joanne M. Braxton and Andrée Nicola McLaughlin. New Brunswick, N.J.: Rutgers UP, 1990. 299–315.

———. *Black Women Writing Autobiography: A Tradition within a Tradition*. Philadelphia: Temple UP, 1989.

———. "Harriet Jacobs' *Incidents in the Life of a Slave Girl*: The Redefinition of the Slave Narrative Genre." *Massachusetts Review* 27.2 (1986): 379–87.

Breau, Elizabeth. "Identifying Satire: *Our Nig*." *Callaloo* 16.2 (1993): 455–65.

Brown, Gillian. *Domestic Individualism: Imagining Self in Nineteenth-Century America*. Berkeley: U of California P, 1990.

Brown, Herbert Ross. *The Sentimental Novel in America 1789–1860*. Durham: Duke UP, 1940.

Brown, William Wells. *Narrative of William W. Brown, A Fugitive Slave, Written by Himself*. Boston: The Anti-Slavery Office, 1847.

Butler, Judith. *Gender Trouble: Feminism and the Subversion of Identity*. New York: Routledge, 1990.

Butterfield, Stephen. *Black Autobiography in America*. Amherst: University of Massachusetts Press, 1974.

Byerman, Keith E. *Fingering the Jagged Grain: Tradition and Form in Recent Black Fiction*. Athens: U of Georgia P, 1985.

Carby, Hazel V. *Reconstructing Womanhood: The Emergence of the Afro-American Woman Novelist*. New York: Oxford UP, 1987.

Chodorow, Nancy. *The Reproduction of Mothering: Psychoanalysis and the Sociology of Gender*. Berkeley: U of California P, 1978.

Christian, Barbara. *Black Feminist Criticism: Perspectives on Black Women Writers*. New York: Pergamon P, 1985.

———. *Black Women Novelists: The Development of a Tradition, 1892–1976*. Westport, Conn.: Greenwood Press, 1980.

Clinton, Catherine, "Caught in the Web of the Big House: Women and Slavery." *The Web of Southern Social Relations*. Ed. Walter J. Fraser Jr., R. Frank Saunders Jr., and Jon L. Wakelyn. Athens: University of Georgia P, 1985. 19–34.

————, ed. *Half Sisters of History: Southern Women and the American Past*. Durham: Duke UP, 1994.

————. *The Plantation Mistress: Woman's World in the Old South*. New York: Pantheon Books, 1982.

————. "Reconstructing Freedwomen." *Divided Houses: Gender and the Civil War*. Ed. Catherine Clinton and Nina Silber. New York, Oxford UP, 1992. 306–19.

————. "'Southern Dishonor': Flesh, Blood, Race, and Bondage." *In Joy and In Sorrow: Women, Family, and Marriage in the Victorian South, 1830–1900*. Ed. Carol Blesser. New York: Oxford UP, 1991. 52–68.

Cole, Phylis. "Stowe, Jacobs, Wilson: White Plots and Black Counterplots." *New Perspectives on Gender, Race, and Class in Society*. Ed. Audrey T. McCluskey. Bloomington: Indiana University P, 1990. 23–45.

Collins, Patricia Hill. *Black Feminist Thought: Knowledge, Consciousness and the Politics of Empowerment*. Boston: Unwin Hyman, 1990.

————. "Shifting the Center: Race, Class, and Feminist Theorizing about Motherhood." *Representations of Motherhood*. Ed. Donna Bassin, Margaret Honey, and Meryle Mahrer Kaplan. New Haven: Yale UP, 1994. 56–74.

Cooper, Anna Julia. *A Voice from the South*. 1892. New York: Oxford UP, 1988.

Cornell, Drucilla. *Beyond Accommodation: Ethical Feminism, Deconstruction, and the Law*. New York: Routledge, 1991.

Cott, Nancy F. *The Bonds of Womanhood: "Woman's Sphere" in New England, 1780–1835*. New Haven: Yale UP, 1977.

————. "Passionlessness: An Interpretation of Victorian Sexual Ideology, 1790–1850." *A Heritage of Her Own: Toward a New Social Hisory of American Women*. Ed. Nancy F. Cott and Elizabeth H. Pleck. New York: Simon & Schuster, 1979. 162–35.

Curtin, Philip. *The Atlantic Slave Trade*. Madison: U of Wisconsin P, 1969.

Dally, Ann. *Inventing Motherhood: The Consequences of an Ideal*. London: Barnett Books, 1982.

Davies, Carole Boyce. *Black Women, Writing and Identity: Migrations of the Subject*. London: Routledge, 1994.

Davis, Angela. "Reflections on the Black Woman's Role in the Community of Slaves." *The Black Scholar* 3.4 (1971): 2–15.

————. *Women, Race & Class*. New York: Random House, 1981.

Davis, Charles T. and Henry Louis Gates Jr., eds. *The Slave's Narrative*. Oxford: Oxford UP, 1985.

Davis, Cynthia J. "Speaking the Body's Pain: Harriet Wilson's *Our Nig*." *African American Review* 27.3 (1993): 391–404.

DeCanio, Stephen J. "*Uncle Tom's Cabin*: A Reappraisal." *The Centennial Review* 34.4 (1990): 587–93.

Diop, Cheikh Anta. *The Cultural Unity of Negro Africa: The Demains of Patriarchy and Matriarchy in Classical Antiquity.* Paris: Presence Africaine, 1962.

Dixon, Melvin. "Singing a Deep Song: Language as Evidence in the Novels of Gayl Jones." *Black Women Writers (1950–1980): A Critical Evaluation.* Ed. Mari Evans. Garden City, NY: Doubleday/Anchor Press, 1984. 236–48.

Doriani, Beth Maclay. "Black Womanhood in Nineteenth-Century America: Subversion and Self-Construction in Two Women's Autobiographies." *American Quarterly* 43.2 (1991): 199–222.

Douglass, Ann. *The Feminization of American Culture.* New York: Alfred A. Knopf, 1977.

Douglass, Frederick. *Narrative of the Life of Frederick Douglass.* 1845. *The Classic Slave Narratives.* Ed. Henry Louis Gates Jr. New York: Penguin Books, 1987.

Doyle, Laura. *Bordering on the Body: The Racial Matrix of Modern Fiction and Culture.* New York: Oxford UP, 1994.

Dubey, Madhu. *Black Women Novelists and the Nationalist Aesthetic.* Bloomington: Indiana UP, 1994.

duCille, Ann. *The Coupling Convention: Sex, Text, and Tradition in Black Women's Fiction.* New York: Oxford UP, 1993.

Epstein, Barbara Leslie. *The Politics of Domesticity: Women, Evangelism, and Temperance in Nineteenth-Century America.* Middletown, Conn.: Wesleyan UP, 1981.

Farnham, Christie. "Sapphire? The Issue of Dominance in the Slave Family, 1830–1865." *"To Toil the Livelong Day": America's Women at Work, 1780–1980.* Ed. Carol Groneman and Mary Beth Norton. Ithaca, N.Y.: Cornell UP, 1987. 68–83.

Fisher, Philip. *Hard Facts: Setting and Form in the American Novel.* New York: Oxford UP, 1985.

———. "Partings and Ruins: Radical Sentimentality in *Uncle Tom's Cabin.*" *Amerikastudien (American Studies)* 28.3 (1983): 279–93.

Fogel, Robert William, and Stanley Engerman. *Time on the Cross: The Economics of American Negro Slavery.* Boston: Little, Brown, 1974.

Foreman, P. Gabrielle. "The Spoken and the Silenced in *Incidents in the Life of a Slave Girl* and *Our Nig.*" *Callaloo* 13.2 (1991): 313–24.

Foster, Francis Smith. "Adding Color and Contour to Early American Self-Portraitures: Autobiographical Writings of Afro-American Women." *Conjuring: Black Women,Fiction, and Literary Tradition.* Bloomington: Indiana UP, 1985. 25–38.

———. "Autobiography after Emancipation: The Example of Elizabeth Keckley." *Multicultural Autobiography: American Lives.* Ed. James Robert Payne. Knoxville: The University of Tennessee Press, 1992. 33–63.

————, ed. *A Brighter Coming Day: A Frances Ellen Watkins Harper Reader.* New York: Feminist Press, 1990.

————. " 'In Respect to Females . . .': Differences in the Portrayals of Women by Male and Female Narrators." *Black American Literature Forum* 15 (1981): 66–70.

————. "Ultimate Victims: Black Women in Slave Narratives." *Journal of American Culture* 1.4 (1978): 845–54.

————. *Witnessing Slavery: The Development of Ante-Bellum Slave Narratives.* 2nd ed. Madison: U of Wisconsin P, 1994.

————. *Written by Herself: Literary Production by African American Women, 1746–1892.* Bloomington: Indiana UP, 1993.

Fox-Genovese, Elizabeth. *Within the Plantation Household: Black and White Women of the Old South.* Chapel Hill: U of N. Carolina P, 1988.

Frazier, E. Franklin. *The Negro Family in the United States.* Chicago: U of Chicago P, 1966.

Freud, Sigmund. "Feminity." *The Standard Edition of the Complete Psychological Works of Sigmund Freud.* Ed. James Strachey. Volume XXII. London: Hogarth P, 1964. 112–35.

Gallop, Jane. "Reading the Mother Tongue: Psychoanalytic Feminist Criticism." *Critical Inquiry* 13.2 (1987): 314–29.

Gardner, Eric. " 'This Attempt of Their Sister': Harriet Wilson's *Our Nig* from Printer to Readers." *New England Quarterly* 66.2 (1993): 226–46.

Gates, Henry Louis, Jr. Introduction. *Our Nig; or, Sketches from the Life of a Free Black.* By Harriet E. Wilson. 1859. New York: Random House, 1983. xi–lv.

Genovese, Eugene D. *Roll, Jordan, Roll: The World the Slaves Made.* New York: Pantheon Books, 1974.

Gessain, Monique. "Coniagui Women (Guinea)." *Women of Tropical Africa.* Ed. Denise Paulme. Trans. H. M. Wright. Berkeley: U of California P, 1963. 17–46.

Getman, Karen A. "Sexual Control in the Slaveholding South: The Implementation and Maintenance of a Racial Caste System." *Harvard Women's Law Journal* 7 (1984): 115–52.

Giddings, Paula. *When and Where I Enter: The Impact of Black Women on Race and Sex in America.* New York: William Morrow, 1984.

Gottfried, Amy S. "Angry Arts: Silence, Speech, and Song in Gayl Jones's *Corregidora.*" *African American Review* 28.4 (1994): 559–70.

Grandy, Moses. *Narrative of the Life of Moses Grandy: Late a Slave in the United States of America.* 1844. *Flight from the Devil: Six Slave Narratives.* Ed. William Loren Katz. Trenton, N.J.: Africa World Press, 1996. 219–48.

Gutman, Herbert G. *The Black Family in Slavery and Freedom, 1750–1925.* New York: Pantheon Books, 1976.

Gwin, Minrose C. *Black and White Women of the Old South: The Peculiar Sisterhood in American Literature*. Knoxville: U of Tennessee P, 1985.

Hafkin, Nancy J. and Edna G. Bay. *Women in Africa: Studies in Social and Economic Change*. Stanford: Stanford UP, 1976.

Harper, Frances E. W. "Colored Woman's Political Future." *World's Congress of Representative Women*. Ed. May Wright Sewall. Chicago: Rand McNally, 1894. 433–438.

———. *Iola Leroy, or Shadows Uplifted*. *Three Classic African American Novels*. Ed. Henry Louis Gates Jr. New York: Vintage, 1990.

Henderson, Mae Gwendolyn. "Speaking in Tongues: Dialogics, Dialectics, and the Black Woman Writer's Literary Tradition." *Changing Our Own Words: Essays on Criticism, Theory, and Writing by Black Women*. New Brunswick, N.J.: Rutgers UP, 1989. 16–37.

———. "Toni Morrison's Beloved: Re-Membering the Body as Historical Text." *Comparative American Identities: Race, Sex, and Nationality in The Modern Text*. Ed. Hortense J. Spillers. New York: Routledge, 1991. 62–86.

Hernton, Calvin C. *Sex and Racism in America*. New York: Grove P, 1965.

Higginbotham, Evelyn Brooks. "African-American Women's History and the Metalanguage of Race." *We Specialize in the Wholly Impossible: A Reader in Black Women's History*. Ed. Darlene Clark Hine, Wilma King, and Linda Reed. Brooklyn: Carlson, 1995. 3–24.

Hine, Darlene Clark. *Hine Sight: Black Women and the Reconstruction of American History*. Brooklyn: Carlson, 1994.

Hirsch, Marianne. "Maternity and Rememory: Toni Morrison's *Beloved*." *Representations of Motherhood*. Ed. Donna Bassin, Margaret Honey, and Meryle Mahrer Kaplan. New Haven: Yale UP, 1994. 92–110.

———. *The Mother/Daughter Plot: Narrative, Psychoanalysis, Feminism*. Bloomington: Indiana UP, 1989.

hooks, bell. *Ain't I A Woman: Black Women and Feminism*. Boston: South End P, 1981.

Hopkins, Pauline. *Contending Forces: A Romance Illustrative of Negro Life North and South*. 1900. New York: Oxford, 1988.

Irigaray, Luce. *Speculum of the Other Woman*. Trans. Gillian C. Gill. Ithaca, N.Y.: Cornell UP, 1985.

Jacobs, Harriet. *Incidents in the Life of a Slave Girl*. 1861. *The Classic Slave Narratives*. Ed. Henry Louis Gates Jr. New York: Penguin, 1987.

Jehlen, Myra. "The Family Militant: Domesticity versus Slavery in *Uncle Tom's Cabin*." *Criticism* 31.4 (1989): 383–400.

Jones, Jacqueline. *Labor of Love, Labor of Sorrow: Black Women, Work, and the Family from Slavery to Present*. New York: Basic Books, 1985.

———. "'My Mother Was Much of a Woman': Black Women, Work, and the Family Under Slavery." *Feminist Studies* 8.2 (1982): 235–69.

———. "Race, Sex, and Self-Evident Truths: The Status of Slave Women during the Era of the American Revolution." *Half Sisters of History: Southern Women and the American Past*. Ed. Catherine Clinton. Durham: Duke UP, 1994. 18–35.

Jones, Gayl. *Corregidora*. Boston: Beacon Press, 1975.

Kaplan, Carla. "Narrative Contracts and Emancipatory Readers: *Incidents in the Life of a Slave Girl*." *Yale Journal of Criticism* 6.1 (1993): 93–119.

Keckley, Elizabeth. *Behind the Scenes. Or, Thirty Years a Slave, and Four Years in the White House*. 1868. New York: Oxford UP, 1988.

King, Wilma. "Suffer With Them Till Death: Slave Women and Their Children in Nineteenth-Century America." *More Than Chattel: Black Women and Slavery in the Americas*. Bloomington: Indiana UP, 1996. 147–68.

Kingston, Maxine Hong. *The Woman Warrior*. New York: Knopf, 1976.

Klein, Herbert S. "African Women in the Atlantic Slave Trade." *Women and Slavery in Africa*. Ed. Claire C. Robertson and Martin A. Klein. Madison: U of Wisconsin P, 1983. 29–38.

Kristeva, Julia. "Stabat Mater." *The Kristeva Reader*. Ed. Toril Moi. New York: Columbia UP, 1986. 160–86.

Kubitschek, Missy Dehn. *Claiming the Heritage: African-American Women Novelists and History*. Jackson: UP of Mississippi, 1991.

Ladner, Joyce A. "Racism and Tradition: Black Womanhood in Historical Perspective." *The Black Woman Cross-Culturally*. Ed. Filomina Chioma Steady. Cambridge: Schenkman, 1981, 269–88.

Lang, Amy Schrager. "Class and the Strategies of Sympathy." *The Culture of Sentiment: Race, Gender, and Sentimentality in Nineteenth-Century America*. New York: Oxford UP, 1992. 128–42.

Lebeuf, Annie M. D. "The Role of Women in the Political Organization of African Societies." *Women of Tropical Africa*. Ed. Denise Paulme. Trans. H. M. Wright. Berkeley: U of California P, 1963. 93–119.

Lerner, Gerda, ed. *Black Women in White America: A Documentary History*. New York: Vintage Books, 1973.

MacCannell, Juliet Flower. "Mothers of Necessity: Psychoanalysis for Feminism." *American Literary History* 3.3 (1991): 623–47.

Margolis, Maxine L. *Mothers and Such: Views of American Women and Why They Changed*. Berkeley: U of California P, 1984.

McDowell, Deborah. "Negotiating Between Tenses: Witnessing Slavery after Freedom—Dessa Rose." *Slavery and the Literary Imagination*. Ed. Deborah E. McDowell and Arnold Rampersad. Baltimore: Johns Hopkins UP, 1989. 144–63.

McKible, Adam. " 'These are the Facts of the Darky's History': Thinking History and Reading Names in Four African American Texts." *African American Review* 28.2 (1994): 223–35.

Meyers, Diana T. "The Subversion of Women's Agency in Psychoanalytic Feminism: Chodorow, Flax, Kristeva." *Revaluing French Feminism: Critical Essays on Difference, Agency, and Culture*. Ed. Nancy Fraser and Sandra Lee Bartky. Bloomington: Indiana UP, 1992. 136–161.

Miller, Randall M. and John David Smith, eds. *Dictionary of Afro-American Slavery*. New York: Greenwood P, 1988.

Morrison, Toni. *Beloved*. New York: Signet, 1991.

———. *Playing in the Dark: Whiteness and the Literary Imagination*. Cambridge: Harvard UP, 1992.

———. "The Site of Memory." *Inventing the Truth: The Art and Craft of Memoir*. Ed. William Zinsser. Rev. ed. Boston: Houghton Mifflin, 1995. 83–102.

Mossell, Mrs. N. F. *The Work of the Afro-American Woman*. 1908. New York: Oxford UP, 1988.

Moynihan, Daniel Patrick. *The Negro Family: The Case for National Action*. Washington, D.C.: Government Printing Office, 1965.

Mullen, Harryette. "Runaway Tongue: Resistant Orality in *Uncle Tom's Cabin, Our Nig, Incidents in the Life of a Slave Girl,* and *Beloved.*" *The Culture of Sentiment: Race, Gender, and Sentimentality in Nineteenth-Century America*. Ed. Shirley Samuels. New York: Oxford UP, 1992. 244–64.

Nichols, Charles H. *Many Thousand Gone: The Ex-Slaves' Account of* Their *Bondage and Freedom*. Bloomington: Indiana UP, 1969.

Nelson, Dana D. *The Word in Black and White: Reading "Race" in American Literature, 1638–1867*. New York: Oxford UP, 1992.

Nudelman, Fanny. "Harriet Jacobs and the Sentimental Politics of Female Suffering." *ELH* 59 (1992): 939–64.

O'Brien, Mary. *The Politics of Reproduction*. Boston: Routledge, 1981.

Okonjo, Kamene. "The Dual-Sex Political System in Operation: Igbo Women and Community Politics in Mid-Western Nigeria." *Women in Africa: Studies in Social and Economic Change*. Ed. Nancy J. Hafkin and Edna G. Bay. Stanford, Calif.: Stanford UP, 1976. 45–58.

Painter, Nell Irvin. "Of *Lily*, Linda Brent, and Freud: A Non-Exceptionalist Approach to Race, Class, and Gender in the Slave South. " *The Georgia Historical Quarterly* 76.2 (1992): 241–59.

Paulme, Denise. *Women of Tropical Africa*. Ed. and trans. H. M. Wright. Berkeley: U of California P, 1963.

Pettis, Joyce. " 'She Sung Back in Return': Literary (Re)vision and Transformation in Gayl Jones's *Corregidora.*" *College English* 52.7 (1990): 787–99.

Phelan, Peggy. *Unmarked: The Politics of Performance*. London: Routledge, 1993.

Prince, Mary. *History of Mary Prince, A West Indian Slave. The Classic Slave Narratives.* Ed. Henry Louis Gates Jr. New York: Penguin, 1987.

Rawley, James H. *The Transatlantic Slave Trade.* New York: W. W. Norton, 1981.

Robertson, Claire. "Africa Into the Americas? Slavery and Women, the Family, and the Gender Division of Labor." *More Than Chattel: Black Women and Slavery in the Americas.* Ed. David Barry Gaspar and Darlene Clark Hine. Bloomington: Indiana UP, 1996. 3–40

Rogers, Susan Carol. "Woman's Place: A Critical Review of Anthropological Theory." *Comparative Studies in Society and History* 20.1 (1978): 123–62.

Roof, Judith. " 'This Is Not For You': The Sexuality of Mothering." *Narrating Mothers: Theorizing Maternal Subjectivities.* Ed. Brenda O. Daly and Maureen T. Reddy. Knoxville: The University of Tennessee Press, 1991. 157–73.

Ryan, Mary P. *Womanhood in America: From Colonial Times to the Present.* New York: Franklin Watts, 1983.

Rushdy, Ashraf H. A. "Daughters Signifying History: The Example of Toni Morrison's *Beloved.*" *American Literature* 64.3 (1992): 567–97.

———. "Reading Mammy: The Subject of Relation in Sherley Anne Williams' *Dessa Rose.*" *African American Review* 27.3 (1993): 365–89.

Sánchez, Marta E. "The Estrangement Effect in Sherley Anne Williams' *Dessa Rose.*" *Genders* 15 (1992): 21–36.

Sánchez-Eppler, Karen. *Touching Liberty: Abolition, Feminism, and the Politics of the Body.* Berkeley: U of California P, 1993.

Silverman, Kaja. *"Histoire d'O*: The Construction of a Female Subject." *Pleasure and Danger: Exploring Female Sexuality.* Ed. Carol S. Vance. Boston: Routledge & Kegan Paul, 1984. 320-349.

Simson, Rennie. "The Afro-American Female: The Historical Context of the Construction of Sexual Identity." *Powers of Desire.* Ed. Ann Barr Snitow, Christine Stansell, Sharon Thompson. New York: Monthly Review Press, 1983. 229–35.

Smith, Valerie. "Form and Ideology in Three Slave Narratives." *Self-Discovery and Authority in Afro-American Narrative.* Cambridge: Harvard UP, 1987.

Spelman, Elizabeth V. *Inessential Woman: Problems of Exclusion in Feminist Thought.* Boston: Beacon Press, 1988.

Spillers, Hortense. "Changing the Letter: The Yokes, the Jokes of Discourse, or, Mrs. Stowe, Mr. Reed." *Slavery and the Literary Imagination.* Ed. Deborah E. McDowell and Arnold Rampersad. Baltimore: Johns Hopkins UP, 1989. 25–61.

———. "Interstices: A Small Drama of Words." *Pleasure and Danger: Exploring Female Sexuality*. Ed. Carol S. Vance. Boston: Routledge & Kegan Paul, 1984. 73–100.

———. "Mama's Baby, Papa's Maybe: An American Grammar Book." *Diacritics* 17.2 (1987): 65–81.

Stampp, Kenneth M. *The Peculiar Institution: Slavery in the Ante-Bellum South*. New York: Vintage Books, 1989.

Starling, Marion Wilson. *The Slave Narrative: Its Place in American History*. Washington, D.C.: Howard UP, 1988.

Stave, Shirley A. "Toni Morrison's *Beloved* and the Vindication of Lilith." *South Atlantic Review* 58.1 (1993): 49–66.

Sterling, Dorothy. *We Are Your Sisters: Black Women in the Nineteenth Century*. New York: W. W. Norton, 1984.

Stevenson, Brenda E. "Gender Convention, Ideals, and Identity among Antebellum Virginia Slave Women." *More Than Chattel: Black Women and Slavery in the Americas*. Ed. David Barry Gaspar and Darlene Clark Hine. Bloomington: Indiana UP, 1996. 167–90.

Stowe, Harriet Beecher. *Uncle Tom's Cabin or, Life among the Lowly*. 1852. New York: Penguin, 1986.

Stuckey, Sterling. *Slave Culture: Nationalist Theory and the Foundations of Black America*. New York: Oxford UP, 1987.

Sudarkasa, Niara. "'The Status of Women' in Indigenous African Societies." *Women in Africa and the African Diaspora*. Ed. Rosalyn Terborg-Penn, Sharon Harley, and Andrea Benton Rushing. Washington, D.C.: Howard UP, 1987. 73–87.

Tanner, Nancy. "Matrifocality in Indonesia and Africa and among Black Americans." *Woman, Culture, and Society*. Ed. Michelle Zimbalist Rosaldo and Louise Lamphere. Stanford, Calif.: Stanford UP, 1974. 97–112.

Tate, Claudia. "Allegories of Black Female Desire; or, Rereading Nineteenth-Century Sentimental Narratives of Black Female Authority." *Changing Our Own Words: Essays on Criticism, Theory, and Writing by Black Women*. Ed. Cheryl A. Wall. New Brunswick, N.J.: Rutgers UP, 1989. 98–126.

———. *Domestic Allegories of Political Desire: The Black Heroine's Text at the Turn of the Century*. New York: Oxford UP, 1992.

———. "Pauline Hopkins: Our Literary Foremother." *Conjuring: Black Women, Fiction, and Literary Tradition*. Ed. Marjories Pryse and Hortense Spillers. Bloomington: Indiana UP, 1985.

Tompkins, Jane. *Sensational Designs: The Cultural Work of American Fiction 1790–1860*. New York: Oxford UP, 1985. 53–66.

Truth, Sojourner. *Narrative of Sojourner Truth; A Bondswoman of Olden Time*. 1878. New York: Arno Press and New York Times, 1968.

Van Allen, Judith. "'Aba Riots' or Igbo 'Woman's War'? Ideology, Stratification, and the Invisibility of Women." *Women in Africa: Studies in*

Social and Economic Change. Ed. Nancy J. Hafkin and Edna G. Bay. Stanford, Calif.: Stanford UP, 1976. 59–85.

Vermillion, Mary. "Reembodying the Self: Representations of Rape in *Incidents in the Life of a Slave Girl* and *I Know Why the Caged Bird Sings*." *Biography: An Interdisciplinary Quarterly* 15.3 (1992): 243–60.

Wallace, Michele. *Black Macho and the Myth of the Superwoman*. New York: Dial P, 1979.

Washington, Mary Helen. *Invented Lives: Narratives of Black Women 1860–1960*. Garden City, N.Y.: Doubleday, 1987.

Welter, Barbara. *Dimity Convictions: The American Woman in the Nineteenth Century*. Athens: Ohio UP, 1976.

White, Barbara A. " 'Our Nig' and the She-Devil: New Information about Harriet Wilson and the 'Bellmont' Family." *American Literature* 65.1 (1993): 19–52.

White, Deborah G. *Ar'n't I a Woman?: Female Slaves in the Plantation South*. New York: W. W. Norton, 1985.

———. "Female Slaves: Sex Roles and Status in the Antebellum Plantation South." *Journal of Family History* 8.3 (1983): 248–61.

Williams, Sherley Anne. *Dessa Rose*. New York: Berkley Books, 1986.

Wilson, Harriet E. *Our Nig; or, Sketches from the Life of a Free Black*. 1859. New York: Random House, 1983.

Winter, Kari J. *Subjects of Slavery, Agents of Change: Women and Power in Gothic Novels and Slave Narratives 1790–1865*. Athens: U of Georgia P, 1992.

Wolff, Cynthia Griffin. " 'Margaret Garner': A Cincinnati Story." *Massachusetts Review* 32.3 (1991): 417–440.

Wyatt, Jean. "Giving Body to the Word: The Maternal Symbolic in Toni Morrison's *Beloved*." *PMLA* 108.3 (1993): 474–88.

Yarborough, Richard. "The Depiction of Blacks in the Early Afro-American Novel." Ph.D. diss., Stanford University, 1980.

———. "Strategies of Black Characterization in *Uncle Tom's Cabin* and the Early Afro-American Novel." *New Essays on Uncle Tom's Cabin*. Ed. Eric J. Sundquist. Cambridge: Cambridge UP, 1986. 45–84.

Yellin, Jean Fagan. "Doing It Herself: *Uncle Tom's Cabin* and Woman's Role in the Slavery Crisis." *New Essays on Uncle Tom's Cabin*. Ed. Eric J. Sundquist. Cambridge: Cambridge UP, 1986. 85–105.

———. Introduction. *Incidents in the Life of a Slave Girl*. By Harriet A. Jacobs. 1861. Cambridge: Harvard UP, 1987. xiii–xxxiv.

———. "Texts and Contexts of Harriet Jacobs' *Incidents in the Life of a Slave Girl Written by Herself*." *The Slave's Narrative*. Ed. Charles T. Davis and Henry Louis Gates Jr. Oxford: Oxford UP, 1985. 262–82.

———. *Women & Sisters: The Antislavery Feminists in American Culture*. New Haven: Yale UP, 1989.

Young, Elizabeth. "Warring Fictions: *Iola Leroy* and the Color of Gender." *American Literature* 64.2 (1992): 273–97.

Zerilli, Linda M. G. "A Process without a Subject: Simone de Beauvoir and Julia Kristeva on Maternity." *Signs*: *Journal of Women in Culture and Society* 18.1 (1992): 111–35.

Index